Also by Rosie Daley

In the Kitchen with Rosie: Oprah's Favorite Recipes

Also by Andrew Weil, M.D.

Eating Well for Optimum Health:
The Essential Guide to Food, Diet, and Nutrition

Eight Weeks to Optimum Health:
A Proven Program for Taking Full Advantage of Your Body's
Natural Healing Power

Spontaneous Healing:
How to Discover and Enhance Your Body's Natural Ability
to Maintain and Heal Itself

Natural Health, Natural Medicine:
A Comprehensive Manual for Wellness and Self-Care

Health and Healing

From Chocolate to Morphine:
Everything You Need to Know About Mind-Altering Drugs
(with Winifred Rosen)

The Marriage of the Sun and Moon:
A Quest for Unity in Consciousness

The Natural Mind:
A New Way of Looking at Drugs and the
Higher Consciousness

The Healthy Kitchen

**Photographs by Sang An, Amy Haskell,
and Eric Studer**

THE HEALTHY KITCHEN

Recipes for a Better Body, Life, and Spirit

Andrew Weil, M.D.
AND Rosie Daley

Alfred A. Knopf   New York   2002

**THIS IS A BORZOI BOOK
PUBLISHED BY ALFRED A. KNOPF**

Copyright © 2002 by Andrew Weil, M.D., and Rosie Daley
Photographs copyright © 2002 by Sang An, Amy Haskell,
and Eric Studer

A portion of this book was originally published in
Body & Soul Guide to Holistic Living.

Library of Congress Cataloging-in-Publication Data
Daley, Rosie.
The healthy kitchen : recipes for a better body, life, and spirit / by
Rosie Daley and Andrew Weil ; photographs by Sang An, Amy Haskell,
and Eric Studer.
p.   cm.
Includes index.
ISBN 0-375-41306-5
1. Cookery (Natural foods)   I. Weil, Andrew.   II. Title.
TX741.D35 2002
641.5'63—dc21   2001050391

Manufactured in the United States of America
First Edition

PHOTOGRAPHIC CREDITS

Sang An: 4, 20, 36, 58, 78, 91, 102, 114, 130, 143, 151, 175, 198, 233,
238, 282, 289. Amy Haskell: xiv, 71, 99, 117, 180, 245, 251, 278, 304.
Bethany Jensen: 203. Eric Studer: 19, 56, 57, 69, 100, 105, 164, 166,
167, 172, 174, 209, 219, 255, 270, 271, 272, 273, 274
All other images are made up of the photographs listed above.

To my friend Barry Bluestein,
who helped me write my first book and encouraged me
to do a second. He is, alas, no longer with us, but his spirit
and his passion for cooking and eating healthy
are here on every page.

—R.D.

To Jenny and Diana

—A.W.

Contents

Acknowledgments

I would first like to thank all the chefs who have inspired me to be a better cook: Miceal Strout, Jeff Hampton, Deborah from Charlie's, Gordon Smith, Cal-a-Vie Spa, and so many more (you know who you are).

Thank you and congratulations to all the professional chefs who have flourished in the public eye and continue to motivate people to cook.

A special thank you to all my friends who came to many recipe-tasting parties, gave me advice, and supplied me with comments about my cooking.

Thanks to my writing team: Rachel Isabell Gomez, for being my main writer and spending enormous amounts of energy and time in rewriting and changing recipes to better suit the public; Judith Jones, my editor, who gave me more than I could ask for—incomparable talent and professionalism, not to mention her love of cooking and unwavering faith in me that lifted my spirits and successfully guided me through two books.

Thanks to Lily Rose Neville, Beverly Lockheart, Marley St. John, Court Stark, Eva David, Natalie and Nicole Thomas, Danny Anderson, the Clinton O'Brien family, Ron Holder, Jill Wilson, Beverly Connors, Nan Self, and Kirt Smidley.

Thanks to the crew at Panikin Coffee for all their hospitality that saw me through my morning and afternoon work sessions.

Thank you always to all my previous employers, who gave me the chance to work with and learn from them. Thank you to Oprah Winfrey for the opportunity to share my love of cooking with such a wide audience and for giving me a reason to create my recipes in the first place.

Thank you to the group at Culinary Concepts Testing in Arizona who tested my recipes.

I am forever grateful to all the people who supported my previous book and for their desire to learn more about cooking.

Thank you to my co-author, Dr. Andrew Weil, for sharing his vast knowledge and understanding of nutrition and the immeasurable benefits that eating well offers all of us.

—R.D.

Thanks to Paul Bogaards at Alfred A. Knopf for making this idea a reality. It has been a pleasure to work with him as well as with my editors Jon Segal and Judith Jones, and, as always, my agent, Richard Pine.

Dr. Jim Nicolai helped me develop and test recipes and did a great deal of work to assist in the completion of the manuscript. It was fun to cook and eat with him. Lynn Willeford also provided recipe ideas.

Thanks to my office staff, especially Michele Hardin and Debra DuBois.

Judith Berger and Suzan Gross and the rest of the staff of Culinary Concepts in Tucson provided invaluable help in testing recipes and calculating their nutritional values.

Finally, thanks to my co-author, Rosie Daley, for showing me new ways of working in the kitchen and for bringing her boundless energy and enthusiasm to this project.

—A.W.

Rosie's Introduction

I have tried to give you throughout this book useful tips about shopping, cooking, planning meals, and making your food look attractive. But, above all, I hope the recipes, which are not only sensible but taste fantastic, will inspire you to cook. This is not a diet cookbook. Eating well is not about dieting, but a life choice. Adopting a healthy lifestyle through food should never leave us feeling deprived. I think most of us agree that eating is one of life's greatest pleasures and every recipe in this book will demonstrate how fulfilling good eating is.

The recipes vary on their level of complexity. Some are simple to prepare. Some take a bit more time and energy to put together. My hope is that you will take on the more advanced recipes when you are ready to. I've shared with you all the techniques that will help you to become more confident in your kitchen. You will notice your skill level growing with each new dish that you make. You will also probably develop a favorite activity in terms of food preparation. I love to make garnishes and to grocery shop. You may love to cut vegetables "julienne" style or poach fish or make spectacular salads or grill outdoors. The beauty of cooking is that everyone already knows how to do it—it is really a matter of just doing it. And, like anything else, the more you do it, the better you get.

Cooking takes some effort, no question, but kitchen stress and time pressures usually arise when certain needed items are not readily available to complete a dish. The first step in making your kitchen truly functional is to plan your shopping. Think about what you want to make, what you have at home, what ingredients can be used for other meals, and what you need to stock up on. Arrange it so that you don't have to shop more than once or twice a week. I buy perishable items only every few days, but I keep lots of frozen or dried foods on hand for whenever I need them. See my tips on Stocking the Pantry.

The one place I always shop is at my local farmers' market. I enjoy the entire process of gathering fresh foods for my meals. A great way to get in touch with the seasons is by becoming aware of what fresh foods are available at specific times of the year. This will also be helpful in your menu planning.

Timing is an essential component to making a great meal. First, review the recipe you want to make, see what can be done ahead of time, and then do it!

Don't be afraid to work with new ingredients, such as cooking with different grains, using tofu, or trying out a variety of peppers, herbs, and spices. Cooking should be varied because that's part of the fun, the creativity, and the learning. Involve your family by planning a meal in a leisurely way on the weekend and use your kids' energy—let them stuff grape leaves, roll up slices of eggplant, knead dough, or cut out cookies.

Perhaps the most significant benefit cooking at home provides, besides quality sustenance, is sitting down in the company of loved ones and sharing a meal that you've made. Everyone's lives are indeed much busier today. But even if you relax at the table with family and friends to enjoy a home-cooked meal just once a week, it will help to relieve the stresses of everyday life and keep you in touch with the people who make life wonderful.

ANDY'S INTRODUCTION

"Good health begins in the kitchen." I agree with that statement, because I believe that good nutrition is one of the most important influences on health. Most of us eat three times a day. Many of us eat more frequently. Each time we do, we have an opportunity to nourish the body, delight the senses, and calm the mind. It is a shame to waste those opportunities by eating food that is neither healthful nor delicious.

It is a fact of contemporary life that people spend less and less time in the kitchen, relying more on prepared food, fast food, and processed food. The statistics on the declining percentage of American families that have even one daily meal together are depressing. Some of this results from the undeniable pressure and fast pace of life in the twenty-first century. Where can we find the time to cook, to make meals from scratch? But some of it also comes from habit, from fear, from lack of knowledge.

Eating habits often develop in early life. For that reason, I encourage parents to involve children in food preparation. Kids love to help in the kitchen, and by having a hand in the creation of meals, they are more likely to want to try new foods, to develop a love of cooking, and to discover the joy of making and eating good food. I have read that most Italian men, by the time they are twenty, have mastered a basic repertory of kitchen skills and can turn out a good tomato sauce, for example. That is a result of their upbringing, of parents encouraging them to take part in cooking at early ages and is quite unlike the situation in America.

I have heard health gurus over the years decry the dangers of various nutrients, foods, and diets—from fat in general and saturated fat in particular to carbohydrates in general and sugar in particular, from milk and meat and fish to soybeans and peanuts, from macrobiotic diets to Beverly Hills diets. All of this makes more people feel that food is the enemy and the dining table a minefield. It makes them throw up their hands and think they will never understand the science of nutrition or the relationship between diet and health. It makes them afraid and confused, and it drives them out of the kitchen and into the arms of fast-food merchants and makers of processed food.

At the same time we are seeing a tremendous upsurge in popularity of cookbooks and of cooking shows on television. I suspect that many people turn to them more for entertainment than for practical information, because most of the books and shows feature celebrity chefs, who are producing food that the average American could never reproduce in a home kitchen.

I am hardly a celebrity chef. I am a home cook and a physician who advocates natural medicine. As I said, I believe that eating well is one important determinant of health. By "eating well," I mean giving your body the fuel it needs, using food to increase your resistance and natural healing power—and not sacrificing the pleasure of eating appetizing, tasty, and satisfying food. In my time I have been served many dreadful dishes that were supposed to be "health food"; I am unwilling to eat food that is boring, artless, and devoid of pleasure even if it's somebody else's idea of healthful.

My purpose in producing this book with Rosie is to show you that good food can be good for you and can also be easy and fun to prepare. Rosie and I do not see eye-to-eye on every culinary issue. (I think you will find that our disagreements make for interesting reading.) But we very much agree that a dish can be only as good as its worst ingredient, that it is worth getting the best and freshest ingredients, that recipes should yield good results without being overly complicated or taxing. Both of us enjoy good food. Both of us enjoy making good food. We want to share that enjoyment with you.

Rosie and Andy picking
vegetables and fruits from his
garden in Arizona

NUTRITION AND HEALTH

The science of nutrition is full of controversy and disagreement. Given the amount of contradictory information from researchers and the media regarding dietary influences on health, it is not surprising that most people are confused. Not long ago we were told that eggs were good for us. Then we learned that eggs were bad. Now, once again, we hear that they are good. For years in the mid–twentieth century, doctors told us to shun butter and eat margarine made from vegetable oils. Now they tell us that margarine may be even worse for the heart than butter. Just as we were learning about the cancer-protective effects of soybeans, some experts began warning us that eating soy could increase cancer risks.

It doesn't help that our health professionals are so poorly educated about nutrition. Medical doctors get next to no training in this most important subject and so are unable to help us navigate through the confusion or interpret all the research findings. And because doctors' eating habits are often less than ideal, they are no better role models for healthful eating than anyone else. And sadly, the food served in most hospitals and medical centers in America is awful.

Rosie and I both believe that our homes should be the best places to eat. We spend a great deal of time in the home kitchen: think how often people gather there, leaving the living room unused. This book would not exist if we did not believe that you can make the home kitchen the source of great food— food that provides optimum nutrition and is also delicious. We will show you how to do that, by giving you recipes, tips on meal planning and shopping, and practical hints for simplifying food preparation. In *The Healthy Kitchen* you will learn how to make dishes that are much more appetizing than those served in "health food restaurants," where people have not yet grasped that eating wonderful food and eating healthy food can be one and the same.

A number of dietary trends in American society are cause for concern. We all know that too many of us are overweight—just sit in an airport and watch who passes by. Even more alarming is the epidemic of obesity in American children; evidently, their weight problems begin very early. Recently, medical journals have reported another alarming trend—the appearance of type-2 diabetes, usually called adult-onset diabetes, in very young children, as young as seven years old. This is a completely new phenomenon. Along with other observations, it suggests that we are eating too much food and too much of the wrong foods (as well as not getting enough physical activity). The reason is that most people do not know how to select foods that will maintain optimum health as well as satisfy and delight the senses. Again, that is just what Rosie and I will help you do in this book.

The primary message given to us by nutritionists and dietitians is to eat a balanced diet—advice so vague as to be meaningless. Some people think it means to eat some of everything, including foods that are distinctly not good for our health. The concept of a balanced diet may be a good one, but to make sense of it, you need practical information about the components of diet and the roles they play in the body.

What we prepare and eat at home and what we eat elsewhere must supply fuel for the body's metabolic engine—that is, enough sources of energy to provide for all the body's needs. It must also supply materials for growth and for the maintenance and repair of the body's structure. And it must supply all other elements needed to keep us in optimum health.

Nutritionists divide dietary needs into two broad categories—micronutrients and macronutrients. Micronutrients are the "little foods" needed in very small quantities to fine-tune our metabolism. They include vitamins, minerals, fiber, and a variety of beneficial compounds from plants called "protective phytochemicals." Eating plenty of fruits and vegetables ensures a proper intake of micronutrients. Macronutrients—carbohydrates, fats, and proteins—are the "big foods" that supply energy needs (calories) as well as materials for growth and repair of tissue. How you choose them can affect how you live, feel, and age.

Macronutrients

Carbohydrates and fats are primarily sources of caloric energy, although the body also uses some special fats as building blocks (for cell membranes, for instance) and starting materials for synthesizing hormones. The body can use proteins as fuel, but it depends on them mainly as raw materials for maintaining and growing body structures. A balanced diet must provide the right number of calories to replace those expended in the course of day-to-day living, and it should provide the right mix of carbohydrates, fats, and proteins to meet the body's needs. This is why daily menu planning is so important—more on that later. In addition, because there are better and worse carbohydrates, good and bad fats, and proteins that are more and less desirable, it should provide the best of the available macronutrients. Let me explain the differences.

Let's start with calories. You can look up in standard tables your average daily caloric need based on sex, body size, and level of activity. Most adults have to consume between 2,000 and 3,000 calories a day. Women, and smaller and less active people, need fewer calories, while men, and bigger and more active people, need more. If you consistently eat more calories than you expend, the chances are you will gain weight, and if you consistently eat fewer calories than you need, the chances are you will lose it. I have to say "chances are" because some people are genetically programmed so that their metabolic rate changes in ways that keep weight constant despite variations in caloric intake. For most of us, unfortunately, the iron-clad rule is that calories in equal calories out, or else weight goes up or down. Most overweight and obese people are simply consuming more calories than they are burning up in their activities of daily living.

"Burning up" is an accurate term. Metabolism is the controlled burning of fuel by living organisms—that is, the chemical combination of foods with oxygen to release the energy they contain. The energy locked up in foods originates in sunlight that is captured by green plants in the process of photosynthesis. The first product of photosynthesis is glucose, a form of sugar and one of the simplest carbohydrates, the basic metabolic fuel of both plants and animals. In animals, glucose circulates in the blood as a ready source of energy that cells can take in and metabolize; one name for it is blood sugar. In addition, both plants and animals can use glucose as a starting material to build other, more complex macronutrients.

In thinking about the relative contributions of different kinds of foods to total caloric intake, it is important to know that fats are almost twice as calorie-dense as either carbohydrates or proteins; fats provide nine calories per gram versus five for the other two macronutrients. Therefore, a simple way to decrease caloric intake is to reduce fat consumption. To do that you need to know what fat is and where it occurs in foods. It is also important to know what carbohydrates and proteins are and where you encounter them.

Carbohydrates

The main sources of carbohydrates in the American diet in decreasing order of magnitude are yeast bread; soft drinks; cakes, cookies, quick breads, and doughnuts; sugar, syrups, and jams; potatoes; ready-to-eat cereal; milk; pasta; rice and other cooked grains; flour; juices and fruit drinks; frozen desserts; and chips and popcorn. Other, less popular carbohydrate-containing foods are beans, sweet potatoes, and winter squash. In general all these foods are relatively inexpensive, filling, and satisfying. Many people crave them. Recently, a number of diet experts have been forcefully telling us to avoid them on the grounds that they are the chief cause of obesity—more of a problem for our waistlines than fat. There is some truth in this statement, but I think it gets badly distorted in many popular diet books. It is unwise to shun carbohydrates.

There are two classes of nutritive carbohydrates, sugars and starches. Sugars include very basic ones like glucose and more complicated ones like sucrose or table sugar. They taste sweet to us, and we seek out that taste. In nature, sugars accumulate in ripe fruit, in some seeds (like sweet corn), and some vegetables (like sweet peppers, which are actually fruits because they contain seeds). They also occur in sap and nectar, which can be concentrated into products like syrup and honey. Starches, more complicated molecules than sugars, are used by plants for storing energy in roots (sweet potatoes), tubers (white potatoes), and seeds (grains). Animals also make a form of starch, glycogen, that is stored in the liver and muscles as a short-term energy reserve.

Nutritionists have told us for years to think of carbohydrates as either simple (sugars) or complex (starches) and to minimize consumption of the former in favor of the latter. That turns out not to be very useful advice. The important way that carbohydrate foods differ from each other is in how fast they convert to glucose and raise the level of it in the blood. Speed of conversion of a carbohydrate food to blood sugar is rated with a quantity called the glycemic index (GI) on a scale from 0 to 100. Glucose has a GI of 100; it need not be digested and goes directly into the bloodstream. Table sugar has a lower GI (65) because it is a compound of glucose and fructose, also known as fruit sugar. The body does not digest fructose very well; it has a very low GI of 23.

Meals full of high-glycemic-index foods like potatoes, bread, and sweet drinks cause rapid rises in blood sugar. They require the pancreas to secrete insulin, the hormone that allows glucose to enter cells. Insulin also affects fat metabolism, weight, and cardiovascular function. Many people who eat diets rich in high-glycemic-index carbohydrates will gain weight, and develop unhealthy levels of fat and cholesterol in their blood. They may also develop high blood pressure and increased risk of diabetes. Too much of these kinds of foods in the American diet probably accounts for a great deal of the obesity we see, including the epidemic of it in our children.

Glycemic index depends on the chemical nature of a carbohydrate food as well as on its physical structure and method of preparation. If whole grains are eaten whole or cracked into large pieces, they convert slowly. The starch they contain gradually becomes glucose and does not provoke a rapid outpouring of insulin. But if grains are stripped of their fibrous coatings (bran) and pulverized into flour, the fine starch particles are easy targets for digestive enzymes that rapidly convert them to glucose, raising blood sugar and forcing the pancreas to work harder.

I like bread, but I much prefer dense, coarse, whole-grain "peasant" breads to those made with finely milled flour, whether white or brown. If I eat oatmeal, I much prefer steel-cut or Irish oatmeal to the usual mushy variety that Americans eat. These preferences guide me toward lower-glycemic-index carbohydrates that are better for me.

Pasta has a lower GI than bread because the starch is in a denser form that resists quick digestion. If pasta is cooked al dente in the Italian manner, it is denser still, with an even lower GI. Beans are also low on the scale, because the fiber they contain slows down digestion of the starch.

In my opinion, diets based on elimination of carbohydrates are not very sensible. Carbohydrates are easily digested sources of energy for the body, and they should provide the largest share of calories you eat. It is important, however, to choose carbohydrate foods wisely and not overdo those at the top of the GI chart. Carbohydrates are certainly not bad in and of themselves, but the way we eat them may be. If you look at the most common sources of them in the American diet, you will note that highly processed and refined foods dominate the list; beans, one of the best sources, with a low GI, are not even on it.

Just think of all the fluffy breads, pastries, crackers, chips, mushy starches, and soft drinks that people consume today. In this book we try to emphasize better carbohydrate choices: whole grains, beans, squash, and fruit. And when we give recipes for waffles or rice pudding, which have higher GI ratings, we recommend topping them with fruit, such as berries or peaches, which have low GIs. The combination brings the glycemic index of the dish down to the moderate zone.

Fats

Fats, also demonized in recent years and blamed by some for all of our dietary woes, are an even more efficient form of storing energy than carbohydrates. Plants pack it into seeds (in nuts, for example), and animals store it under the skin, both to insulate themselves and to provide a source of energy when food is scarce. Of course, many of us never lack for food, and we keep accumulating fat rather than burning it up.

Here are the main sources of fat in the American diet in descending order of magnitude: beef; margarine; salad dressings and mayonnaise; cheese; milk; cakes, cookies, quick breads, and doughnuts; poultry; oils; yeast bread; chips and popcorn; sausages; eggs; nuts and seeds; butter; ice cream. This is an interesting and, to me, distressing list. The first two items on it represent two sources of bad fat that offer two different kinds of dangers to health. The fat in beef, like that in other animal flesh, poultry, and milk, is saturated fat. Saturated fat is solid at room temperature. The body can easily burn it as fuel, but, in many people, excessive consumption of it drives up levels of cholesterol and blood fats and increases the risk of cardiovascular disease. If the major source of fat in the diet is saturated fat, risks of heart attacks and arterial problems increase in most people. The easiest way to reduce these risks through diet is to cut down on red meat and dairy products made from whole milk and to remove the skin (and accompanying fat) from poultry. Only a few vegetable fats are saturated—palm and coconut oils especially—and you are only likely to encounter them in some manufactured foods, so read the labels (see page xxxvii).

Most vegetable oils are unsaturated to one degree or another. The more unsaturated ones are called polyunsaturated and remain liquid and pourable even at cold temperatures. The less unsaturated ones are called monounsaturated and turn translucent and thick in the refrigerator but not completely hard like saturated fat. Margarine is made from liquid vegetable oils that are artificially saturated (with hydrogen) to make them semisolid. This process changes the fat molecules in ways that make them very unhealthful. Margarine and other partially hydrogenated oils damage arteries and raise the risk for heart attack. I believe they also promote cancer, inflammation, damage to the immune system, and premature aging. Some of this harmfulness is due to their content of trans-fats, which are unnatural fat molecules created in the hydrogenation process.

Look again at the list of fat sources in the American diet. At the top of the list you'll find mostly foods containing saturated animal fat or processed vegetable oils, both undesirable, as I have said. Some of the best fats are those found in nuts like walnuts, almonds, and cashews, and in seeds like sesame and pumpkin. Nuts and seeds are near the very bottom of the list of what people eat.

In recent years, Americans have repeatedly been told to "get the fat out," and they have been eating more and more low-fat and nonfat foods. In my opinion, telling people to avoid fat is as misguided as telling people to avoid carbohydrates. As fat-free foods have proliferated in our society, people have grown steadily fatter, probably because they have been eating more calories, especially from low-quality carbohydrate foods. When food has too little fat, it very often just doesn't taste good. That isn't the kind of food you—or we—want to put on our tables. Fat conveys flavors to our taste buds and contributes to the pleasurable "mouth feel" of good food. The problem is not to get the fat out but to avoid bad fat and get the good fat in.

From the standpoint of health, the best fats are the monounsaturated ones found in nuts, seeds, olives, and avocados. Most of the recipes in this book that call for oil specify olive oil, and many use nuts and seeds. Olive oil is a mainstay of the Mediterranean diet, one of the best ways of eating in the world (more on that later, too). Fortunately, it is now easy to find good quality (extra virgin) olive oil in ordinary supermarkets. If you don't want too strong a flavor of olive oil in a dish, you can try one of the "light" brands or use a good, neutral-flavored oil. My current favorite is grapeseed oil.

Never heat oils to the smoking point, and never breathe the smoke of burning oil; it is highly toxic and carcinogenic. (One of the reasons I favor grape-seed oil is that it has a high smoking point—that is, it can be heated to higher temperatures before it begins to smoke.) Also beware of rancid oils—those that have oxidized as a result of exposure to air, light, and heat. They not only have an unpleasant smell (like that of oil paint) that will make food taste bad, but they, too, are toxic and carcinogenic. Buy oils in smaller rather than larger con-tainers, protect them from light and heat, use them up quickly, and throw them out if they smell odd. These same recommendations apply to foods that contain oils, like nuts, seeds, crackers, chips, and baked goods.

One special group of good fats deserves particular attention. Omega-3 fats are a group of polyunsaturated fats that are absolutely essential for opti-mum health. The body needs them on a regular basis to synthesize hormones and build cell membranes, including those of nerve cells in the brain. Dietary sources of omega-3s are few, and, probably, most Americans are deficient in them. That deficiency may underlie our susceptibility to heart disease, inflam-matory diseases (including forms of arthritis and autoimmunity), some forms of cancer, and a variety of nervous and mental disorders. Research on the preven-tive and therapeutic potential of omega-3 fats is currently a very active area of medical investigation.

The main food source of these good fats is fish, especially fatty fish from cold waters: salmon, mackerel, herring, sardines, and (to a lesser extent) albacore tuna. Non-fish sources are few: walnuts, flax seeds, hemp seeds, and the oils extracted from them. There are smaller amounts in soybeans and sea vegetables (such as nori and arame). A new source is fortified eggs produced by chickens fed dietary supplements rich in omega-3s. I cannot overemphasize the importance of including these foods in your diet and preparing them regularly. *The Healthy Kitchen* offers many recipes that will help you accomplish that.

If you keep your saturated-fat intake to a minimum and avoid partially hydrogenated and other processed vegetable oils, concentrate on using olive oil and other monounsaturated fats, and make sure to eat enough omega-3 sources, you do not have to follow an ascetic, ultra-low-fat diet to enjoy optimum health. In fact, you can allow enough fat in your diet to make food delicious and yet also be assured that you are reducing disease and promoting general health.

Protein

The last category of macronutrients is protein. A lack of it results in severe wasting, especially in children, because the body needs protein to grow, maintain, and repair itself. Many people worry about whether they are getting enough protein and think that meals have to be built around dense portions of animal protein, like a steak or a roast—in other words, that a meal without meat would be nothing but side dishes and accompaniments. One of the things Rosie and I hope to accomplish in this book is to change your thinking on this, and to suggest ways you can build meals on far healthier protein sources that are delicious—meals that can be prepared easily and that you'll be proud to serve.

Here are the main sources of protein in the American diet today, again in decreasing order of magnitude: beef; poultry; milk; yeast bread; cheese; fish and shellfish (excluding canned tuna); eggs; pork (fresh); ham; pasta; cakes, cookies, quick breads, and doughnuts. Who would have thought that bread would be so high on the list? Wheat and other grains contain protein along with their starch, and some bread contains milk, but most of it provides a great deal of high-glycemic-index carbohydrate. And most people eat bread with fat, often a bad fat like margarine. Beans, an excellent protein source with low-glycemic-index carbohydrate and no fat, do not appear on the list, because they contribute a maximum of only 1 percent of the protein in the American diet.

There are several problems with relying on meat, poultry, milk, and cheese as primary protein sources. Meat and unskinned poultry contain a great deal of saturated fat and cholesterol, both of which increase risks of cardiovascular disease. Commercial meat and poultry also contain residues of drugs and hormones used to promote the growth of animals, and the raising of animals for food is very damaging to the environment (see page 149). Milk and cheese are also significant sources of saturated fat, and milk, especially, is associated with a number of common health problems (see page 34). For all these reasons, I recommend moving away from dependence on animal foods for your protein and looking more to fish and vegetable sources.

If you eat salmon, sardines, herring, and albacore tuna regularly, you can get omega-3 fats along with your protein. But take care when eating fish, too (see page 176); you want to select wisely the varieties you eat and learn to cook them in healthful ways. Rosie and I have included a number of fish dishes that we think are easy and delicious as well as good for you. We also give recipes for vegetarian dishes that are high in protein because they use beans, soy foods, and whole grains.

More and more enlightened dietitians recommend that people move toward "plant-based" diets to reduce disease risks and improve well-being. That does not mean forgoing all animal foods and sticking to salad bars when you eat out. It does mean unlearning the habit of organizing meals around centerpieces of meat and poultry and becoming acquainted with the great variety of satisfying protein-rich dishes that can be made from vegetarian ingredients. Populations that eat plant-based diets live longer and enjoy better health than populations whose protein sources match those on the list above. We hope this book can inspire you to move in that direction.

By the way, far from not getting enough protein, most Americans get too much, often taking in their whole day's needs with a typical breakfast of eggs, bacon, toast, and milk. Protein deficiency is very rare in our society except among very poor people, the elderly, and some people on bizarre diets. If you eat more protein than your body needs to make and maintain tissue, the excess goes into the metabolic furnace to provide caloric energy. Protein is not as good a fuel as carbohydrate or fat, however. It is neither an efficient nor a clean-burning fuel, requiring more work on the part of the digestive system, especially the liver, and more work for the kidneys to eliminate the residues of its combustion. Those residues can irritate the immune system. Protein needs are increased in growing children, nursing mothers, and those recovering from illness and injury, but even for them the typical American diet probably provides too much.

So how should the optimum diet break down in terms of macronutrients? I recommend the following percentages of total calories: 50 to 60 percent from carbohydrates, 30 percent from fat, and 10 to 20 percent from protein. At the end of this chapter I will give more detailed recommendations.

Micronutrients

I want to start by reminding you that it is not necessary to worry about the details of these important elements, needed by the body in much smaller amounts for optimum functioning. All you have to do is be sure to eat a variety of fruits and vegetables, of good quality and in sufficient quantities (ideally five to nine half-cup servings a day). They will supply all of your micronutrient needs.

Vitamins are essential nutrients obtained from food that are necessary for health and growth. Vitamins C and E occur mainly in plants, the B-complex occurs mainly in animal tissue, and others are in both plant and animal foods. The body can make vitamin D with exposure to sunlight, and bacteria in the gut make small amounts of B-vitamins and vitamin K. Of course, you can make sure you are getting all your vitamins by taking a supplement, and there are good reasons for doing so (see page 145). Nonetheless it is useful to know that you can get all the vitamins you need by eating a varied diet that includes some animal foods (such as cheese and fish) and that is rich in fresh fruits and vegetables. People who avoid animal foods entirely are at risk for developing deficiency of vitamin B-12, which can cause severe illness in children and pernicious anemia in adults; these people must take this vitamin in supplement form.

A number of minerals are also essential micronutrients and, again, their sources are mostly fruits and vegetables. Two that deserve special comment are iron and calcium. If you cut down on red meat, as Rosie and I suggest, you eliminate a major dietary source of easily assimilable iron. You can make up for this by eating more dried beans, dried fruit (prunes, raisins, figs), molasses, cocoa, and dark, leafy greens, as well as by doing some cooking in cast-iron pots. Be aware that iron is an oxidant that can promote undesirable changes in the body; it can raise the risk of heart disease, for example. Therefore, you should never take supplemental iron unless a blood test shows you to be iron-deficient.

Calcium, on the other hand, probably should be supplemented, especially in women at risk for bone loss and osteoporosis, such as those with family histories of these conditions. The problem may not be that the diet does not provide enough of this mineral but that other factors prevent its absorption and use or promote its loss. For example, inadequate vitamin D in the diet hampers the body's ability to use calcium, and high intakes of carbonated soft drinks, salt, caffeine, and alcohol all promote loss. Diets top-heavy in animal protein also lead to calcium loss. Dairy products are good sources of this mineral, as are collards, kale, broccoli, sea vegetables, sesame seeds, and some fortified foods like orange juice, soy milk, and tofu.

Fiber, another micronutrient, is necessary for proper intestinal function and may reduce risks of cardiovascular disease and some cancers. It is simply the indigestible part of food, otherwise known as roughage, that makes up much of the bulk of stool. There are various types of fiber, and all of them are "resistant carbohydrates"—that is, carbohydrates too complex to be broken down by the human digestive system. Vegetarians take in a lot of fiber; people who eat mainly meat, potatoes, and white bread do not. Cooked beans are a good source, as are whole grains, nuts, and many vegetables and fruits. Berries are particularly rich in fiber, which occurs in the tiny seeds they contain. I do not recommend taking fiber supplements, because they can cause gas and bloating and interfere with absorption of minerals. If you eat more fruits, vegetables, whole grains, seeds, and nuts, you will get all the fiber your body needs.

The final category of micronutrients, and to me the most interesting, is the protective phytochemicals. These are a large and very diverse group of compounds found in fruits, vegetables, and mushrooms that strengthen our natural defenses against agents of disease, reducing risks of cancer and other serious illnesses. Scientists keep discovering new ones, and research on them is very promising.

One class of protective phytochemicals acts as antioxidants, blocking chemical reactions in the body that can damage tissues and promote cancer and premature aging. For example, the red and purple pigments in berries, cherries, red grapes, and red cabbage are powerful antioxidants with many beneficial effects. So are the carotenoid pigments that give color to carrots, pumpkins, winter squash, sweet potatoes, tomatoes, cantaloupes, and other yellow and orange fruits and vegetables. They also occur, but are not visible, in dark, leafy greens. This family of compounds is strongly cancer-protective. Another natural antioxidant, called EGCG, accounts for most of the health-promoting effects of green tea.

Again, you don't need to know the details of the chemistry or pharmacology or even the names of all the protective phytochemicals now known to medical science. Just remember to eat your fruits and vegetables.

Before ending this overview of nutrition and health, and moving on to how you can make use of this information in your everyday cooking, I would like to summarize for you the information about the optimum diet I recommend. This is the way of eating that I believe will help you attain maximum health and longevity. It should also give you all the enjoyment you want when you sit down to eat.

The optimum diet should:

- Supply all of your needs for calories, macronutrients, and micronutrients
- Support general health throughout life and maximize longevity
- Provide the pleasure you expect from eating.

General Characteristics of the Optimum Diet

- *Variety.* Cover all nutritional bases and minimize the intake of any harmful elements in foods.
- *Freshness.* The higher the percentage of fresh foods in the diet the better.
- *Unprocessed foods.* The lower the percentage of processed foods in the diet the better.
- *Abundance in fruits and vegetables.* The more fruits and vegetables you eat, the more protective phytochemicals you take in.

Calories

Depending on sex, body size, and activity level, most adults need to consume between 2,000 and 3,000 calories a day. Women, and smaller and less active people, need fewer calories; men, and bigger and more active people, need more. If you are eating the appropriate number of calories and not varying your activity, your weight should not fluctuate greatly.

The recommended distribution of calories is: 50 to 60 percent from carbohydrates, 30 percent from fat, and 10 to 20 percent from protein.

Carbohydrates

Adult women should eat about 225 to 270 grams of carbohydrates a day, while men should eat about 288 to 345 grams. The majority of this should be in the form of whole, unprocessed foods with a low (i.e., below 60) glycemic index, and everyone should try to eat some low-GI carbohydrate with each meal (whole grains, beans, vegetables, and nontropical fruits). If you eat high-GI carbohydrates, try to include them in meals that also contain some low-GI foods.

Try to reduce your consumption of foods made with wheat flour and sugar and increase your consumption of beans.

Fat

On a 2,000-calorie-a-day diet, 600 calories can come from fat—that is, about 67 grams. Ideally, this should be in a ratio of 1:2:1 of saturated to monounsaturated to polyunsaturated fat, meaning that no more than 100 calories should come from saturated fat. You should reduce saturated fat by eating less butter, cream, cheese, and other full-fat dairy products, unskinned chicken, fatty meats, and products made with palm and coconut oil. Use olive oil as a principal oil in cooking. Limit your consumption of polyunsaturated vegetable oils (safflower, sunflower, corn, sesame) and avoid margarine, vegetable shortening, and all products made with partially hydrogenated oils. Also avoid fried foods in restaurants, especially fast-food restaurants.

Be sure to eat sources of omega-3 fats: oily fish, fortified eggs, soy foods, walnuts, flax, and hemp seeds.

Protein

Your daily intake should be between 50 and 100 grams on a 2,000-calorie-a-day diet. Eat less protein if you have liver or kidney problems, allergies, or autoimmune disease. Eat more vegetable protein, especially from beans, in general, and soybeans, in particular, and less animal protein, except for fish and reduced-fat dairy products. Avoid protein supplements.

Vitamins and Minerals

Eating a diet high in fresh foods with plenty of fruits and vegetables will provide most of the micronutrients you need. In addition, I recommend supplementing the diet with the following:

- vitamin C, 100 mg twice a day
- vitamin E, 400 to 800 IU of a natural form (d-alpha tocopherol together with other tocopherols)
- selenium, 200 mcg of a yeast-bound form
- mixed carotenoids, 25,000 IU
- a B-complex vitamin providing at least 400 mcg of folic acid
- calcium, 1,200 to 1,500 mg, preferably as calcium citrate.

Fiber

The optimum diet should provide 40 grams of fiber a day. You can achieve this by increasing your consumption of fruits (especially berries), vegetables (especially beans), and whole grains. Ready-made cereals can be good fiber sources, but read labels to make sure they give you at least 4, and preferably 5, grams of bran per one-ounce serving.

Protective Phytochemicals

To get the maximum natural protection against cancer, degenerative diseases, and environmental toxicity, eat a variety of fruits, vegetables, and mushrooms, and drink tea, especially green tea.

Water

Try to drink six to eight glasses of pure water a day or drinks that are mostly water (tea, very diluted fruit juice, sparkling water with lemon). Use bottled water or get a home water purifier if your tap water tastes of chlorine or other contaminants or you live in an area where the water is suspected of being contaminated (see page 31). I recommend that you drink tea regularly for its antioxidant effects, especially green tea. Decaffeinated forms are available.

If you drink alcohol, red wine is probably the best choice because of the antioxidant effect of the red pigments (see page 39). I do not recommend using any form of alcohol excessively or on a daily basis.

Now, how can you put all of this information into practice? The recipes that Rosie and I have devised for this book are mostly consistent with the recommendations for the optimum diet, except for some desserts, which should be reserved for special occasions. You also have to think about shopping, menu planning, time management in the kitchen, and the storage and use of leftovers. Throughout *The Healthy Kitchen* you will find sidebars that address some of these matters. In her recipes, Rosie frequently offers tips from her kitchen to help you simplify food preparation and make the most efficient use of time in your kitchen. Before I end this chapter, I'd like to give you some general advice on putting meals together that take account of the facts of human nutrition.

A first consideration is whether the day's meals approximate the number of calories you need and the right amounts of macronutrients and micronutrients. For example, if you are going to have a main course of chicken or fish for dinner, you may not want to serve a protein-rich breakfast. If you are going to have a dish with a high-fat content, try to cut back on fat in the other dishes you eat. If you are serving a high-glycemic-index carbohydrate food like waffles, make sure to serve berries with them to lower the GI of the meal.

Where will you get your omega-3 fatty acids today? From fish? Walnuts?

Fortified eggs? Flax seeds? Ask yourself how you can get the recommended number of servings of fruits and vegetables in a day. Here is one possibility: have a banana and a glass of orange juice with breakfast, two cups of salad and some vegetable juice at lunch, a cup of broccoli with dinner, and some berries and a slice of melon for dessert. That will easily take care of your needs for micronutrients.

In planning menus, think about the preparation time involved, so that you do not find yourself in a last-minute frenzy. What can you prepare in advance? If you are making an elaborate main dish, you might want to serve simple sides to accompany it. Do you expect to have leftovers? If so, think about how you can use them in later meals. By getting in the habit of planning in this way, you can make your healthy kitchen an efficient one also.

Rosie and I want you to have fun in the kitchen, not to knock yourself out. We hope this book will help you discover the pleasure of making, serving, and eating food that is both good and good for you. **—A.W.**

Stocking the Pantry

In general, most all of my recipes call for ingredients that are readily available, but occasionally you'll come across something that has to be bought in a specialty store, such as an Asian, Middle Eastern, or health food market. In those instances I have alerted you and indicated where the item is to be found. But there are certain ingredients that I use frequently which you will want to have on hand on your pantry shelf or in your refrigerator so you'll know they are there when you want to make a recipe from this book.

So let's stock the pantry before we begin.

Oils

Toasted-sesame oil and olive oil are essential for sautéing and adding flavor and texture to a dish. Grapeseed and walnut oil are optional but good to have for salad dressings and for sautéing, particularly grapeseed because of its high smoke threshold. Note that we always call for toasted-sesame oil, which is the Asian variety but it is readily available these days in supermarkets. Store oils in a cool, dark place and don't buy more than you can use up in a month or so.

Asian Products

Soy sauce: We always call for a natural soy sauce, such as tamari (see Andy's comments on page 58). Available at supermarkets. Get a good supply; it keeps indefinitely.

Mirin: A sweet, low-alcohol rice wine that adds an aromatic flavor to many dishes. Probably available at most supermarkets, but you may have to get it at an Asian grocery store. Keeps well, unrefrigerated.

Rice vinegar: Milder than Western-style vinegars, although you could substitute apple cider vinegar. Available at most supermarkets these days; otherwise try an Asian market.

Coconut milk: Available in cans in most supermarkets—low-fat variety preferred. Store in a lidded jar and refrigerate after opening; keeps for up to ten days.

Wasabi: This is a fiery root-herb that resembles horseradish, although it is not related to it. It is used frequently in Japanese dishes. Available in specialty and Asian stores in either powder or paste form. Use sparingly. Refrigerate well-sealed after opening.

Miso paste: Made from soybeans. Available in Asian grocery stores. Organic, brown-rice miso or light yellow preferred. Refrigerate after opening. Keeps a long time.

Pasta

I have recipes using buckwheat and bean-thread noodles as well as Italian-style pasta. Look for the former in Asian grocery stores.

Rice and Grains

You'll need brown, basmati, jasmine, and (optional) wild rice. Also, quinoa, bulgur wheat, cornmeal, couscous, oat bran, and millet. All these are best bought at a health food store where you can get organic products; buy them in bulk if you have a big household and are going to use them a lot, and store them in tightly sealed jars on the pantry shelf, except during very hot, humid weather when you might want to refrigerate the grains.

Flour

I use both all-purpose white flour and whole wheat flour as well as whole wheat pastry flour. Pastry flour is a high-starch, fine-textured flour that makes delicate pastries and cakes.

Nuts and Seeds

Walnuts, almonds, pine nuts, sesame seeds, and sunflower seeds are frequently used. Try to get organic nuts and seeds in health food stores and keep them tightly sealed, in the refrigerator or freezer.

Herbs and Aromatics

Some herbs are so much better when used fresh that it is worth growing your own. (See Rosie's Tips on Growing Herbs, page 100, and Andy's About Herbs, page 98.) But some keep their character and aroma very well when dried, and I would recommend that you have the following dried herbs on hand: thyme, sage, oregano, mint, rosemary, and tarragon. Dried basil loses a lot of its character but when combined with seasonings as in the Cajun mixture below, it is acceptable. Keep your fresh herbs in tightly sealed jars in a cool, dark place, preferably the refrigerator. Dried herbs do not have to be refrigerated. Replace them when they lose their bloom (your nose is your best guide); if they've lost their aroma, throw them out.

Seasonings and Spices

Again, if you cook a lot, you may want to buy the spices you use most frequently in bulk at a health food store. Store in tightly sealed containers in the refrigerator.

Italian seasoning: I call for this quite a lot. If you don't have it on hand, you can make up a batch by crushing and mixing together 1 teaspoon sage, 1 tablespoon thyme, and 1 tablespoon oregano.

Mexican seasoning: You can buy this in a jar or make your own by combining 1 tablespoon garlic powder, 1 tablespoon cumin, and 1/2 teaspoon each black pepper, paprika, onion, and crushed thyme.

Cajun spice blend: Available in jars or make your own by mixing 1 tablespoon paprika, 1/2 tablespoon cayenne pepper, 1 tablespoon salt, 1/2 tablespoon oregano, 1/2 tablespoon basil.

Curry powder: Indian cooks would mix their own but since it is made up of about twenty spices, I recommend that you buy a good prepared brand.

Turmeric: One of the principal spices that go into curry, it is what produces the deep yellow-orange color; it can be a little bitter if you use too much.

Saffron: Very expensive, but a little goes a long way and gives a dish a deep yellow color and a subtle flavor.

Cumin: A spice that gives a distinct flavor to Mexican foods, which I use to give a kick to all kinds of dishes.

Chili pepper: You can buy it powdered, as cayenne, red pepper, or chili powder; as flakes; as chili oil; or as chili paste (the latter should be kept in the refrigerator after opening). If you don't have exactly what is called for you can use the above interchangeably, but it is hard to give exact measurement equivalents, so you will have to let your tastebuds guide you. Add a little, taste, and then use more if you like it hot.

Paprika: A Hungarian sweet chili powder that gives subtle flavor and brilliant color.

Fennel: A spice with a licorice flavor (but not as sugary sweet as licorice suggests). It is better to buy it whole and grind or crush it as needed. (I call for it sprinkled on tofu and on some vegetables.)

Cinnamon, ginger, cloves, nutmeg, and allspice: These aren't just limited to sweets and baked goods in our recipes, so you'll want to have them on hand to add interesting flavor to some sauces, soups, and stews. Unless used in baking, the ginger we call for is fresh ginger root and it should always be available in the vegetable drawer of your refrigerator. (Allspice is aptly named because it tastes like cinnamon, cloves, and nutmeg combined.)

Nutmeg should be bought whole so you can grate it fresh (the small holes of any grater will do) because once powdered it loses its flavor rapidly. Freshly grated nutmeg perfumes not only sweets but many a savory dish of ours.

Sweeteners

When you want to sweeten desserts or drinks, sugar isn't the only way to go. I use honey, maple syrup, crystallized ginger, and natural fruit preserves.

Onions and Garlic

Fresh is always best. We use these aromatics a lot, so be sure to have them in your vegetable bin (no need to refrigerate). Avoid powdered onion and garlic in any form and never buy the peeled and sometimes chopped garlic you find in jars at supermarkets these days. It's easy to peel a clove of garlic: just smash it with the flat side of a big knife and the skin will split so that it can be pulled off. If you don't like the smell of garlic on your hands, rub some salt on them to remove it.

Fruits

Always try to have lemons, oranges, and limes when in season in your refrigerator. Both of us use them a lot in our recipes. It is also useful to have dried fruits on hand, such as mangoes, apricots, figs, currants, and golden raisins, which keep well in tightly sealed plastic bags.

—R.D.

READING FOOD PRODUCT LABELS

The most important piece of advice I can give you about shopping for food is to read product labels. We are fortunate to live in a country where a great deal of information about food products must be disclosed on labels. It is foolish not to take advantage of that in deciding what to buy.

You can start by reading the list of ingredients on a product. These will be in descending order, from those present in the greatest amount to those present in the least. I recommend that you reject any product whose list of ingredients is too long, the print too fine, or the space on the label barely adequate to contain it. If you do not recognize a lot of the ingredients, that should also be cause for rejection. And think about how you would make something equivalent at home; if the ingredients on the label differ markedly from what you would use in your own kitchen, do not buy the product. Finally, look for the presence of unhealthy ingredients, such as partially hydrogenated oils and artificial colors. (Below, I'll list some other additives to watch out for.)

Next, check the information under Nutrition Facts, starting with calories per serving. Make sure that the serving size is realistic. A bag of chips might say it contains eight or more servings, but you might eat half of it all at once. Consider the breakdown into macronutrients. Note the percentage of fat calories and the kinds of fat present. Also note cholesterol and sodium content. Check the total carbohydrates and the amount of sugar and fiber, if any. Also look for the presence of vitamins and key minerals like iron and calcium.

Here are the basic rules to follow when you are trying to be good label detectives:

- Try to buy foods that contain the same ingredients you would use at home.
- Avoid products that have many unfamiliar ingredients or just too many ingredients.
- Avoid products containing partially hydrogenated oils, artificial colors, artificial sweeteners, nitrites or nitrates, sulfites, potassium bromate, and brominated vegetable oil. In my opinion, all of these pose health risks.

- Minimize consumption of products containing MSG (monosodium glutamate), aluminum, and the preservatives BHA, BHT, and TBHQ. In my opinion, these may pose health risks.
- In checking Nutrition Facts on food labels, make sure the serving size is what you would actually eat, and adjust the arithmetic if it is not.

—A.W.

ALL COMMENTS AND RECIPES FROM DR. ANDREW WEIL ARE PRINTED ON A GREEN BACKGROUND. THE RECIPES AND TIPS FROM ROSIE DALEY APPEAR ON WHITE AND BEIGE.

Breakfast

Eggs Florentine with Orange and Dill Sauce

Scrambled Eggs with Fresh Salsa

Scrambled Tofu

Vegetable "Quiche"

Frittata

Pancakes and Waffles

Frosted Orange Ginger Fruit Salad

Two-Colored Fruit Gazpacho

Granola

Muesli

Multi-Grain Scones

Applesauce Muffins

BREAKFAST

I always eat breakfast, and recommend that you do too. We all need food in the morning to resupply ourselves with sources of glucose, which is not stored in the body and is needed to fuel the brain. Studies show that those who eat breakfast are more productive at school and work than those who skip it. But there is disagreement over what should be eaten for the first meal of the day.

I myself like leftovers. I've never cared for most of the common American breakfast foods and feel just terrible if I eat some of them (pancakes, sweet rolls, and fried potatoes, for example). I do fine on a traditional Japanese breakfast of steamed rice, broiled fish, miso soup, pickled vegetables, seaweed, and green tea. I also like fruit, nuts, some fresh cheese, and olives. You will have to experiment to find out what you like and what works best for you.

In any case, eating breakfast makes it easier to meet your daily nutritional requirements. Research shows that people who eat breakfast get more vitamins A, C, and E, folic acid, calcium, iron, and fiber than those who skip it. They also do better with weight control, because they are less prone to overeat at other meals or load up on high-calorie snacks later in the day.

Perhaps the most common excuse for skipping breakfast is lack of time; but considering the nutritional importance of the first meal of the day, you should try to find ways of eating something in the morning that is quick and easy to prepare. (And I don't mean a cup of coffee and a doughnut.) Breakfast should provide one-quarter to one-third of your day's protein, some good (i.e., low-glycemic-index) carbohydrate, and some fat. Here are some ideas:

- A bowl of whole-grain cereal with calcium-fortified soymilk and some fruit. The most nutritious fruits are kiwi, cantaloupe, papaya, mango, blueberries, strawberries, and bananas. Add a tablespoon of freshly ground flax seeds as a source of essential fatty acids.
- A soy shake: blend one-half cake of silken tofu, 1/2 cup apple juice, 1 cup frozen, organic strawberries, and one banana.
- Keep some hard-boiled eggs on hand, or scramble up a few eggs to eat with whole-grain toast. Include a glass of calcium-fortified orange juice or a container of plain yogurt to which you can add some berries or other fruit.

Finally, if all you take in the morning is coffee, try switching to green tea for the protection it provides against cancer and heart disease. —**A.W.**

Eggs Florentine with Orange and Dill Sauce

The orange-dill sauce drizzled over the poached eggs has a faint fruit flavor due to the orange juice, a spiciness from the balsamic vinegar, and a hint of the exotic, penetrating flavor of turmeric—a spice relative of ginger. This dish makes a vibrant breakfast—colorful, easy, and healthy.

SERVES 6

PER SERVING:

CALORIES 236.2

FAT 12.5 G
  SATURATED FAT
  5.5 G
(46.5% OF CALO-
  RIES FROM FAT)

PROTEIN 11.6 G

CARBOHYDRATE
  20.7 G

CHOLESTEROL
  266 MG

FIBER 2.6 G

❉

1 pound washed spinach, stems removed

ORANGE AND DILL SAUCE

1 egg yolk
1/4 cup freshly squeezed orange juice
1 teaspoon balsamic vinegar
2 teaspoons lemon juice
1/2 teaspoon turmeric
1/2 teaspoon salt

3 tablespoons butter at room temperature
2 teaspoons chopped fresh dill

1 teaspoon white vinegar
6 eggs
3 English muffins, split in half
2 beefsteak tomatoes, sliced

GARNISH

Fresh cracked black pepper (optional)

Fill a medium pot with water and bring it to a boil. Drop in the washed spinach and cook for 3 minutes, stirring several times. Drain the spinach in a colander. Put a bowl or plate directly on top of the spinach, inside the colander, and press down to squeeze all excess water from the leaves. Cover and set aside.

Fill the bottom of a double boiler halfway with water and place over medium heat. Set the top pot over the water and drop in the egg yolk. Add the orange juice and stir until blended. Stir in the balsamic vinegar and the lemon juice, then the turmeric, salt, and butter. Add 1 teaspoon of the dill and whisk until all the ingredients are thoroughly blended and the sauce has a thick creamy consistency (approximately 2 minutes).

Remove the top part of the double boiler and set aside. Pour

Eggs Florentine with Orange and Dill Sauce

the white vinegar into the water in the bottom pot and heat it just to the boiling point. Gently crack the eggs one by one into the simmering water, and poach for 3 minutes. Remove the eggs with a slotted spoon and let the water drip from the spoon so they aren't watery. Transfer the eggs to a warm platter and cover.

Toast the English muffins on the middle rack under the broiler. Remove them from the oven and put them on plates. Place 1 tomato slice on each muffin half and spoon 1/4 cup of the cooked spinach on top. Arrange 1 poached egg on top of that and drizzle a spoonful or so of the orange-dill sauce over everything. Sprinkle some of the remaining 1 teaspoon of chopped dill and black pepper (optional) over the sauce as garnish. Serve immediately.

Tips from Rosie's Kitchen

This recipe uses a double boiler. If you do not have one, you can improvise by setting a medium stainless-steel bowl inside a large saucepan, so that the top of the bowl fits snugly onto the top of the pot. If you use this setup, be careful not to burn yourself—the steam from the bottom pot gets very hot!

ANDY SUGGESTS

I would happily substitute olive oil for the butter in the Orange and Dill Sauce.

ARE EGGS GOOD FOR YOU?

It's hard to keep up with medical opinion about eggs. First they were good, then they were bad, now they're good again. Egg yolks contain a dazzling array of essential vitamins and minerals, particularly vitamins A, D, E, and K and iron, while the whites are a great source of high-quality protein. The egg's once-tarnished reputation had to do with its yolk, a source of saturated fat and cholesterol. As fat and cholesterol became Public Health Enemies Numbers One and Two, health-conscious consumers scratched eggs off their shopping lists. The egg industry then launched advertising campaigns to tell us exactly how many eggs a week are safe to eat without increasing the risk of heart disease. The really interesting news, however, is that certain eggs can actually improve cardiovascular health because they provide omega-3 fatty acids.

My favorite source of omega-3s is fish, particularly salmon and sardines. Flax seeds, hemp seeds, and walnuts are other sources. Eggs may now join these foods, provided that hens get omega-3s in their diets, which in turn will be incorporated in the yolks of their eggs. Most of the eggs in grocery stores come from factory-farmed chickens, which do not get to eat the required sources, such as soybeans and greens. In order to obtain the benefits you want from eggs, choose those from free-ranging, organically fed hens.

Recently, farmers have begun to produce "designer" eggs, containing more omega-3 fatty acids than regular ones. They do this by fortifying chicken feed with a meal made from algae or flax. These new eggs taste better than regular eggs—and they're better for you. They also cost more, but I think they're worth the extra money.

Even if you eat only the best eggs, you should still not eat them with abandon. Dietary cholesterol may not be as great a culprit as many people think—its negative effect on serum cholesterol is dwarfed by the effect of saturated fat in most people's diets—but whole eggs turn up in so many prepared dishes and processed foods that we can easily end up eating too many of them, especially in combination with sugar, milk, cream, butter, and cheese, classic recipes for atherosclerosis and heart disease. You can often substitute egg whites for whole eggs in recipes or even leave out eggs altogether. Experiment. If you like eggs, I think it's fine to eat one or two a day, as long as you cook them without a lot of fat and use them in dishes that are consistent with the guidelines for healthy eating. **—A.W.**

Scrambled Eggs with Fresh Salsa

There are two words for this dish: easy and nourishing. Everybody has time to make scrambled eggs! This meal is a good combination of protein from the eggs and carbohydrate from the bread. If you want to forgo the toast, wrap the scrambled eggs inside of a warm whole-wheat tortilla to make an egg burrito. No matter how you serve the scrambled eggs, the fresh salsa is what really makes this traditional breakfast food better than usual.

Keep in mind that if you are concerned about cholesterol, you can make this dish using only egg whites and get just as much nutritional value from it.

SERVES 6

PER SERVING:

CALORIES 204.9

FAT 8.2 G
  SATURATED FAT
  2 G

(33.3% OF CALORIES FROM FAT)

PROTEIN 10.2 G

CARBOHYDRATE
26.5 G

CHOLESTEROL
216 MG

FIBER 4.6 G

SALSA

1 bunch cilantro (1/2 cup cilantro
  leaves)
1 cup chopped tomatoes
1/4 cup diced red bell pepper
1/4 cup diced red onion
1 small jalapeño pepper, seeded
  and minced
2 tablespoons freshly squeezed
  lime juice

1 tablespoon olive oil
1/2 cup sliced mushrooms

1/2 cup sliced green onions or
  scallions
1/2 cup chopped red bell pepper
1/2 cup chopped yellow or green
  bell pepper
6 whole eggs
1 teaspoon salt
1/4 cup skim milk

GARNISH

6 slices whole grain bread
6 slices honeydew melon

Make the salsa: Hold the cilantro under running water to wash off the dirt. Pinch the leaves off the stems, coarsely chop the leaves, and put them in a small bowl with the remaining salsa ingredients. Toss thoroughly until everything is blended together. Cover and refrigerate until ready to use.

Smear a nonstick medium sauté pan with 1/4 teaspoon of the oil and set it over medium heat. Sauté the mushrooms, onions, and peppers in the pan, tossing them occasionally, until limp, about 2 minutes. Remove from the heat.

Whisk the eggs, salt, and milk together in a small bowl. Coat the bottom of a separate pan with the remaining olive oil, set it over low heat, pour in the eggs, and partially cook them for 3 minutes, stirring with a wooden spoon until they are no longer runny. Transfer the partially cooked eggs to the pan with the vegetables and cook everything together for 1 minute, stirring with a wooden spoon or spatula. Remove from the heat and cover to keep warm.

Cut each bread slice diagonally, put them on a cookie sheet, and toast them under the broiler on the lower rack for less than 30 seconds on each side. Serve the eggs with toast, a slice of honeydew melon, and a small ramekin of salsa.

Scrambled Tofu

Don't worry, you egg eaters, you aren't deprived of flavor here. So have some variety in your breakfasts, alternating between eggs and tofu (see more about tofu from Andy on page 192). This dish is light, well seasoned, and, like eggs, full of protein for get-up-and-go energy. Turmeric is what lends the color and mild flavor to this dish.

SERVES 6

PER SERVING:

CALORIES 98.3

FAT 7.5 G
    SATURATED FAT
    1 G
(65.9 % OF CALO-
    RIES FROM FAT)

PROTEIN 5.5 G

CARBOHYDRATE
    3.5 G

CHOLESTEROL
    0 MG

FIBER 1.3 G

16-ounce block firm tofu
3 cloves garlic, peeled and sliced
    thin (1 1/2 tablespoons)
3 tablespoons diced red bell
    pepper
2 tablespoons olive oil
1/2 teaspoon turmeric
1/2 teaspoon salt
1/4 teaspoon freshly ground
    black pepper

3/4 cup sliced green onions, scal-
    lions, chives, or 1/2 cup minced
    onion
2 teaspoons soy sauce

GARNISH

Fresh salsa (page 8)
Corn tortillas

Drain the tofu and crumble it, using clean hands. Sauté the garlic and diced pepper with the olive oil in a medium sauté pan on medium heat, for about 2 minutes. Stir in the crumbled tofu first, then add turmeric, salt, pepper, green onions (scallions, chives, or onions), and soy sauce. Cook the tofu for 3 more minutes, stirring occasionally. Serve with salsa and warm corn tortillas.

Tips from Rosie's Kitchen

You can use the scrambled tofu to make a "tofu-salad sandwich" with lettuce and tomato, as opposed to an egg-salad sandwich, or you can mix the scrambled tofu with a little bit of the Pesto (page 160) for more of a side-dish type food.

Vegetable "Quiche"

This fresh vegetable "quiche" is made with a light, crispy potato crust and a filling of vegetables and herbs and spices.

This "quiche" makes a wonderful morning brunch or lunch or a simple dinner, served with a salad and a small, toasted baguette. If you should not be eating egg yolks, you can make it using only the egg whites.

1/2 cup purified water
1/4 cup sun-dried tomatoes
1/2 pound asparagus (about 2 cups chopped) or broccoli florets
1/2 medium onion, chopped
2 cloves garlic, sliced
2 tablespoons olive oil
1 carrot, cut in small cubes (about 1 cup)
5 mushrooms, sliced
1 tablespoon chopped fresh basil, or 1 teaspoon dried
1 tablespoon chopped fresh parsley
1/8 teaspoon chili flakes
1/8 teaspoon freshly grated nutmeg
1/2 teaspoon salt
1 teaspoon freshly ground black pepper
3 small red potatoes, washed and thinly sliced
1/2 cup grated cheese, Pepper Jack or Swiss
1/4 cup milk
1/2 cup low-fat sour cream
6 eggs
1 medium tomato, sliced (seeds squeezed out)
3 tablespoons freshly grated Parmesan cheese

SERVES 8

PER SERVING:

CALORIES 205

FAT 12.6 G
  SATURATED FAT
  4.9 G
  (53.8% OF CALO-
  RIES FROM FAT)

PROTEIN 10 G

CARBOHYDRATE
  14.3 G

CHOLESTEROL
  175 MG

FIBER 2.3 G

Preheat oven to 375°F.

Boil the water, pour over the sun-dried tomatoes, and allow to soak for about 15 minutes until they become soft and plump. Strain off any remaining liquid, and coarsely chop.

Cut off about 1 inch of the coarse ends of the asparagus stalks and discard or save them for soup. Cut the remaining stalks into about 6 pieces or chop coarsely. If you are using broccoli, cut into florets. Blanch the asparagus by boiling it in a medium pot of water for 2 minutes or less. Asparagus should be bright green and firm to the bite. Drain, rinse the asparagus in cold water, and drain again in a colander.

Sauté the onions and the garlic in the olive oil over low heat until the onions are transparent, approximately 10 minutes. Add the carrots, mushrooms, basil, parsley, chili flakes, nutmeg, salt, and pepper and continue to cook for 5 more minutes. Remove from the heat.

Lightly grease the bottom and sides of a 9-inch pie pan. Line the bottom with the potato slices, overlapping them slightly. Whisk together the cheese, milk, sun-dried tomatoes, sour cream, and the eggs in a large bowl. Mix in the sautéed vegetables and the blanched asparagus, coating everything with the cheese, milk, and egg liquid, then pour into the potato-lined pie pan. Arrange the tomato slices on top and sprinkle with Parmesan cheese. Bake for 1 hour, covering after 45 minutes if top browns. Completely baked quiche should be very firm. Let cool 15 minutes before slicing and serving. Leftovers can be wrapped and kept in the refrigerator for up to 3 days.

Tips from Rosie's Kitchen

Try to grate fresh nutmeg and Parmesan cheese yourself because it makes a noticeable difference in the flavor.

Drop the potato slices in cold water to prevent them from discoloring.

To Blanch Fruits and Vegetables: *Boil them for about 2 minutes and then plunge them into cold water—this stops the cooking and sets the color. Blanching is also done to loosen the skins of fruits or vegetables such as plums or tomatoes.*

SPICES AND SPICY FOOD

Skillful use of spices is a mark of a good cook. Once precious beyond measure for their ability to preserve food and mask off-tastes in days before refrigeration, the spices of the world are now available to anyone in the nearest supermarket. You just have to learn how to work with them.

A good starting point is to take one at a time. Get to know its aroma and flavor and think about which foods you would want to taste it in. Try allspice, the tiny dried fruit of a West Indian tree, so called because it is reminiscent of clove, nutmeg, and cinnamon. Recipes often tell you to add allspice to sweets like cookies, but it is quite wonderful in savory dishes like beans and soups. Cumin is a major spice in Latin America, the Middle East, and India, extremely versatile, and a good one to experiment with. In India it is usually used with coriander, the two together forming a backbone of the aromatic personality of curry. Chinese cooks often use ginger and garlic together in stir-fries. Try that combination—both are assertive flavors and somehow complement each other.

After you gain familiarity with individual spices and have a sense of how and when you want to employ them, you can play with combinations. It is also important to develop a sense of how much spice to add, because too little will not command attention and too much can detract from the dish as a whole. A tomato sauce made too pungent with marjoram and oregano is a disaster, as is a stuffing with too much sage. Knowledge here comes with practice and a lot of tasting along the way. Remember: You can always add more.

When most people talk about spicy food, they mean hot and spicy, particularly from the presence of chile, black pepper, mustard, ginger, and other hot spices. But food can be spicy without being pungent. In Ayurveda, the traditional system of lifestyle medicine from India, food is generally prepared without the hot spices but with liberal amounts of aromatic ones like cardamom, cumin, and coriander. Some people say that spicy food does not agree with them, failing to notice that the hot and spicy food they have encountered may have been poorly prepared, greasy, or otherwise likely to cause digestive distress. Most authorities agree that judicious and balanced use of spices stimulates appetite and digestion, and that many spices have specific beneficial effects. For example, ginger and turmeric are powerful anti-inflammatory agents, and garlic is a natural antibiotic.

Make sure the spices you use are fresh. Protect them from light and heat (I keep mine in the refrigerator), and throw them out if their colors and aromas fade. I can't imagine cooking without spices. They enable me to enhance, adjust, and balance the flavors of my dishes and are essential to me when I cook. —**A.W.**

Frittata

Frittatas, or Italian omelets, are a bit easier to make than omelets, though the techniques are similar. I like frittatas because they are a substantial dish—dense with eggs, vegetables, and seasonings. You can eat a slice or two for breakfast, brunch, or lunch, or you can warm up a slice for a quick dinner on those evenings when you get home late from work. I like to serve the frittata with a mixed green salad.

SERVES 6

PER SERVING:

CALORIES 166.4

FAT 13 G
  SATURATED FAT
  3.3 G
(67.8 % OF CALO-
  RIES FROM FAT)

PROTEIN 7.9 G

CARBOHYDRATE
  6 G

CHOLESTEROL
  183 MG

FIBER 1.7 G

5 eggs
2 tablespoons grated Parmesan
  cheese
1 clove garlic, finely chopped
1/4 cup chopped onion
1 tablespoon olive oil
1 teaspoon Italian seasoning
1/2 teaspoon freshly ground black
  pepper
1/2 teaspoon salt
1/4 cup sliced mushrooms

1/2 cup sliced zucchini
1/2 cup asparagus, coarse ends
  removed, spears cut into 2-inch
  pieces
2 tablespoons grated cheddar
  cheese

GARNISH

1 avocado, cut into wedges
1 tomato, cut into wedges

Preheat broiler.

Lightly beat eggs and Parmesan cheese in a bowl. Put the garlic, onions, and olive oil in an ovenproof sauté pan and cook over medium heat until the onions become limp. Add the spices. Add the mushrooms, zucchini, and asparagus and sauté until the onions are limp and transparent, about 2 1/2 to 3 minutes. Pour the egg batter over the vegetables, shaking the pan to keep the eggs from sticking to the bottom. Loosen the edges of the omelet with a spatula and tilt the pan so that the uncooked part runs around the pan. Just before the eggs are about to set, sprinkle the grated cheddar cheese on top and remove from the heat. Put the pan under the broiler on the highest shelf until the top becomes brown, about 2 minutes. Slide the frittata onto a platter and cut into wedges. Garnish with avocado and tomato wedges. Serve immediately.

Tips from Rosie's Kitchen

For a denser version of this frittata, I replace the zucchini with artichoke hearts and the asparagus with diced potato.

Pancakes and Waffles

The aroma and taste of homemade pancakes or waffles is irresistible! The batter in this recipe makes feathery light pancakes, or light and crispy golden waffles.

You'll definitely want to make these for a breakfast or brunch with friends or family, or on that free weekend morning.

4 eggs
1/3 cup freshly squeezed orange juice
1 teaspoon pure vanilla extract
1 1/4 cups milk
1 1/2 cups unbleached white flour
1/2 cup whole wheat pastry flour
1 teaspoon baking powder
1/4 teaspoon salt

FOR MEDALLION-SIZED BLUEBERRY PANCAKES

1 pint blueberries, washed

FRESH FRUIT COMPOTE FOR PLAIN PANCAKES

1 pint strawberries, washed, hulled, and sliced in half
1 pint blueberries, washed
1/2 cup pure maple syrup

WAFFLE TOPPING (Per Serving)

1/2 banana, sliced
1/4 cup walnuts
1 tablespoon pure maple syrup

Crack the eggs, letting the whites fall into a clean, dry mixing bowl and dropping the yolks into a separate bowl. Beat the whites with a mixer, on high speed, or whip with a balloon whisk for about 2 minutes until the egg whites become fluffy and then firm. Be careful not to overmix, or they will flatten out.

Mix the egg yolks with a fork. Add the orange juice and vanilla and whisk everything together until it becomes foamy. Add the milk, barely stirring.

Place the dry ingredients together in a separate bowl and stir with a wooden spoon until everything is thoroughly blended. Slowly stir the dry ingredients into the egg-yolk mixture and continue to mix until all the dry ingredients are wet and there are no clumps of flour. Slowly fold in the egg whites and stir only once or twice.

Prepare the fruit compote by mixing all the ingredients together until all the fruit is completely coated with syrup.

To make medallion-sized blueberry pancakes: Coat the bottom of a flat griddle or large frying pan with 1/4 teaspoon butter or grapeseed oil and set it over medium heat for about 1 minute. Drop 2 tablespoons of batter onto the hot grill, placing them far enough apart so that the pancakes don't touch. Distribute 1 tablespoon (about 5) blueberries on top of each pancake, letting the berries sink into the batter. When bubbles begin to appear on the surface, in about 2 minutes, flip the pancakes over. Cook the blueberry side for 3 minutes. Transfer pancakes to a hot platter and stack them to keep them warm. Continue cooking the pancakes until all the batter is used up. (You do not need to add more butter to the pan.) Serve immediately. Makes 30 medallion-sized pancakes.

To make regular-sized plain pancakes: Coat the bottom of a flat griddle with 1/4 teaspoon butter and set it over medium heat for about 1 minute. Pour 3 tablespoons of batter onto the griddle and cook until bubbles start to form on top of each pancake. Turn them over and cook for about 2 minutes more. Transfer the pancakes to a hot platter and stack them to keep them warm. (No butter is needed after the first set of pancakes.)

When all the batter is used up, top each of 3 pancakes with 3 tablespoons of the fruit compote. Makes 12 regular-sized pancakes.

To make waffles: Preheat the waffle iron until the signal comes on indicating it is ready. Pour enough of the batter evenly over the iron to fill it (usually about 1/2 cup) and let the batter cook until the edges are golden brown. Turn out onto a warm plate and top with the banana, chopped walnuts, and maple syrup.

Tips from Rosie's Kitchen

The orange juice in the batter acts like a natural sweetener, alleviating the need for more syrup.

Separating the eggs is important, because the beaten whites make the pancakes puff up to perfection and the waffles light on the inside and slightly crunchy on the outside. Be sure to incorporate the egg whites slowly into the batter.

If you prefer, you can take some of the blueberries and spoon them into the smaller pancakes as they are cooking. You'll need about 2 tablespoons of blueberries to sprinkle on each pancake.

Frosted Orange Ginger Fruit Salad

For the same reasons this fruit salad makes a great breakfast, it also makes a great snack. It is light, naturally sweetened, and smothered in a smooth yogurt and ginger topping. Often, we find ourselves so busy that we quickly grab less-healthy foods to satisfy us. Make this ahead of time and keep it in the refrigerator, or take it to work in a covered container.

SERVES 12

PER SERVING:

CALORIES 84.6

FAT 0.9 G
  SATURATED FAT
  0.5 G
(12.3% OF CALO-
  RIES FROM FAT)

PROTEIN 1.3 G

CARBOHYDRATE
  13.8 G

CHOLESTEROL 9 MG

FIBER 2 G

2 cups washed and sliced fresh strawberries
2 cups grapes
1 cup washed, cored, and diced apples
3 oranges, peeled, seeded, and cubed
1/4 cup freshly squeezed orange juice (from the 3 peeled, seeded, and cubed oranges)

1 cup plain low-fat yogurt (optional)
1/2 cup chopped crystallized ginger
2 tablespoons honey

GARNISH

12 sprigs mint

Toss all the fruit together in a medium bowl. Whisk the orange juice, yogurt, ginger, and honey in a separate bowl. Pour the dressing over the fruit. Cover and refrigerate for at least 2 hours to marry the flavors.

Spoon the coated fruit into 12 small dessert dishes or parfait glasses. Garnish each with a sprig of mint.

Tips from Rosie's Kitchen

Crystallized ginger can be bought at most health-food stores in the bulk-food section. It gives the yogurt a subtle tangy yet sweet taste. If you choose not to use the yogurt, just mix the orange juice, crystallized ginger, and honey to make a glaze for the fruit.

Use a serrated knife when you peel, seed, and cube the oranges, because its edge will cut the flesh cleanly and precisely. Put an orange on a shallow dish or plate to catch the juice; then cut off the top and bottom so both ends are flat. Cut off the rounded parts of the orange, being careful not to slice too much into the meat. You will have an orange with square corners. Pull the orange open and you'll be able to see the seeds. Pick them out and discard. Save all the juice.

Frosted Orange Ginger Fruit Salad

Two-Colored Fruit Gazpacho

What is more pleasurable to eat than a fruit soup? This isn't only great to eat; it is good to look at because of the color. This gazpacho will cool you and your friends and family off on any warm afternoon.

Serves 6

Per serving:

Calories 208.7

Fat 0.9 g
   Saturated fat
   0 g
(3.7% of calories
   from fat)

Protein 2.4 g

Carbohydrate
   52.1 g

Cholesterol 0 mg

Fiber 9.7 g

11/2 pints fresh raspberries (about 31/2 cups)
20 ounces packaged unsweetened frozen raspberries, defrosted
3 tablespoons sugar
16 ounces lime-flavored sparkling water
6 fresh mint leaves, cut into thin strips

5 kiwi fruits, peeled
2–3 tablespoons freshly squeezed lime juice
1 cup finely diced honeydew melon
1 cup finely diced cantaloupe

Process the raspberries and sugar in a food processor until they are smooth. Strain the raspberry puree through a colander to trap the seeds and transfer it to a big bowl. Add the sparkling water and mint and stir.

Process the kiwis and the lime juice in the food processor until smooth. Pour equal amounts of the raspberry puree into each of 6 small, chilled soup bowls. Pour equal amounts of the kiwi–lime juice puree in the middle of the raspberry purée in each of the 6 bowls. Sprinkle equal amounts of the honeydew melon and the cantaloupe into each soup bowl.

Two-Colored Fruit Gazpacho

FRUIT

Nature clearly intends us to eat fruit. Juicy fruits have evolved into attractive and nutritious foods so that animals, including us, will eat them and disperse their seeds. Natural toxins occur commonly in roots, stems, and leaves to deter predators from eating the plants; they occur very rarely in fruits. Not only does fruit offer quick energy in the form of sugar, it is a cornucopia of health-protective elements: vitamins, minerals, fiber, antioxidant pigments, and other phytochemicals that reduce risks of disease. We all know we should eat fruit, even without nutritionists constantly telling us so.

The problem is often how to get good fruit. The quality of much of the fruit sold in supermarkets in this country is not great. Usually it is unripe, picked in a condition that is favorable to the shippers and distributors but not to those eating it. Worse, the varieties of fruits selected for mass production are often those that merely look good rather than taste good and that again offer more benefits to growers and distributors than consumers. The Red Delicious apple is a case in point. It looks the way people think an apple should, but more often than not it is mealy and insipid, distinctly inferior to varieties produced elsewhere, like the Fuji apple from Japan. I am not sorry to see the American apple industry in trouble as a result of trying to foist the Red Delicious variety on us for so many years—people are no longer buying.

Then there is the problem of residues of agrichemicals. I try to get organic fruit if I can. If I can't, I peel fruit when possible or wash it in a weak soap-and-water solution to remove what's on the surface. In my discussion of organic produce (see page 107), I mention that with some crops, such as strawberries, dangerous systemic pesticides are used that permeate the fruit and cannot be washed off.

Some diet gurus tell people to avoid fruit because of its sugar content. This is nonsense. The nutritional benefits of fruit far outweigh any problems related to the sugar in it. Do keep in mind, though, that fruit juices are concentrated sugar sources, both natural and, in many cases, added. It is not a good idea to let kids drink them to excess or to think of fruit juice as a substitute for water. Dried fruits also contain concentrated sugar. Enjoy them in moderation, but don't overdo.

I am very fond of berries, and am delighted to have read research findings that confirm their nutritional benefits. Not only are they low on the glycemic index, they are full of micronutrients, especially fiber. (Raspberries are one of the best sources; the fiber is in the little seeds.) Berries are particularly rich in pigments called proanthocyanidins that are strong antioxidants and cancer fighters. Blueberries help fight urinary tract infections and have anti-aging properties. But I don't think about all this when I sit down to eat a bowl of berries. I just think about how beautiful and delicious they are. And I am happy that I can keep bags of frozen organically grown berries on hand year-round. Thawed slightly, they make a fine dessert, with or without a scoop of fruit sorbet. **—A.W.**

Granola

Homemade granola makes a great snack alone, as a topping for yogurt or vanilla ice cream, or as a cereal with cold milk or rice milk, topped with bananas or peaches. You can mix anything you want with it, such as raisins, currants, or a different type of nut, to create your own homemade version of granola.

2 tablespoons grapeseed or
   expeller-pressed canola oil
1/2 cup sesame seeds
1/2 cup honey
1 tablespoon pure vanilla extract

2 cups old-fashioned rolled oats or
   milled 3-grain hot cereal
1/2 cup slivered almonds
1 tablespoon orange zest
1/2 cup unsweetened coconut
1 tablespoon cinnamon

Preheat oven to 350°F.

Put the oil, sesame seeds, honey, vanilla, oats, almonds, orange zest, and coconut in a large bowl. Stir everything together until thoroughly coated. Turn out onto a greased baking pan with a rim, and spread out the ingredients. Sprinkle the cinnamon on top and bake for 20 minutes, moving everything around a couple of times with a spatula until all the oats are evenly browned. Let cool for 5–10 minutes. Store in a zip-lock plastic bag in the freezer until ready to eat.

SERVES 6

PER SERVING:

CALORIES 403.3

FAT 20 G
  SATURATED FAT
  4.1 G
(42.8% OF CALO-
  RIES FROM FAT)

PROTEIN 8.7 G

CARBOHYDRATE
  51.4 G

CHOLESTEROL
  0 MG

FIBER 4.5 G

Muesli

SERVES 4

PER SERVING:

CALORIES 193.6

FAT 3.4 G
  SATURATED FAT
  0.8 G
(14.8% OF CALO-
  RIES FROM FAT)

PROTEIN 5.6 G

CARBOHYDRATE
  38.1 G

CHOLESTEROL
  2 MG

FIBER 4.4 G

Instead of eating ordinary breakfast cereals, which can be laden with sugar—or, worse, skipping breakfast altogether—treat yourself. The combination of fruits in this natural cereal makes it sweet to perfection, and the walnuts provide a splash of protein. You will have to soak the oats and the fruit overnight, so plan ahead if you want to take this to work when you anticipate a busy morning. Or enjoy it any day of the week for breakfast.

1 cup old-fashioned rolled oats
4 sun-dried black mission figs,
    pitted prunes, or apricots,
    chopped
4 pitted dates, chopped
2 tablespoons sun-dried raisins or
    dried cranberries
8 almonds, chopped

1/2 teaspoon cinnamon
1 pinch ground nutmeg
1 cup apple juice
1/2 medium apple

GARNISH

1 banana, sliced
1 1/2 cups plain low-fat yogurt

Mix the oats, figs, dates, raisins or cranberries, almonds, cinnamon, and nutmeg together in a large bowl. Pour in the apple juice and soak overnight. After the oats and fruit have absorbed all the apple juice, grate the apple, with the skin, and stir it into the oat mixture until it is thoroughly distributed throughout. Divide evenly among 6 bowls. Garnish each serving with a few slices of banana, top with 1/4 cup yogurt, and serve.

Tips from Rosie's Kitchen

I sometimes use Irish oatmeal or 4-grain cereal to make muesli. Irish oatmeal has a chewier consistency than rolled oats. What I especially like about the 4-grain cereal is that it contains cracked wheat, cracked rye, cracked barley, and rolled oats, so you get a lot of fiber from the cracked grains and a good amount of vitamins B-1, B-2, and E from the rolled oats.

Multi-Grain Scones

These scones are the perfect answer for the morning rush! Unlike a lot of low-fat foods, which can be so loaded with sugar that you feel hungry soon after eating them, these are quite filling—you can eat just half of one and still satisfy the need for morning sustenance. Plus, you get in a nice amount of bran for the day, an appropriate source of roughage.

1 egg
1/2 cup sugar
5 tablespoons grapeseed or
   expeller-pressed canola oil
1/8 teaspoon lemon zest
1/2 cup oatmeal, not instant
1/4 cup wheat bran
1 1/2 cups unbleached white flour
2 tablespoons millet
2 tablespoons poppy seeds

1/2 teaspoon salt
1 tablespoon baking powder
1/2 teaspoon cinnamon
1/2 cup milk

ZESTY LEMON TOPPING

3 tablespoons freshly squeezed
   lemon juice
1/4 cup confectioners' sugar

MAKES 6 SCONES

PER SERVING:
CALORIES 375.3
FAT 10.7 G
  SATURATED FAT
  1.5 G
(25.4% OF CALO-
RIES FROM FAT)
PROTEIN 8.6 G
CARBOHYDRATE
62 G
CHOLESTEROL
23 MG
FIBER 5.2 G

Preheat oven to 375°F.

Whisk the egg, sugar, and oil together in a bowl. Mix the lemon zest and all the dry ingredients together in a separate bowl and stir with a wooden spoon until all of them are evenly dispersed throughout. Slowly add the dry ingredients into the egg, sugar, and oil, and mix to create a thick dough. Add the milk and mix well.

Lightly grease a baking pan. Scoop up tablespoonfuls of the dough and drop them one by one in mounds onto the baking pan, leaving 2 inches of space between. You should have 10 scones. Bake for 15–20 minutes, just until the crust is barely golden brown and the dough is dry. Remove from the oven and let cool for 10 minutes.

With a fork mix the Lemon Topping ingredients until the sugar is completely melded in. Drizzle 1 tablespoon over each scone.

Tips from Rosie's Kitchen

If you want to make these scones completely dairy-free, substitute soy milk for regular milk. I also sometimes add 1 cup of walnuts for crunch and texture.

Applesauce Muffins

These are light and moist because of the applesauce, and they have a surprising blast of chewy fruit and smooth preserves in the middle. I make them to eat with a cup of coffee or tea in the morning, or I'll cut one in half to satisfy a midday or late-afternoon sweet tooth.

MAKES 12 MUFFINS

PER SERVING:

CALORIES 152.8

FAT 1.3 G
  SATURATED FAT
  0.2 G

(8.1% OF CALORIES
  FROM FAT)

PROTEIN 4.1 G

CARBOHYDRATE
  36 G

CHOLESTEROL
  18 MG

FIBER 3.8 G

1 1/2 cups whole wheat pastry flour
1 cup oat bran
2 teaspoons baking powder
1/2 teaspoon baking soda
1 teaspoon cinnamon
1 teaspoon allspice
1 egg

1/2 cup brown sugar
1/2 cup chopped dates
1 1/4 cups Fresh Applesauce (page 249), or ready-made
1/4 cup raspberry or any all-fruit jam

Preheat oven to 350°F.

Mix the flour, bran, baking powder, baking soda, cinnamon, and allspice in a large bowl. Make a well in the center and add the egg, brown sugar, and dates. Gradually stir in the applesauce. Mix thoroughly.

Fill 12 muffin molds with 1/3 cup of the batter, then drop 1 teaspoon of jam on top of the batter. Drop another 1/3 cup of batter on top of the jam. The jam will fall into the batter when it bakes. Bake for 25–30 minutes, until the tops are light brown.

EATING MINDFULLY

An exercise in mindfulness training, a Buddhist meditation practice, is to put a raisin in your mouth and see how long you can keep it there while paying attention to its taste and texture. Mindfulness is the technique of bringing all of our awareness to the here and now, to the sensations in our bodies and our breathing, for example, rather than letting much of it slip away in contemplation of the past and future or of other subjects that are not real. The assumption is that when we act with full awareness, our actions are more likely to achieve what we intend, and that when we feel with full awareness, we are more likely to feel fulfilled.

Many people perform the act of eating semiconsciously, swallowing food without really tasting it or focusing their attention on the next bite before they have enjoyed the present one. Others talk, read, or watch television while eating, directing their attention incompletely to their food. One consequence of unmindful eating is overeating. Who has not mindlessly shoveled in quantities of popcorn or chips while watching a movie or staring at a television screen? Another consequence of unmindful eating is failure to get full sensory pleasure from food.

I notice that if food is really good, conversation at the table is reduced to a minimum, and people concentrate on the enjoyment of the moment. Then they are likely to eat less and enjoy it more.

We eat automatically out of habit. To break the habit requires motivation and practice. Try the raisin exercise to see how long you can go without chewing it up or swallowing it. When food is served to you, take a moment to fully appreciate its appearance and aroma before starting to eat. When you first taste it, try to give it your full attention. I think you will find, as I have, that eating mindfully heightens the pleasure of the experience. **—A.W.**

Beverages

Frozen Fruit Smoothie

Citrus Mango Freeze

Pineapple Almond Shake

Sunrise Orange Grapefruit Juice

Honey Ginger Lemonade

Lemon Cayenne Tonic

Cranberry Barley Tonic

Mulled Cider or Red Wine

Berry Herbal Tea with Orange Slices

Spiced Tea

Matcha

Yogurt-Lime Drink

Low-Fat Vanilla Shake

Raspberry Evening Spritzer

THE IMPORTANCE OF WATER

We hear a lot about the importance of drinking water. Mostly we are told about the quantity of water we should drink, rarely about quality. To my mind water quality is all-important, not only for drinking but also for use in preparing food. If your tap water contains impurities that can hurt you—arsenic or lead, for example—food that you make with it will put those impurities into you, even if you use bottled water for drinking. I have rejected otherwise excellent bread because it tasted of chlorine to me, obviously from the chlorinated water used to make the dough.

I might use tap water to boil pasta or steam or boil vegetables. In these cases the water is mostly not consumed. But if I'm making soup or adding water to a recipe, I want it to be free of toxic impurities as well as unpleasant odors.

Bottled water is convenient, but over time it is expensive. And unless the manufacturer provides good information about its purity—in Europe they are more rigorous about this, and we should be in America too—you may be paying for a product that is not significantly better than tap water. I have long had a water-purifying system in my home and enjoy having an adequate supply of pure water for both drinking and cooking at reasonable cost. Because many different types of systems are available, I recommend that you do some homework before investing in one. A good first step is to have your water tested to determine what kind of impurities it contains.

I use a steam distiller to purify my water, because I believe distilled water is the cleanest you can get. Home distillers are efficient and convenient, but the initial cost is higher than that of other methods. If the main problem is off-odors or tastes, as from chlorine, you may be happy with a simple carbon filter. Another system I recommend is a carbon-block–KDF unit, which fits under the sink and runs the water through two cartridges (which must be changed periodically), one containing solid carbon, the other an alloy of copper and zinc. It removes most of the common impurities and is reasonably priced.

You can find more information on toxins in water and ways to remove them by consulting my book *Eight Weeks to Optimum Health*.

And remember to drink enough water—six to eight glasses a day. This can include tea, mineral water, or sparkling water with a hint of fruit juice. —**A.W.**

Frozen Fruit Smoothie

SERVES 3

PER SERVING:

CALORIES 75.7

FAT 0.3 G
  SATURATED FAT
  0.1 G
(3.1% OF CALORIES
  FROM FAT)

PROTEIN 0.6 G

CARBOHYDRATE
  19.1 G

CHOLESTEROL 0 MG

FIBER 1.3 G

Frozen fruit smoothies are great for snacks, breakfast, or an after-dinner pleasure. You'll need to freeze the bananas for a couple of hours in a zip-lock bag or lidded plastic container. Frozen bananas act like fruity ice cubes, giving the smoothie a thick consistency that makes it so much fun to drink.

1 cup peeled and sliced bananas, frozen

1 cup peeled and sliced fresh peaches, or washed, hulled, and sliced strawberries

1 1/2 cups unfiltered apple juice

GARNISH

1 sprig mint or a small handful fresh berries

Put all the ingredients in the blender. Cover and blend on low speed until smooth. Pour into 3 large wineglasses and serve immediately. Garnish with mint leaves or berries.

Tips from Rosie's Kitchen

You may need to pulse the fruit when blending to break it up. You can also turn off the blender and use a wooden spoon to shift the fruit around, and then blend again until smooth. To cut down a little on the acidity of the fruit, and to add some calcium and protein to the smoothie, you can add 2 tablespoons yogurt or your favorite soy/whey protein powder. Most blenders have only the capacity to make 3 servings of this smoothie at a time. If you want more just repeat the procedure.

   To Blanch Almonds (to remove their skins): *Drop them into a small saucepan of boiling water, and boil for 5 minutes. Strain the almonds and rinse with cold water to cool them. With your fingers, rub and squeeze the almonds to remove the brown skin, which will slide off easily. This is the part that children love. Sometimes the almonds pop out of their skins so readily that they skid across the floor.*

Citrus Mango Freeze

I serve this with Chicken Tostadas (pages 217–18) because it has the same kind of festive feel to it, but you can make this any time you're in the mood for a cold blast of blended fruit.

3 mangoes, sliced (about 4 cups), or 4 cups frozen mango slices
3/4 cup freshly squeezed orange juice
1/4 cup freshly squeezed lime juice
1/4 cup freshly squeezed lemon juice

1/2 cup ice, crushed or cubes
1/2 cup seltzer water

GARNISH

6 fresh strawberries, hulled
1 lime, sliced

Put the mango slices and the juices in a blender. Add the ice and seltzer and blend until smooth. Divide among 6 small martini glasses. Drop 1 strawberry in the middle of each and garnish the rims with a lime slice. Add fancy straws for added color and fun.

SERVES 6

PER SERVING:

CALORIES 133.1

FAT 0.9 G
    SATURATED FAT
    0.1 G
(5.4% OF CALO-
    RIES FROM FAT)

PROTEIN 1.8 G

CARBOHYDRATE
    33.9 G

CHOLESTEROL 0 MG

FIBER 5.9 G

Pineapple Almond Shake

The almonds in this invigorating shake make it a terrific source of protein, and blanching your own almonds is a great kitchen activity for kids.

1/4 cup blanched almonds
1 cup roughly chopped fresh pineapple
1/2 cup ice, crushed or cubes

1/2 teaspoon pure maple syrup
1/4 cup rice milk or soy milk
1/2 cup pineapple juice

Grind the almonds in a blender to a fine powder, as for making Andy's nut milk (pages 34–5). Add all the ingredients and blend until smooth. Pour into 3 large drinking glasses. (If you want to make more, repeat the recipes. Most blenders will accommodate only enough for 3.)

SERVES 3

PER SERVING:

CALORIES 96.7

FAT 5.2 G
    SATURATED FAT
    0.5 G
(45.5% OF CALO-
    RIES FROM FAT)

PROTEIN 2.5 G

CARBOHYDRATE
    11.6 G

CHOLESTEROL 0 MG

FIBER 1.3 G

GOT (TOO MUCH) MILK?

A great deal of propaganda from the dairy industry tells us that we never outgrow our need for milk and that milk is nature's perfect food. I'm sure it is for baby cows, but even they quickly outgrow their need for it. In nature, animals drink milk only in infancy. And throughout the world a great many people consider it distinctly unwise to drink milk. In fact, most people, other than those of Northern European origin, cannot digest lactose, the sugar in milk. As they grow out of childhood, they stop making the enzyme needed to break it down and experience major digestive upsets—bloating, cramps, and diarrhea—if they drink milk.

Butterfat, the fat in cow's milk, is the most saturated fat in our diet. In many dairy products, such as cream, sour cream, butter, ice cream, and cheese, the percentage of butterfat is much higher than that of milk. Butterfat is a principal contributor to high cholesterol levels in the blood and to atherosclerosis, the artery-clogging disease that leads to heart attacks and strokes.

The protein in milk, casein, irritates the immune system in people with certain inherited predispositions (such as a propensity for allergy and autoimmunity). Casein also stimulates mucus production and so tends to aggravate chronic bronchitis, sinusitis, and ear infections. Introduced too early in life to susceptible people, cow's milk can trigger the onset of juvenile diabetes, asthma, eczema, and a variety of allergic conditions.

In addition, most commercial milk contains residues of antibiotics, drugs, and hormones, which are used to keep dairy cows producing abundantly. Milk also contains environmental toxins that cows concentrate in their fat. So clearly I have reservations about the dairy industry's contention that milk is a health food.

A number of milk substitutes—made from soybeans, rice, oats, potatoes, and almonds—are on the market. Except for soy milk, these are not protein sources, which must be kept in mind if they are given to children in place of cow's milk. Many of them are fortified with calcium, none contain lactose or casein, and all have fats that are much better than butterfat for our bodies. Some are sweetened and flavored and work well on cereal or in beverages; others taste insipid or unpleasant. The best work well in recipes—soups or sauces, for instance—that call for milk or cream. To cut down on your intake of cow's milk, experiment with these products to find ones you like.

One option is nut milk, which you can make yourself.

To Prepare Nut Milk: Grind raw nuts (cashews and blanched almonds are delicious) to a fine powder in a blender or food processor, then add water and blend at high speed for two minutes. The ratio of water to nuts determines the richness of the end result—the "milk"—which can be made as heavy as cream for pouring over berries or as lean as skim milk. You can improve the texture of nut milk by straining it through a fine sieve, pressing as much liquid as possible from the residue, and discarding the residue. You can then use the nut milk in any recipe, such as a cream soup. It offers these advantages: no lactose, no casein, and monounsaturated fat instead of saturated. I use cashew milk instead of coconut milk in Thai curries. It is delicious and much better for you than the saturated fat of coconut. **—A.W.**

Sunrise Orange Grapefruit Juice

The cool, invigorating flavor of this fresh-squeezed citrus fruit juice will liven up your morning. Just a small amount will give you your daily supply of vitamin C without any added preservatives, sugars, or acids that you might find in store-bought juices. You'll be amazed at the intensity of the taste that just-squeezed juice offers. Pink grapefruits are my favorite because the pink they add to the orange juice puts the sunrise in each glass. I like the way they taste and they are higher in vitamin A than their other grapefruit relatives. The sweetness of the oranges and the mildly bittersweet taste of the grapefruit make a spirited drink.

4 oranges   2 grapefruits

Cut the oranges and grapefruits in half and squeeze, using a hand juicer. Mix both juices together in a small pitcher, serve in small (4-ounce) juice glasses, and enjoy!

MAKES 6 SERVINGS

PER SERVING:

CALORIES 86.3

FAT 0.4 G
  SATURATED FAT
  0.1 G
(3.7% OF CALORIES
  FROM FAT)

PROTEIN 1.8 G

CARBOHYDRATE
  22.6 G

CHOLESTEROL 0 MG

FIBER 4.1 G

Front: Berry Herbal Tea with Orange Slices; rear left: Citrus Mango Freeze; rear right: Frozen Fruit Smoothie

Honey Ginger Lemonade

Capture the essence of the summer sun and the natural goodness it brings in this invigorating beverage. I like to combine fresh honey my neighbor gives me with fresh-squeezed lemon juice and a twist of ginger to add a unique kick to this old-time favorite summer refresher.

1 cup freshly squeezed lemon
   juice
1/2 cup honey
1/4 cup peeled fresh ginger slices

7 sprigs fresh mint
2 cups purified water
4 cups ice cubes

Put the juice, honey, ginger, and 1 chopped sprig of the mint in a large pitcher and stir, pressing the mint and ginger to release flavor. Add the water and stir until the honey dissolves, then add the ice. Pour into six 10-ounce glasses and garnish each glass with a sprig of mint and a fancy straw.

Tips from Rosie's Kitchen

Children three years old and younger can become seriously ill from honey, so please don't give them a glass of this lemonade. However, you can use local honey to help battle against seasonal allergies for older children and adults. Honey's thick coating with the vitamin C in lemons combine perfectly to soothe a sore throat and help treat a cold. To really combat a cold try Lemon Cayenne Tonic:

Lemon Cayenne Tonic

3/4 cup freshly squeezed lemon
   juice
1/4 cup honey

1 cup purified water
1/2 teaspoon cayenne

Mix everything together to create a syrupy, feel-good tonic. Drink hot or cold.

SERVES 6

PER SERVING:
CALORIES 104.8
FAT 0.1 G
  SATURATED FAT
  0 G
(0.8% OF CALORIES
  FROM FAT)
PROTEIN 0.5 G
CARBOHYDRATE
  28.7 G
CHOLESTEROL 0 MG
FIBER 0.3 G

MAKES 6 SHOT-SIZE
SERVINGS

PER SERVING:
CALORIES 51
FAT 0 G
  SATURATED FAT
  0 G
(0.5% OF CALORIES
  FROM FAT)
PROTEIN 0.2 G
CARBOHYDRATE
  14.4 G
CHOLESTEROL 0 MG
FIBER 0.2 G

Cranberry Barley Tonic

Barley was one of the first grains harvested and cultivated by man. Throughout time, it has been used in breads, cereals, soups, and even curative drinks. This is a very clean beverage that is excellent for those times when you feel you haven't eaten well and want to cleanse your system, or if you want to drink something purifying yet flavorful.

SERVES 8

PER SERVING:

CALORIES 77.7

FAT 0.3 G
  SATURATED FAT
  0.1 G
  (3.7% OF CALORIES
  FROM FAT)

PROTEIN 1.5 G

CARBOHYDRATE
  17.8 G

CHOLESTEROL 0 MG

FIBER 1.8 G

1/2 cup barley   2 cups cranberry juice
3 cups purified water   2 tablespoons raspberries

Put the barley and the water in a large saucepan, cover, and simmer for 1 hour. Remove from the heat and let the water cool briefly. Strain the barley through a fine sieve, reserving the liquid. Mix the barley water with the cranberry juice and pour it into eight 8-ounce glasses. Garnish with 3 raspberries in each glass.

Tips from Rosie's Kitchen

Don't throw away the cooked barley! Use it in place of pasta in the Mixed-Bean-Minestrone Stew (page 126), or to make a barley pilaf, which you can flavor with sun-dried tomatoes.

WINE

Many people throughout the world drink wine with their meals. I am not one of them, I'm afraid. I am not a great consumer of alcohol in any form, and if I am going to drink, I usually prefer premium Japanese sake, which I like cold. (Sake is made from rice and so is technically not wine.) I find it agrees with me more than other alcoholic beverages, never giving me a sour stomach, a headache, or a hangover, all symptoms I experience, not infrequently, from wine.

For some years I have followed the debate about the health benefits of alcohol in general and wine in particular. Here are some of my thoughts on the matter:

Alcohol is known to be toxic to liver and nerve cells. It is also addictive, and the addiction can be hard to break. Many people use alcohol to relax, especially at the end of the workday, and as a social lubricant because of its disinhibiting effects. Used moderately for these purposes, the benefits of alcohol may well outweigh its risks, especially since most of us need to relax. Recently, wine has received a lot of attention for possible beneficial effects on health—especially cardiovascular health, and especially red wine. If red wine, in fact, is heart healthy in ways that white wine and other forms of alcohol are not, the reason must be that there are unique elements in red wine, elements other than alcohol. Likely candidates are the red pigments, because these have significant antioxidant properties and can retard the oxidation of cholesterol in the blood that damages arteries. You can include these same antioxidant pigments in your diet by drinking red grape juice or eating red and purple fruits, especially berries. By doing so you would avoid risks of addiction to alcohol and any of its toxicity. Of course, you would not then get the pleasure that so many people experience from wine.

It is also possible, however, that alcohol itself has healthful as well as harmful properties and that all forms of it provide them, including white wine and spirits. Aside from its relaxing effects, alcohol appears to raise HDL cholesterol, the so-called good cholesterol that circulates in the blood and counteracts the influence of bad LDL cholesterol. Regular aerobic exercise also increases the HDL fraction; otherwise, it is hard to raise good cholesterol without resorting to pharmaceutical drugs.

Whether alcohol improves health directly by some biochemical mechanism or indirectly as a result of relaxing us, the key to using it wisely is moderation. A glass or two of wine with a good meal can be a good thing. Much more than that day in and day out may not be so good. Try saving wine for special occasions or for out-of-the-ordinary meals. Be conscious of the amount you consume at any one meal. If you drink wine regularly, try to give your body one or two alcohol-free days a week.

Finally, be aware that wine contains many additives that do not have to be listed on labels. In general, inferior wines have more of them than superior wines. I think that the unpleasant symptoms I develop from drinking wine are the result of sensitivities to additives, and I experience fewer of them from expensive wine. In recent years more organically produced wines have appeared in both America and Europe, some of very good quality. I prefer them and find that they are much less likely to cause unwanted effects.

My bottom line: Used moderately and with awareness, wine can add to the pleasure of eating and improve both physical and emotional well-being.

—A.W.

Mulled Cider or Red Wine

SERVES 6

PER SERVING:

CALORIES 188.8

FAT 3 G
  SATURATED FAT
  0.6 G
(12.4% OF CALO-
  RIES FROM FAT)

PROTEIN 1.2 G

CARBOHYDRATE
  46.2 G

CHOLESTEROL
  0 MG

FIBER 7.2 G

This smooth and yummy beverage is perfect to serve in the autumn and straight through the holidays for a Christmas brunch or a cold winter evening by the fire. You can use either wine or apple cider. It depends on what you feel is appropriate for the occasion and your guests.

31/2 cups apple cider or 1 bottle
    red wine
1 cup purified water
1/2 cup sugar

2 cinnamon sticks
1/2 lemon, cut into slices
12 whole cloves

Put all the ingredients into a saucepan and bring to a low boil, then reduce the heat and simmer for 3 minutes. Strain and serve in cups or heat-resistant clear glasses.

Berry Herbal Tea
with Orange Slices

I love the idea of fresh fruit in a drink! I use it a lot in the summer when I make tea for my friends and family, and it is always a big hit. You can serve this drink cold during the heat of the day, or warm during the cool of the evening.

3 cups purified water
4 Red Zinger tea bags
1/2 orange, sliced
1 cup apple or cranberry juice

1/2 cup fresh strawberries, washed and hulled, or frozen strawberries, cut in half, or fresh raspberries, washed

Bring the water to a boil in a medium saucepan. Drop in the tea bags and orange slices. Pour in the apple or cranberry juice. Remove from heat. Cover and let the tea steep for 3 minutes. Remove the tea bags. Drop an orange slice into each of 6 heat-resistant glasses, distribute the berries evenly among them, and then pour the tea over. Serve hot or chilled.

SERVES 6

PER SERVING:

CALORIES 28.4

FAT 0.1 G
    SATURATED FAT
    0 G

(3.0% OF CALORIES
    FROM FAT)

PROTEIN 0.2 G

CARBOHYDRATE
    7 G

CHOLESTEROL 0 MG

FIBER 0.5 G

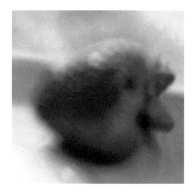

Spiced Tea

SERVES 6

PER SERVING:
CALORIES 39

FAT 0.1 G
  SATURATED FAT
  0 G
(2% OF CALORIES
  FROM FAT)
PROTEIN 0.1 G
CARBOHYDRATE
  9.7 G
CHOLESTEROL 0 MG
FIBER 0.1 G

Drinking hot tea is a pleasure guaranteed to take the chill from your bones in the dead of winter. The ambrosia of spices will warm your kitchen and welcome your guests in from the cold or complete an evening meal.

6 cups purified water
2 chamomile tea bags or 2 tablespoons bulk chamomile tea in a
  tea infuser

2 apple-spice tea bags
2 cups apple juice
Cinnamon sticks (optional)

Bring the water to a boil in a small pan, then remove from the heat. Drop in the tea bags or the infuser and let the tea steep for 5 minutes. Pour in the apple juice and stir. Pour into large coffee mugs and serve. If you wish, add 1 cinnamon stick to each mug.

Tips from Rosie's Kitchen

A tea infuser is a stainless steel mesh basket that holds loose tea leaves and can be bought at any grocery store. If you don't have one, you can just strain the tea through a fine mesh strainer after it has steeped.

COFFEE AND TEA

Coffee is a strong stimulant that can be addictive and can cause or aggravate a number of medical problems. It can irritate both the upper and lower digestive tract, disturb urinary and prostate function, cause or worsen cardiac arrhythmias, and wreak havoc with moods, energy cycles, and sleep patterns. If you enjoy coffee, if it does not affect your physical or mental health, and if you can use it nonaddictively—meaning without suffering withdrawal when you stop— go ahead and drink it. But I'm going to try to persuade you that tea is better for you.

Even though tea leaves contain more caffeine than coffee beans, not as much of it winds up in the finished brew. Most people find tea to be less jangling than coffee and less likely to cause any unwanted symptoms. And more people are becoming aware of its health benefits.

Both green and black teas are made from the same plant, *Camellia sinensis,* an attractive shrub. For green tea the leaves are briefly steamed, then dried. For black tea, the leaves are heaped up and "sweated" before being dried, a natural fermentation process that changes their color, chemistry, aroma, and flavor. Oolong tea, now produced mainly on Taiwan, is in between; shorter fermentation gives it qualities intermediate between green and black tea. Scented teas are mixed with dried flower petals (as in jasmine tea) or essential oils (as in Earl Grey). Herbal teas are made from plants other than *Camellia sinensis* and do not have the beneficial properties of that species.

A number of recent studies on tea—some quite extensive—show that both green and black tea offer significant protection against both heart disease and cancer. This is so because tea has strong antioxidant activity, mainly due to its content of polyphenols, one of which, EGCG, is among the most powerful antioxidants known. Green tea contains more of it than black tea, which is why I recommend it as a daily beverage. Green tea also contains L-theanine, an amino acid that produces a state of relaxed alertness and may account for the difference in the quality of stimulation from that of coffee.

Much of the green tea I see in America is more yellow or brown than green and often tastes like hay. The green tea I drink in Japan is really green and has a rich, aromatic taste with a slight bitterness. The highest quality, *gyokuro,* has a deep, rich flavor. Another form I like very much is *matcha,* powdered green tea that is whisked to a froth in a tea bowl and used in the Japanese tea ceremony. And I sometimes drink *genmaicha,* a mixture of green tea and toasted brown rice that gives the tea a nutty taste. All of these are now available in America at tea shops, from mail-order catalogs, and from online tea suppliers on the Internet. I often order iced tea as a beverage when I eat out, not just in summer but year-round. And I enjoy trying new varieties of tea. I'm currently experimenting with some delicious oolongs and a rare Chinese "white tea" that brews into an almost colorless infusion with a very delicate taste but appears to have even more antioxidant activity than green tea.

Japanese research suggests that for the best effect on health, one should drink about four cups of green tea a day. If you don't want so much caffeine, you can find decaffeinated forms. At the moment, far more Americans are drinking coffee than are drinking tea, but more of us are learning how to select and make good tea, and more high-quality tea is obtainable here—a far cry from the tea bags most of us grew up with. If you are a coffee drinker, try substituting tea on occasion and see how you feel. I predict that we will see a great increase in tea drinking in our land, which I think will be a good thing. —**A.W.**

MATCHA (Japanese Powdered Green Tea)

Matcha is the special green tea used in the Japanese tea ceremony. It is my favorite tea, and I drink a bowl of it every morning. Along with the special utensils used to make it, matcha is becoming more available here. It comes in small cans, usually containing 20 or 40 grams of bright-green, finely powdered tea grown under special conditions. You can order it on the Internet or find it at better Japanese grocery stores. One source of high-quality matcha and kits for preparing it is www.drweil.com.

To reduce the possibility of the matcha powder forming lumps with the addition of hot water, it is best to pass it through a fine sieve (tea strainer). Sift the contents of the can onto waxed paper and then return the sifted powder to the can.

Bring a small quantity of purified water to a boil and remove from heat. Pour a small quantity of this water (about 1/2 cup) into the tea bowl *(cha-wan)* to warm it. Soften the bamboo tea whisk *(cha-sen)* by immersing the end in the hot water for about 10 seconds, then remove it. Empty the bowl and dry it with a paper towel.

Using the bamboo tea scoop *(cha-shaku)* place two heaping scoops (about 1 level teaspoon) of matcha powder in the bottom of the bowl.

Add approximately 1/3 cup of less-than-boiling water (about 180° F.) to the bowl. (By the time you have warmed and dried the bowl the water in the kettle should be about the right temperature.) Boiling water is too hot for matcha; it will damage the flavor of the tea.

Using the tea whisk, first incorporate any stray bits of powder into the water with slow circular or figure-8 strokes, then agitate the mixture vigorously with a back-and-forth motion of the wrist for approximately 15 seconds. The surface of the tea should be completely frothy. *Caution:* To protect the tea whisk, do not rub it or press it against the bottom or sides of the bowl. After each use, rinse it under running cold water. You may wipe the tea scoop clean with a paper towel.

Drink the matcha immediately. In the tea ceremony, Japanese quaff a bowl in three audible slurps, but you can enjoy it at your own pace. It is pleasant to nibble on something sweet while sipping the tea.

Yogurt-Lime Drink

This is a versatile beverage because you have the choice of making it with just yogurt; adding fruit and blending it just enough to transform the drink into a whipped, frothy, chunky fruit beverage; or adding frozen fruit to create a dessert drink. This drink is festive, yet the coconut milk flavored with cinnamon and cloves gives it a mellow flavor.

SERVES 6

PER SERVING:

CALORIES 132.4

FAT 2.6 G
  SATURATED FAT
  2.4 G

(6% OF CALORIES
  FROM FAT)

PROTEIN 2.1 G

CARBOHYDRATE
  21.2 G

CHOLESTEROL 2 MG

FIBER 0.1 G

1/3 cup freshly squeezed lime juice
1 cup plain low-fat yogurt
1/3 cup honey
2 cups purified water
1 tablespoon pure vanilla extract

1/8 teaspoon ground cloves
1/8 teaspoon ground nutmeg
14 ounces canned light coconut
  milk
1/8 teaspoon ground cinnamon

Mix the ingredients together in a bowl. Chill for 2 hours. Pour into 8-ounce glasses, sprinkle cinnamon on top, and serve.

Tips from Rosie's Kitchen

To Create a Low-Fat Tropical Shake: *Add 2 cups frozen fruit, or 1 cup fresh fruit and 1 cup ice. I recommend papaya or peeled and sliced peaches (about 1/2 papaya or 3 peaches). Use a blender to blend everything together. Garnish with a sprinkling of cinnamon and a straw.*

Peach-Yogurt Lime Drink: *For a different kind of fruit taste and some festivity, add 1 pitted peach, sliced in half, to the yogurt-lime drink and pulse it in the blender just enough to blend the fruit but maintain some chunks. Pour 1/2 cup into each of 6 cups and serve. The delicate chunks of peach will color the frothy coconut milk with hues of red, pink, and yellow.*

ANDY SUGGESTS

I would substitute cashew milk (pages 34–5) for the coconut milk.

Low-Fat Vanilla Shake

I came up with this concoction when my diabetic niece was craving a sweet cool treat. The banana, honey, and ice are a good substitute for ice cream, as they thicken, sweeten, and chill this creamy dessert drink. This is a great way to satisfy a sweet tooth without all the fat and sugar you'll find in a regular shake. And this delicious delight is a great way to sneak some calcium, protein, and potassium into your kids, as well as yourself.

1 cup peeled sliced banana (see Tips)
2 tablespoons pure vanilla extract
2 cups ice

2 cups skim milk (or prepared milk alternative)
2 tablespoons honey
2 tablespoons unsweetened cocoa powder (optional)

Put the sliced banana, vanilla, ice, milk, and honey into the blender and blend until smooth. Pour into 6 glasses and add a straw—a shake just isn't complete without a fun straw!

MAKES SIX 1-CUP SERVINGS

PER SERVING:

CALORIES 98.3

FAT 0.3 G
  SATURATED FAT 0.2 G
(3.1% OF CALORIES FROM FAT)

PROTEIN 3.2 G

CARBOHYDRATE 19.9 G

CHOLESTEROL 1 MG

FIBER 0.9 G

Tips from Rosie's Kitchen

When you have more bananas than you know what to do with, don't throw them away! Just peel, slice, and freeze them while they're ripe and put each banana in its own sealed baggie. Not only does this buy you some time for using them all up, but frozen bananas are useful in chilling and thickening this shake and other blended drinks. If you would like a non-dairy drink, you can substitute 1/2 pound silken tofu instead of skim milk (if you do use this substitution, the maple syrup and cocoa combinations really hit the spot). The cocoa powder is a great way to tempt kids into this healthy drink, and if you love a maple flavor, you can substitute maple syrup for the honey in this recipe. Use your imagination and adapt this recipe here and there to suit your own tastes and preferences.

Raspberry Evening Spritzer

This simple blend of fruit, natural sweeteners, tea, and seltzer water is an ideal afternoon or evening drink for a casual gathering with friends or an afternoon surprise during the workweek.

MAKES 8
SPRITZERS

PER SERVING:

CALORIES 144.1

FAT 0.1 G
  SATURATED FAT
  0 G
(0.6% OF CALORIES
  FROM FAT)

PROTEIN 0.4 G

CARBOHYDRATE
  38.6 G

CHOLESTEROL 0 MG

FIBER 1.1 G

1 cup purified water
6 ounces raspberries
1 teaspoon herbal or black tea
  leaves

1 cup honey
1 small orange, washed and cut
  into 8 thin slices
8 cups chilled seltzer water

Bring the water to a boil in a saucepan and drop in the raspberries. Lower heat and simmer for 3 minutes. Remove from heat and sprinkle the tea into the pan. Cover and let steep for 2 minutes. Strain the warm liquid through a fine mesh strainer into a small saucepan, using the back of a large spoon to break up the pulp of the berries and push the liquid through. Add the honey. Stir for about 2 minutes, then chill in the refrigerator.

Place 1 orange slice at the bottom of 8 tall glasses. Pour 1 tablespoon of the chilled raspberry syrup and 1 cup of cold seltzer water into each glass. Stir, add ice, and serve immediately. If you wish, stick a couple of colorful straws in each glass for added color and fun.

Appetizers

Chicken Satay with Peanut Dipping Sauce

Baked Vegetable Wontons

Mediterranean Stuffed Grape Leaves

Broccoli Pancakes

Spanish Seafood Cocktail, Gazpacho Style

Steamed Alaskan Crab Legs

Smoked Fish with Horseradish Sauce

Horseradish Sauce

Thai Shrimp Brochette

Vegetable Nori Rolls

Spinach Toasts

Polenta Triangles with Roasted Bell Peppers

Eggplant Dip

Miso Pâté

White Bean Spread

Goat Cheese Toasties with Sun-dried Tomato and Basil

Stuffed Mushroom Caps with Couscous

OUTDOOR COOKING

Cookouts are more popular than ever, especially since the advent of efficient gas grills that are much easier to use than charcoal-burning devices. I love grilling food outdoors, and I can do it almost year-round in southern Arizona, where I live. But there are some health pitfalls to this kind of cooking.

The typical American barbecue emphasizes large portions of meat and usually skimps on vegetables and whole grains. On my grill, you will find fish, vegetables, and mushrooms. And research findings have clearly established that high-temperature grilling (or broiling) of foods that contain fat and protein produces carcinogenic compounds called heterocyclic amines (HAs) that can raise the risk of colo-rectal cancer in those with a genetic predisposition for it. HAs probably increase risks of other cancers as well.

I have a number of recommendations for protecting yourself from exposure to them. First of all, grill more vegetables and fish and less meat. Animal flesh is more likely to become carcinogenic when it is exposed to high heat. Second, try not to cook animal foods, including fish, to the point of charring. Blackened fish and other animal foods are popular but not healthful. If you are served food this way, try not to eat the blackened outer layer. Third, if you do grill meats, choose leaner cuts, because the more fat, the likelier the grill is to smoke, and the smoke from burning fat is carcinogenic. (Don't inhale it!) Finally, be aware that marinating flesh foods before cooking them may help reduce the formation of HAs, probably because common marinade ingredients act as antioxidants. This is true of citrus juice and spices like turmeric, ginger, and garlic, for example.

Never use charcoal-lighter fluid or self-starting packages of briquettes in a charcoal grill. If you do, you will wind up with residues of toxic chemicals in your food. Instead, use an inexpensive chimney lighter that uses a small amount of newspaper to ignite a mass of charcoal in a large metal cylinder. Some chefs feel that charcoal grills give better results, but gas grills offer great convenience. They are much faster to light and heat and much less polluting of the atmosphere.

Grilled vegetables can be terrific if they are well flavored and well cooked—still crunchy but also tender and sweet. I can't get enough of thick slices of sweet onion, brushed with olive oil, salt, pepper, and maybe sprinkled with herbs, then grilled to perfection. Sweet peppers and mushrooms are also great. In fact, with a portion of grilled salmon or tuna, a green salad, and maybe some rice, I find it hard to imagine a more satisfying experience of outdoor cooking.—**A.W.**

SERVES 6

PER SERVING:

CALORIES 34.4

FAT 0.4 G

    SATURATED FAT
    0.1 G

    (10.2% OF CALO-
    RIES FROM FAT)

PROTEIN 6.4 G

CARBOHYDRATE
    0.5 G

CHOLESTEROL
    16 MG

FIBER 0 G

PEANUT DIPPING
SAUCE

SERVES 6

PER SERVING:

CALORIES 157.1

FAT 9.7 G

    SATURATED FAT
    1.7 G

    (50.6% OF CALO-
    RIES FROM FAT)

PROTEIN 6.6 G

CARBOHYDRATE
    15.2 G

CHOLESTEROL 0 MG

FIBER 8.4 G

Chicken Satay with Peanut Dipping Sauce

Satay, or bite-sized pieces of skewered meat or fish, originated in Indonesia. Traditionally, a peanut sauce is served with satay, but you can serve it with Pineapple Dipping Sauce (page 67) if you or your guests don't like nuts or peanut butter.

PEANUT DIPPING SAUCE

1 cup chopped onions

2 cloves garlic, sliced

3 tablespoons toasted sesame oil

2 cups vegetable stock (page 122)

2 tablespoons natural soy sauce
    (such as tamari)

1 tablespoon Thai chili sauce or 1
    tablespoon chili flakes

1 tablespoon paprika

1 1/2 teaspoons ground cumin

3 tablespoons grated fresh ginger

1 tablespoon honey

1/2 cup natural peanut butter

3 tablespoons chopped fresh
    parsley

3 tablespoons chopped chives

1 tablespoon chopped fresh mint
    leaves

CHICKEN

2 whole boneless, skinless chicken
    breasts, or 4 halves

1/4 cup freshly squeezed orange
    juice

1 tablespoon red or green Thai
    curry paste or 1/8 teaspoon chili
    flakes

Twelve 6-inch wooden skewers,
    submerged in water for 1 hour

Make the Peanut Dipping Sauce: Sauté the onions and garlic in the sesame oil in a sauté pan over medium heat. Cook for 4 minutes, until the garlic turns golden brown. Add the vegetable stock, soy sauce, chili sauce or flakes, paprika, and cumin and whisk until completely blended. Add the ginger, honey, and peanut butter, stir, and simmer for 10 minutes or until the sauce becomes thick. Remove from heat and add the parsley, chives, and mint. Pour 3/4 cup of the sauce into a bowl. Store the remainder in the refrigerator to use later with Slow-Baked Tofu with Stir-Fry or another dish.

Preheat broiler or grill.

Cut each chicken breast into 3 sections by making 2 vertical slices through each one. Mix the orange juice and the curry paste or flakes together in a large bowl and drop in the chicken. Mix well with a spoon, coating the chicken pieces. Cover and refrigerate for 30 minutes.

After the chicken has marinated, secure 1 slice of meat on each skewer by puncturing 1 end of it with the point of the skewer. Sliding the meat down a bit on the skewer, puncture the other end of the meat and pull the chicken piece tight across the skewer. The chicken should lie flat on the skewer. (It is almost as if you are threading the chicken slices.) Repeat the process for all the skewers. Put the chicken on a baking sheet and broil for 2 minutes on each side, or grill over medium heat, spooning a little sauce over each skewer.

Serve the chicken satay on a platter with a sprinkling of chopped mint and the bowl of peanut sauce in the middle for dipping. Makes 12 skewers—2 per person—with 1 tablespoon peanut sauce for each skewer.

Tips from Rosie's Kitchen

Wooden skewers come in lengths of 12 inches and 6 inches. You'll want 6-inch skewers for this recipe, but sometimes it's hard to find this size (they seem to be the most popular), so you can buy the large ones and cut them in half. Soaking them in water keeps them from burning while on the grill. When you are putting the chicken on the skewer, be sure to pierce the meat at the pointed end, not on the end that you cut.

This peanut sauce is a favorite dipping sauce of mine. I often serve it with a stir-fry tofu dinner. If you think the dipping sauce is too thick and you want to change the consistency to more of a dressing, add 1/4 cup rice vinegar. You can double the Peanut Dipping Sauce recipe so you'll have extra on hand in the fridge to top off your favorite stir-fry. It also goes well with Slow-Baked Tofu (page 193).

POULTRY

One of the differences in Rosie's style of cooking and eating and mine is that she uses chicken and turkey and I do not. Poultry is a popular and versatile animal food that offers one great advantage over meat: its fat is mostly external to muscle and can be removed by skinning. In terms of its effect on human hearts and arteries, skinned chicken is a more healthful choice than beef, veal, lamb, or pork, provided you cook it without a lot of added saturated fat. Simple broiling and baking are good ways to prepare it, and Rosie's recipes show you how to do this. Duck and goose have much more fat in them and are more challenging to turn into healthy fare, because the fat of these fowl is highly saturated and contains cholesterol. Wild fowl have much less fat, so little, in fact, that recipes often call for generous amounts of butter or bacon fat to keep their meat moist during roasting.

You will see that I suggest substituting baked tofu for the chicken and turkey in some of Rosie's creations. I do this to show that it is possible to make very acceptable vegetarian versions of them, which I enjoy. I avoid poultry for two reasons, one more personal than the other. I know that I live at the expense of other living things, both animal and vegetable. My daughter, a strict lacto-ovo vegetarian, says she will not eat anything that would run away from her. She will not eat fish because she identifies too much with them. I draw my own line between fish and fowl, recognizing the arbitrariness of that decision.

Aside from the moral question of eating other creatures, I have a number of concerns about the health risks of commercially raised poultry. Free-range chickens and turkeys—those that are allowed to run around and peck for food—are more nutritious than birds that spend all of their lives caged, often in crowded, appalling conditions. The fat from free-range poultry has a better spectrum of fatty acids, and the flesh tastes better. Also, the common birds sold in supermarkets contain significant residues of drugs and hormones used to stimulate their growth. People who eat a lot of them increase health risks—for hormonally driven cancers, such as breast cancer, among others. If you are going to eat chicken and turkey, I urge you to buy organically raised birds that are certified to be free of drugs and hormones. These are more expensive, of course. They are also becoming more available at better supermarkets as well as from catalogs and natural-food stores.—**A.W.**

Baked Vegetable Wontons

I serve these a lot as an appetizer or light finger food when I'm having a small, informal gathering of friends. They are light with barely a touch of crunch on the outside. Enjoy them with the simple Soy and Ginger Dipping Sauce described below or with the Pineapple Dipping Sauce (page 67). You can use it with the Chicken Satay (page 52) or with the fish from the Grilled Fish Tacos (page 210).

This is another great recipe in which to involve kids. Gather them in the kitchen after the preparation of the vegetables is complete and let them help you with the stuffing and folding. It is actually fun and it will make the process move faster.

SERVES 10

PER SERVING:

CALORIES 101.8

FAT 8.4 G
   SATURATED FAT
   1.2 G

(72.8% OF CALO-
   RIES FROM FAT)

PROTEIN 0.8 G

CARBOHYDRATE
   6.7 G

CHOLESTEROL
   0 MG

FIBER 1.4 G

SOY AND GINGER DIPPING SAUCE

1 cup purified water
1/2 cup dried mango
1 tablespoon natural soy sauce
   (such as tamari)
2 tablespoons mirin (sweet rice
   wine)
1 tablespoon rice vinegar
1 teaspoon finely grated ginger
1/4 teaspoon chili paste

VEGETABLE WONTON FILLING

1 cup grated carrot
1/2 cup thinly sliced shiitake,
   oyster mushrooms, or button
   mushrooms

1 cup finely shredded Napa
   cabbage (about 1/4 head)
2 tablespoons toasted sesame oil
1/4 cup chopped scallions or green
   onions
1/2 tablespoon freshly grated
   ginger
1/2 tablespoon curry powder
1 tablespoon mirin (sweet rice
   wine)
1 tablespoon natural soy sauce
   (such as tamari)
1 package 30 small, square
   wontons (uncooked)
1/4 cup toasted-sesame oil (for
   brushing)

SOY AND GINGER
DIPPING SAUCE
SERVES 20

PER SERVING:

CALORIES 19.3

FAT 0 G
   SATURATED FAT
   0 G

(20% OF CALORIES
   FROM FAT)

PROTEIN 0.3 G

CARBOHYDRATE
   4.4 G

CHOLESTEROL
   0 MG

FIBER 0.3 G

Make the Soy and Ginger Dipping Sauce first.

Boil the water and pour over the dried mango and let sit for about 30 minutes or until the fruit softens. Strain the water and use 1/2 cup of the fruit-flavored water as a base for the sauce. Add the soy sauce, mirin, rice vinegar, ginger, and chili paste.

Preheat oven to 375°F.

Brushing a border of sesame oil on each wonton wrapper

Filling and folding the wontons

Make the filling: Sauté the carrot, mushrooms, and cabbage in the sesame oil in a large sauté pan over medium heat, until limp, about 5 minutes. Add the scallions or green onions and ginger. Sprinkle the vegetables with curry powder, then stir in the mirin and soy sauce. Remove from the heat.

Lay out 12 wonton sheets at a time on a clean surface and with a pastry brush lightly brush all along the edges of the sheet using some of the sesame oil (see illustrations). You will be folding the sheet at an angle, so drop 1 tablespoon of the vegetable mixture a touch off the center of the diagonal fold so that you can close the wonton. After the filling is in place, fold 1 corner of the sheet over to the opposite corner. Press the 2 sides of the wonton down with a fork to seal it. Fold in the 2 pointed edges, which jut out from the folded side of the triangle. Brush the tops with sesame oil. Repeat this process for the remaining wonton sheets. Put the stuffed wontons on a baking sheet lightly greased with olive or grapeseed oil and brush the tops of the wontons with the remaining sesame oil. Bake for 6 minutes, turn them over, and continue baking until the tops are brown, about another 6 minutes.

Serve the dipping sauce in a bowl in the middle of a platter with the wontons arranged around it. Makes 30 wontons—3 per person.

Left: Securing the seals with the tines of a fork; below left: Brushing sesame oil on the filled wonton

Sampling the baked wonton

Tips from Rosie's Kitchen

Wontons can keep in the refrigerator for up to 3 months. Wrap about 5 of them carefully in wax paper, and then seal the package tight with plastic wrap. They are good to have on hand. All you need to do is heat them up for a few minutes in the oven and eat!

SOY SAUCE:
SHOYU AND TAMARI

"Shoyu" is the Japanese word for soy sauce, a universal condiment and ingredient in the cooking not only of Japan but also of China, Korea, and other countries of East and Southeast Asia. Rosie and I both like to use soy sauce in our cooking, often using it in place of salt, but we are careful about the brands we buy.

Soy sauce is a traditional fermented food, made originally from soybeans, rice starter (koji), wheat, salt, and water. Good-quality Japanese soy sauce is still brewed traditionally from all-natural ingredients, but mass-produced Chinese and American soy sauce is made by a chemical process that results in a distinctly inferior product. Instead of saying "naturally fermented" or "naturally brewed," the imitations will list "hydrolyzed soy protein" as a main ingredient. It not only tastes bad, it may not be good for you; dangerous toxins have recently been found in popular Chinese brands.

The real soy sauce will usually be called shoyu or tamari, though the latter word is inaccurate. ("Tamari" properly refers to the liquid drained from vats of miso, a fermented soybean paste; it is now used to indicate a high-quality shoyu brewed without wheat.) Be aware that soy sauce contains a lot of salt— too much for both Rosie's taste and mine. We prefer reduced-sodium varieties, with up to one-third less salt. Again, look for naturally brewed brands with only the ingredients listed above.

Soy sauce can be a base for dipping sauces and marinades, flavored with vinegar, sugar, ginger, garlic, toasted sesame oil, or chile. You can use it to deepen the flavor of soups and gravies or to season grain dishes. Add it carefully, always tasting to avoid making dishes too salty. You will find it to be a versatile and welcome addition to the kitchen.—**A.W.**

Mediterranean Stuffed Grape Leaves

Mediterranean Stuffed Grape Leaves

This easy, exotic Greek treat makes a fine appetizer, but it can also be enjoyed as a side dish with lunch or dinner. The raisins and mint give the rice a sweet and aromatic taste, and the simplicity of chive "ribbons" wrapped around the grape leaves dresses them up a bit. For hors d'oeuvres, use 36 leaves and 1 1/2 tablespoons of filling for each leaf.

SERVES 12

PER SERVING:

CALORIES 110.9

FAT 4.4 G
  SATURATED FAT
  0.7 G
(34.4% OF CALO-
  RIES FROM FAT)

PROTEIN 2.5 G

CARBOHYDRATE
  16.6 G

CHOLESTEROL 0 MG

FIBER 1.3 G

❋

FILLING

2 cups vegetable stock (page 122)
  or purified water
1 cup brown rice
1 teaspoon salt
1/3 cup grated radish
1/3 cup chopped scallions or green
  onions
1/2 cup minced celery
3/4 cup chopped fresh mint leaves
2 tablespoons olive oil
2 teaspoons white wine vinegar
2 teaspoons freshly squeezed
  lemon juice

1/3 cup currants or yellow raisins
1/4 cup pine nuts
1/4 teaspoon freshly ground black
  pepper
1 pinch salt (optional)
1 tablespoon capers

36 grape leaves
1 bunch chives
1 teaspoon olive oil
1 tablespoon lemon juice

Bring the stock or water to a boil in a large pot. Add the rice and salt. Reduce heat and simmer, covered with a tight-fitting lid, for 45 minutes. All the water should be absorbed. Fluff the rice with a fork.

Mix together the rice and all the other filling ingredients in a large bowl, tossing thoroughly with a spoon. Rinse the grape leaves (see Tips). Spread the grape leaves out and spoon 1 1/2 tablespoons of the filling on the end of each leaf, and then roll up, folding the outer edges in. Take three 5-inch-long chives and dip briefly in boiling water to make them more pliable. Tie them around each stuffed grape leaf. Place the leaves in a small casserole dish and drizzle 1 teaspoon olive oil and 1 tablespoon lemon juice over them. Cover with foil and bake for 10 minutes at 350°F. Serve warm or cold. Makes 36 grape leaves—3 per person.

Tips from Rosie's Kitchen

Grape leaves are not readily available fresh, so you will have to buy them bottled or canned. They are packed in brine, a salty solution that you'll want to rinse off before using. Gently lift the leaves out of the jar, lay them in a bowl, and run them under a soft stream of water, letting the water completely drench the leaves. To dry, lay the leaves in a colander and let them drain, or lay them on a flat surface and pat dry with a clean cloth.

Broccoli Pancakes

Even if your kids don't like broccoli, they will eat these pancakes. I serve them as a side dish with the Thai Shrimp Brochette (page 67), alongside the Mock Sour Cream; however, they are certainly a meal on their own if you want to serve them as an entrée.

1 large head broccoli
1/4 cup coarsely chopped onion
1/2 small hot chili pepper or 1 teaspoon chili paste
1 large garlic clove, peeled and sliced
1/4 cup vegetable oil
2/3 cup whole wheat pastry flour
1/8 teaspoon dried dill weed
1 pinch salt
1 large egg or 2 egg whites
1/4 cup low-fat milk
Sprinkling paprika

MOCK SOUR CREAM

1 cup plain non-fat yogurt
1 tablespoon freshly squeezed lime or lemon juice
1/2 small onion or large shallot, finely chopped
1/2 teaspoon Tabasco sauce, or to taste
Sprinkling chopped fresh dill

Cut the florets off the head of the broccoli and separate them by cutting the large ones in half so they are all more or less the same size. You should have about 3 cups. Discard the stalks, or save them along with any remaining florets to use in soup or a vegetable stir-fry.

Bring 1/2 cup water to a boil in a medium pan, then drop in the broccoli florets, cover, and let steam as they cook, for 3 minutes. Strain in a colander.

Put the steamed broccoli, onions, chili, and garlic in a food processor and pulse on and off to chop (do not purée the vegetables), or chop by hand. Transfer the chopped ingredients to a mixing bowl and stir in the oil, flour, dill, and salt. Add the egg or egg whites and milk and mix thoroughly with a wooden spoon.

Smear the bottom of a large, nonstick skillet with 1/4 teaspoon of butter and set it over medium heat for about 1 minute. Drop tablespoonfuls of the batter into the hot skillet, placing

Tips from Rosie's Kitchen

If you don't want to bother to make the Mock Sour Cream, plain low-fat yogurt is fine as a topping.

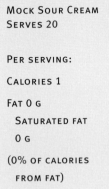

MOCK SOUR CREAM
SERVES 20

PER SERVING:

CALORIES 1

FAT 0 G
    SATURATED FAT
    0 G

(0% OF CALORIES
    FROM FAT)

PROTEIN 0 G

CARBOHYDRATE
    0.3 G

CHOLESTEROL 0 MG

FIBER 0 G

them far enough apart so that the pancakes don't touch, and cook over low to medium heat for about 1 minute. Turn the pancakes and cook the other side for 1 minute. Transfer them to a hot platter to keep warm while you continue making the rest until all the batter is used up.

Mix all of the ingredients for the Mock Sour Cream together and spoon 1 teaspoonful on top of each pancake, then top with a sprinkle of paprika.

Makes twenty 1-inch pancakes—2 per person.

Spanish Seafood Cocktail, Gazpacho Style

Peeled shrimp are easy to cook and take no time at all. However, if you find yourself without time to spare, you can get bay shrimp, which are already peeled and cooked. If you buy them raw, cook the shrimp first and then toss the cocktail ingredients together while the shrimp is chilling on ice. Cut the fruits and vegetables in bite-sized portions so you and your guests will easily be able to take a stab at a little bit of everything and taste all the flavors in one bite.

SERVES 6

PER SERVING:

CALORIES 300.8

FAT 8.1 G
  SATURATED FAT
  1.3 G
(23.8% OF CALO-
  RIES FROM FAT)

PROTEIN 33.7 G

CARBOHYDRATE
  24.8 G

CHOLESTEROL
  230 MG

FIBER 3.7 G

SHRIMP

2 pounds small to medium-sized
  raw shrimp, peeled and
  deveined
1 1/3 cups purified water

1 large grapefruit
12 ounces pineapple juice
1/4 cup freshly squeezed lime juice
2 fresh jalapeño peppers, finely
  chopped

1/8 teaspoon chili powder
1/4 teaspoon salt
12 ripe avocados diced
2 cups peeled and chopped celery
1/2 cup chopped cilantro leaves
1 cup finely chopped green onions
  or scallions, or red onion
1 cup chopped leaf lettuce

GARNISH

2 limes

Fill a large pot with water. Steam the shrimp in a steamer basket until they turn pink. Strain them in a colander and pour ice over them to chill them and stop the cooking. After the shrimp are chilled, cut each one into 4 sections.

Peel the grapefruit and separate the sections. Cut the sections into bite-sized pieces. Put them in a large bowl with the pineapple juice. Toss to coat the grapefruit sections with the juice. Add the remaining ingredients except the lettuce and limes. Toss gently to mix everything together. Lay a bed of lettuce on the bottom of each of 6 martini glasses. Scoop an equal portion of the seasoned salad mixture on top of the lettuce. Cut the limes into 6 slices, and then cut a small slit in each so that you can insert a slice on the rim of each martini glass.

Steamed Alaskan Crab Legs

Alaskan crab is best when bought frozen. Keep it frozen until you are ready to use it, or defrost it overnight in the refrigerator. Crab has a sweet, mellow flavor, and it's light, so it makes a great late-night dinner served with mixed field greens.

11/2 cups purified water
6 large frozen crab legs (approximately 2 pounds)

GARNISH

6 lemon wedges
Cocktail sauce
Horseradish Sauce (page 66)

Pour the water into a large pot with a steamer basket inside. Bring the water to a boil and lay the crab legs in the basket. If the legs are frozen, steam them for 16 minutes. If they have been defrosted, steam them for 7 minutes. Remove the legs from the pot using kitchen tongs and let cool briefly, until you are able to touch them with your fingers. Cut them in half using clean kitchen scissors, then cut them down the leg for easy access to the meat. Serve 1 leg per person with lemon wedges and dishes of cocktail sauce and Horseradish Sauce on the side.

SERVES 6

PER SERVING:

CALORIES 127.1

FAT 0.9 G
  SATURATED FAT
  0.1 G
(6.9% OF CALORIES
  FROM FAT)
PROTEIN 27.7 G
CARBOHYDRATE
  0 G
CHOLESTEROL
  64 MG
FIBER 0 G

Tips from Rosie's Kitchen

You may come across a transparent cartilage inside the crab legs. Pull it out, and don't eat it.

SMOKED FISH WITH HORSERADISH SAUCE

SERVES 4

PER SERVING:

CALORIES 170

FAT 3 G
   SATURATED FAT
   2 G
(16% OF CALORIES
   FROM FAT)

PROTEIN 30 G

CARBOHYDRATE
   5 G

CHOLESTEROL
   47 MG

FIBER 0.5 G

❋

If you have never dealt with a fresh horseradish root, be prepared for an experience. In the days before food processors, grating the root by hand was just like being exposed to tear gas. Freshly ground horseradish with vinegar and a little salt completely outclasses the prepared varieties sold in stores, and mixed with low-fat sour cream, it becomes a wonderful condiment for fish, boiled or baked potatoes, and other cooked vegetables.

1/2 cup low-fat sour cream
2 tablespoons Horseradish Sauce
   (recipe follows), or more to taste

Smoked fish, such as salmon, trout, or whitefish, 2–4 ounces per person
1 medium sweet onion, finely chopped

Mix the sour cream with the prepared horseradish.
   Serve individual portions of smoked fish, accompanied by the chopped onion and additional Horseradish Sauce.

Horseradish Sauce

1 cup fresh horseradish root, peeled and cut into 1/2-inch cubes (see *Note*)

1/4 cup white vinegar, or more if necessary
1/2 teaspoon salt

Put the horseradish root cubes in a food processor and grind them to fine particles. This will take 3–4 minutes. Be careful not to inhale the very irritating fumes.
   Pour the white vinegar onto the ground horseradish until it is thoroughly moist. Season with salt and mix well.
   Store the prepared horseradish in the refrigerator in a tightly covered container and use it as a condiment.

Note: Horseradish roots are available in the produce sections of most supermarkets. Choose a root that is firm, not one that is shrunken, limp, or dried out. Use a vegetable peeler to remove the outer brown layer and a paring knife to trim out any remaining peel. Then cut the firm, white flesh with a heavy knife.

Thai Shrimp Brochette

There are many diverse flavors on the skewer in this recipe, but none of them competes. The fruit sweetness in contrast to the chili gives this dish an exotic flair. The shrimp can be broiled or grilled and served hot or cold.

MARINADE

1/3 cup sesame oil
2 tablespoons prepared chili paste
1/2 teaspoon salt
1/2 cup freshly squeezed lime juice
4 tablespoons washed and finely
    chopped cilantro leaves

12 large raw shrimp, cleaned and
    deveined

BROCHETTE

1 green or yellow bell pepper,
    seeded and cut into 1 1/2-inch
    pieces
1 red onion, quartered
2 small zucchinis, cut in rounds
12 cherry tomatoes

PINEAPPLE DIPPING SAUCE

1 tablespoon cornstarch
1/4 cup cold purified water
2 cups pineapple juice
1/4 cup finely chopped red or
    green pepper
1/4 teaspoon chili flakes
1 cup finely chopped fresh
    pineapple

GARNISH

1/2 bunch washed cilantro,
    stemmed

SERVES 6

PER SERVING:

CALORIES 291

FAT 14 G
  SATURATED FAT
  2 G

(40.3% OF CALO-
  RIES FROM FAT)

PROTEIN 9.5 G

CARBOHYDRATE
  37 G

CHOLESTEROL
  40 MG

FIBER 5.3 G

❋

Submerge twelve 6-inch wooden skewers in water for 1 hour.

Mix all of the marinade ingredients in a medium-size mixing bowl. Put all the shrimp in another bowl, and all the vegetables in a third bowl. Use half of the sauce to coat the shrimp completely, turning them with a spoon. Use the remaining half of the sauce to coat all the vegetables. On each skewer thread 1 piece of pepper, 1 coated shrimp, 2 chunks of red onion, 1 zucchini round, and 1 cherry tomato (feel free to make all-vegetable skewers if you have vegetarian guests). Discard the remaining marinade used to coat the shrimp (to avoid contamination); use the vegetable-coating sauce to baste the brochettes while cooking to keep everything extra moist and spicy. Lay the skewers on the grill, baste, and cook 2$1/2$ minutes. Turn them over, baste, and cook for an additional 2$1/2$ minutes.

If you are using a broiler, lay the brochettes on a baking tray and broil them on the middle rack in the oven. Follow the instructions for cooking over the grill.

Meanwhile make the Pineapple Dipping Sauce: Mix the cornstarch with the water together in a small bowl until the cornstarch is completely dissolved. Bring the pineapple juice, peppers, and chili flakes to a boil in a small saucepan, then pour in the cornstarch and water mixture. Stir with a whisk until

Tips from Rosie's Kitchen

To Prepare Shrimp: You'll want to rinse and devein the shrimp because the intestinal tract that runs along the back sometimes contains sand and grit. First, remove the shell by cutting down the back of the shrimp and peeling it off. Remove and discard the vein that runs down the back, then rinse the shrimps.

When you are cutting the vegetables, try and be consistent with the size of each piece. It's a good way to ensure that they cook evenly.

Preheat the grill at least 15–20 minutes in advance so that the heating unit or the coals are hot and the intensity of the heat is consistent.

You can use the same method as for the Thai Shrimp Brochettes, using a variety of marinated vegetables and shrimp, chicken, or tofu.

it thickens, about 3 minutes. Cool and fold in the chopped pineapple.

Serve the skewers on a platter on top of a bed of the cilantro leaves with a side of the Pineapple Dipping Sauce. Makes 12 skewers—2 per person.

Here, Rosie is threading marinated shrimp and eggplant on skewers, and Andy is preparing tofu, summer squash, and other vegetables.

Grilling the brochettes on Rosie's outdoor grill

THE PLEASURES
OF PEPPERS

Peppers, sweet and hot, belong to the genus *Capsicum* and are native to the New World. Most are green when unripe and go through various color changes as they mature. Most end up bright red, some orange or yellow. Purple and chocolate-brown sweet peppers are not fully ripe. Ripe peppers are sweeter, softer, and more digestible, with a high content of vitamins C and A. Hot peppers also contain variable amounts of capsaicin, the pungent principal ingredient that gives a sensation from a mild tingle to a searing burn. Birds cannot taste capsaicin, which may have evolved to deter animals other than birds from eating the fruits and chewing up the seeds. Birds excrete the seeds and help propagate the plants.

Despite the violent effect of capsaicin in the mouth, it has several health-promoting aspects that have led herbalists to recommend hot peppers for a number of conditions. Hot peppers stimulate blood circulation and sweating, increase metabolism, and actually promote healing of tissues in the mouth, esophagus, and stomach. Capsaicin is also a long-acting local anesthetic, now used in medicine, both as an injectable preparation and a topical cream (especially for the long-lasting pain that sometimes follows an attack of shingles). Eating hot peppers can cause an endorphin high that many people enjoy, and some take very seriously.

It is a common belief that spicy food upsets the stomach. Usually it is not the hot peppers that are responsible. It may be other spices, such as black pepper and mustard, that irritate, or too much fat, or poor preparation. I grow many varieties of hot as well as sweet peppers in my garden, drying some of them to use in cooking throughout the year and turning others into hot sauces that I freeze. If I want to tame the heat, I remove the placental tissue (the whitish ribs to which the seeds adhere), which contains the most capsaicin. I always wear rubber gloves when handling very hot peppers and I am careful not to let any of the juice get in my eyes.

I don't like heat in my food just for the sake of heat. I find some varieties of chilis and some dishes made with them just too hot without any redeeming flavor. But I am a great fan of chili peppers and recommend them for health as well as pleasure. —**A.W.**

Vegetable Nori Rolls

Nori is dried, sweet-tasting seaweed that is used quite a bit in Japanese cuisine, such as in sushi. It is high in protein, calcium, and iron. This recipe is an example of how simple ingredients such as vegetables and rice, with a combination of just the right seasonings, can exceed our expectations. When that happens, inspiration kicks in and you start to think of additional ways to use what you already have in your kitchen.

SERVES 12

PER SERVING:

CALORIES 126.2

FAT 2 G
  SATURATED FAT
  0.3 G
(15.3% OF CALO-
  RIES FROM FAT)

PROTEIN 3.9 G

CARBOHYDRATE
  24.3 G

CHOLESTEROL 0 MG

FIBER 3.4 G

2 cups purified water
1 cup uncooked brown, white, or
  basmati rice
1 tablespoon rice vinegar
1 tablespoon mirin (sweet rice
  wine)
6 sheets nori
1/2 medium carrot, peeled and cut
  into thin strips
1/2 medium cucumber, seeded
  and cut into thin strips
1/2 avocado, thinly sliced

5 green onions or scallions, cut
  into strips
2 tablespoons plum paste
2 tablespoons wasabi (hot, green
  horseradish paste)

GARNISH

1/2 head red cabbage, shredded (2
  cups)
2 cups shredded daikon radish
2 tablespoons natural soy sauce
  (such as tamari)

Bring the water to a boil in a medium pot. Add the rice, reduce heat, cover, and simmer. For brown rice, simmer for 45 minutes; white rice, 20 minutes; basmati, 25 minutes. Rice should be firm and all the water absorbed. Dump the rice into a bowl and add the vinegar and the mirin. Fluff the rice with a wooden spoon and let it cool completely.

You will toast, fill, and roll each nori sheet one at a time. Hold the first sheet 10 inches above a low flame, lightly waving it with your hand until it discolors slightly. Lay the nori sheet on top of a sushi mat. Using a flat wooden spoon, drop 1/2 cup of cooled rice on one of the narrow ends of the toasted sheet, flattening the rice to create a slab. About 1/2 inch up the rice slab, make a lengthwise gutter or groove, using a chopstick or the dull edge of a knife, to cradle the vegetable strips so they don't roll off

the rice. Lay a strip of each cut vegetable in the trench, then
spread 1 teaspoon plum paste and 1 teaspoon wasabi across the
vegetables. Roll the sheet up from the filled end. When you get
to the other end of the roll, wet the inside edge of the sheet like
an envelope, and seal in the contents. Wrap the roll tightly in
plastic wrap. Do not remove or cut it until you are ready to
serve, or it will dry out. Repeat the process with the remaining 5
rolls. Refrigerate.

Right before serving, remove the rolls from the plastic wrap
and cut them into six 1-inch sections. Serve on a platter gar-
nished with a bed of shredded red cabbage and daikon radish.
Place a dish of natural soy sauce in the center of the platter.
Makes 6 rolls—3 slices per person.

Spinach Toasts

Cooking spinach takes very little time, but you need to wash and drain it carefully, and remove tough stems first, which may take 5 or 10 minutes. Plan accordingly.

The spinach on these little appetizers is a great source of iron and vitamins A and C.

SERVES 12

PER SERVING:

CALORIES 115.5

FAT 3.3 G
  SATURATED FAT
  0.6 G
(24.2% OF CALO-
  RIES FROM FAT)

PROTEIN 4.4 G

CARBOHYDRATE
  18.8 G

CHOLESTEROL 1 MG

FIBER 3 G

3/4 cup purified water
2 bunches fresh spinach (about 2 pounds), stemmed
9 pieces thinly sliced whole wheat bread
1 small onion, minced
1 clove garlic, minced
1 tablespoon canola or grapeseed oil
2/3 cup low-fat plain yogurt
1/8 teaspoon freshly ground nutmeg
1 tablespoon chopped fresh mint
Freshly ground pepper to taste
1 1/2 tablespoons chopped toasted walnuts (page 112)

GARNISH

1 red apple, cut in thin wedges

Preheat oven to 300°F.

Pour the water into a large stainless steel pot and bring it to a boil. Drop in the washed spinach and cook for 3 minutes, stirring several times. Drain the spinach in a colander over a pan to catch all the water, which you can save to make vegetable stock (page 122). Put a bowl or plate on top of the spinach, inside the colander, and press down to squeeze excess water from the leaves.

Trim the crusts from the bread slices, cut on the diagonal to create 2 triangular pieces, then cut again to make 4 triangles. Put them on a cookie sheet and bake until lightly toasted, about 5 minutes.

Meanwhile, sauté the onions and garlic in canola or grapeseed oil in a medium nonstick sauté pan over low heat until onions are softened, about 2 minutes. Remove from heat.

Put the spinach leaves into a medium bowl, along with the onions and the garlic. Add the yogurt, mint, pepper, and nuts and toss thoroughly with a fork.

Spread the spinach mixture on the toasts just before serving. Garnish with apple wedges. Makes 36 pieces—3 triangles per person.

Tips from Rosie's Kitchen

To Prepare Spinach: *Remove the stems from the spinach leaves by holding the sides of the leaf and pulling the stem upward and off the leaf. Wash the spinach by dunking it in a large pot filled with water. Swish it around on the surface with your fingers to separate the leaves and loosen the dirt. Do this for about 5 minutes. Lift a few leaves at a time out of the water and shake off any excess water before dropping them into a bowl. If the leaves are still gritty, change the water and repeat the process.*

Polenta Triangles with Roasted Bell Peppers

Polenta, or cornmeal, is made from dried corn kernels that have been ground into fine, medium, and coarse textures. It is cooked to a thick and moist consistency and either served hot right out of the cooking pot or cooled in a baking pan and cut into triangles. Here it is cooked with cheese to give it added flavor. I find that the simple act of roasting peppers for the roasted purée spread gives them a sweet, smoky taste— just right for mild tasting polenta.

This dish makes not only a substantial appetizer, but it can also be eaten for breakfast, a snack, or lunch.

SERVES 6

PER SERVING:

CALORIES 111.6

FAT 10.4 G
  SATURATED FAT
  1.5 G
(82.5% OF CALO-
  RIES FROM FAT)
PROTEIN 0.8 G
CARBOHYDRATE
  4.2 G
CHOLESTEROL 0 MG
FIBER 0.5 G

POLENTA

3 cups purified water
1 cup cornmeal (polenta),
    medium ground
1 teaspoon salt
1 tablespoon finely chopped basil
1/4 cup freshly grated cheddar or
    Parmesan cheese

ROASTED BELL PEPPER PURÉE

3 large red bell peppers, seeded
    (about 11/2 pounds)
11/2 tablespoons olive oil
1 tablespoon balsamic vinegar
1/8 teaspoon hot sauce (such as
    Tabasco)
2 shallots, peeled and roughly
    chopped
1/4 teaspoon salt
1/8 teaspoon freshly ground black
    pepper

GARNISH

2 tablespoons chopped parsley
11/2 tablespoons additional
    Parmesan cheese
6 fresh basil sprigs

Prepare the polenta. Bring the water to a boil in a saucepan. Slowly pour in a continuous stream of cornmeal, stirring constantly. Add the salt. Reduce the heat to low and cook uncovered, stirring occasionally, until the polenta begins to pull away from the sides of the pan, about 20 minutes. Shut off the heat and stir in the basil and cheese. Working quickly, grease with olive oil a medium-size (approximately 9 × 7 inches) shallow casserole dish or pan and pour in the cornmeal, spreading it out over the whole surface. Let the polenta set and cool for 1 hour.

Preheat oven to 400°F.

Prepare the Roasted Bell Pepper Purée. Cut the sweet red peppers into large pieces. Smear a little of the olive oil over the bottom of an ovenproof casserole dish and lay the peppers inside. Cover and bake for 20 minutes until they become soft. Remove from the oven (leave the oven on to bake the polenta) and let cool. Put the peppers in a food processor and process until smooth. Add the remaining ingredients including all but a teaspoon of the remaining olive oil, and process until thoroughly blended. Scrape the dip into a serving bowl.

When the polenta has cooled completely, cut two vertical lines through it, so you have three rectangles. Make diagonal cuts from corner to corner of each rectangle to make an "X," creating 4 triangles within each of the 3 rectangles. Smear some olive oil over a baking sheet and with a spatula remove each of the 12 triangles and arrange them on the sheet, leaving space around each one so that the edges can crisp. Bake on the top rack in the oven for 15 minutes, or until browned.

To serve, pour 2 tablespoons of the Roasted Bell Pepper Purée on each of 6 serving plates. Arrange 2 Polenta Triangles alongside, sprinkle some chopped parsley and Parmesan over them, and place a basil sprig on the side. Makes 12 triangles—2 per person.

Tips from Rosie's Kitchen

If you plan to serve polenta as a side dish, spoon it out of the cooking pot immediately after it is removed from the heat into 1/2 cup serving sizes. As a side dish it could be served as a bed for the Cornish Hens (page 150). If you are serving it as an appetizer, you must let it set for at least 1 hour before it is cut into individual servings. For leftovers, warm the remainders in a baking pan under the broiler for a few minutes, then serve.

ANDY SUGGESTS

I prefer Parmesan to the cheddar in the polenta— I think it gives a more authentic Italian flavor.

Eggplant Dip

Eggplant Dip has a great texture with a tangy, vinegary, seasoned taste that is mellowed with the pita. I also like to smear the dip inside warm crepes (page 170) for a different kind of presentation.

1 eggplant (1 1/2 pounds)
1/2 medium onion, grated or finely chopped
2 tablespoons capers
2 tablespoons freshly squeezed lemon juice
1/4 cup olive oil
1/2 teaspoon dried oregano
1/2 teaspoon salt or to taste

3/4 teaspoon freshly ground black pepper
1 tablespoon red wine vinegar
4 pitas
1 tomato, peeled, seeded, and diced
1 tablespoon chopped fresh parsley

SERVES 8

PER SERVING:

CALORIES 169.3

FAT 7.3 G
  SATURATED FAT
  1 G
(38% OF CALORIES
  FROM FAT)

PROTEIN 3.8 G

CARBOHYDRATE
  23.1 G

CHOLESTEROL 0 MG

FIBER 2.7 G

Preheat oven to 375°F.

Set the eggplant on a baking pan or dish and pierce it a few times with a knife. Bake it until it becomes soft, about 30 minutes; it should pierce easily with a fork. Remove it from the oven and let cool. When completely cooled, peel the skin off and put the flesh into a blender or food processor. Add the onions, capers, and lemon juice. Turn on the machine, then gradually add the olive oil. Continue to blend until the eggplant is smooth and creamy. Transfer to a bowl and stir in the oregano, salt, pepper, and vinegar.

Warm the pitas briefly on a baking sheet, then cut each of them into 8 wedges. Arrange them on a plate or platter. Just before serving, stir the tomato and parsley into the dip. Makes 32—4 wedges per person.

Top: Goat Cheese Toasties with Sun-Dried Tomato and Basil
Front: left, White Bean Spread; right, Polenta Triangles with Roasted Bell Peppers

MISO PÂTÉ

This appetizer is a bit more complicated than the other dishes I've devised for this book, but it's worth making for a fancy dinner. It's a vegetarian answer to chopped liver that will make the chickens thank you. It also happens to be a heart-healthy treat, since it has none of the saturated fat of pâté made from meat or poultry. The texture and flavor will develop as the mixture rests for a day after you put it together, so please resist the temptation to dig into it prematurely!

SERVES 10

PER SERVING:

CALORIES 266

FAT 14.2 G
    SATURATED FAT
    2 G

(48% OF CALORIES
    FROM FAT)

PROTEIN 9 G

CARBOHYDRATE
    28 G

CHOLESTEROL 0 MG

FIBER 5 G

1 loaf good-quality whole wheat bread, sliced (OK if stale)
1 cup unsalted vegetable broth
1 cup tahini
1¹/₂ tablespoons red, mugi, or hatcho miso
1 tablespoon toasted-sesame oil
2 cloves garlic, mashed

1 medium onion, finely chopped
¹/₂ cup chopped fresh parsley
3 tablespoons dry sherry, more as needed
Dashes of thyme, sage or rosemary, and allspice
Freshly ground black pepper to taste

Preheat oven to 250°F.

Place the bread slices on a baking sheet and bake them until they are thoroughly dry, about 45 minutes. Let the bread cool, then break it into pieces. You should have about 4 cups of pieces. Put the bread and broth in a bowl and work it with your hands until evenly moist.

In a separate bowl, mix the tahini, miso, sesame oil, and garlic, until well blended. Add to the moistened bread and work everything together well using your hands. Add the onions, parsley, and sherry. Season well with thyme, sage or rosemary, allspice, and pepper. Add a few more tablespoons of sherry if needed and knead with your hands until pâté is well blended. Add a little more liquid (broth or water) if necessary, to make a moist, sticky consistency. Pack the pâté firmly into a small loaf pan or bowl. Cover and refrigerate for 24 hours. (This is important!)

Remove the pâté from the refrigerator at least a half hour before serving. Unmold it and serve with crackers.

White Bean Spread

Most of us love bread. When thinking of great taste accompaniments to bread, challenge the butter and olive oil and balsamic vinegar routine with this herby spread. What you have here is a versatile spread for toasted baguettes or warm crepes. You can also use it as a dip made for thick chunks of French bread or pita sandwiches. Plan one day in advance in order to soak the beans overnight. Of course, you always have the option of using canned beans if you're really pressed for time, but I encourage you to prepare them from scratch. The difference is in the taste and the feeling you get when you've really made something yourself.

SERVES 12

PER SERVING:

CALORIES 156.1

FAT 4.1 G
    SATURATED FAT
    0.7 G
(23.1% OF CALO-
    RIES FROM FAT)
PROTEIN 8.6 G
CARBOHYDRATE
    22.3 G
CHOLESTEROL 1 MG
FIBER 5.4 G

2 cups Great Northern or can-
    nellini beans, soaked overnight
    in 6 cups of water to cover and
    1 teaspoon baking soda
1 bay leaf
1 teaspoon dried basil or pesto
    (page 160)
2 teaspoons freshly squeezed lime
    juice
1 clove garlic, coarsely chopped
1 teaspoon ground cumin
1 teaspoon salt
2 tablespoons freshly grated
    Parmesan cheese
3 tablespoons extra virgin olive oil
1 whole grain
    baguette

Do not drain the water that the beans have been soaking in overnight. Bring it to a boil and cook for 45 minutes. The beans should be easily pierced with a fork.

Preheat the broiler.

Drain and transfer the cooked beans to a food processor or blender. Add the basil or pesto, lime juice, garlic, cumin, salt, Parmesan cheese, and 1 tablespoon of the olive oil and process or blend until smooth. Cut the baguette into 1-inch slices and brush the remaining tablespoons of olive oil over them, then broil on the lower rack until lightly browned.

Put the toasted baguette slices on a platter. Scrape the spread into a nice bowl and set it in the middle of the platter and serve.

ANDY SUGGESTS

I much prefer the pesto to the dried basil.

Tips from Rosie's Kitchen

As long as you are preparing beans from scratch, you could double the amount, using half to make White Beans and Fusilli (page 160).

CHEESE

I love cheese, and so do most people I know. We love it for its unctuous texture and complex range of flavors that include notes of earth, mushrooms, and, in stronger varieties, distinctly animal tones that in other contexts might be disagreeable. I especially like cheeses from England, Ireland, France, Switzerland, and Italy. I'm afraid I'm not much of a fan of most of the anemic varieties made for the American mass market. But I am encouraged by the growth of new artisanal and farmstead cheeses made in the United States, some of them honest and robust enough to satisfy cheese lovers.

For years, I ate cheese sparingly and with guilt, because I was afraid of its effect on my cholesterol levels and cardiovascular health. My continuing study of nutrition has reduced my anxiety and given me confidence to make cheese a regular part of my diet. I'm encouraged that it occurs in the Mediterranean diet, which is associated with some of the best health on the planet, including low incidence of cardiovascular disease. Mediterranean peoples eat cheese often, but the cheeses they like are natural, not processed, and they do not favor varieties with extremely high fat content, like Brie and triple cremes. Furthermore, they eat cheese in the context of a diet rich in monounsaturated fat from olive oil and omega-3 fatty acids from fish. The Mediterranean diet also provides a wealth of antioxidants and other protective phytochemicals from an abundance of fresh fruits and vegetables of high quality. All of this neutralizes any adverse impact of the butterfat in cheese.

Sometimes I make a meal of cheese with a green salad. I always have a wedge of Parmesan on hand, which I grate as a seasoning on many dishes. I keep other cheeses, like Gruyère, for snacking. And I often put several varieties out at the end of a meal, usually with fruit, instead of a sweet dessert.

Some people cannot tolerate dairy products. The protein in cow's milk (casein) may aggravate such conditions as asthma, eczema, bronchitis, sinusitis, allergies, and autoimmunity. Cheeses made from the milk of goats and sheep do not represent that problem; they have a different kind of protein. I like most sheep's milk cheeses (Roquefort is probably the most famous) for their sharp, full flavors, and I believe that the fat in sheep's milk is less likely to raise levels of cholesterol in the blood than butterfat. Goat cheese, in my experience, runs the gamut from luscious to nasty depending on the breed of goat, the handling of the milk, and the age of the product. Once rare in America, it has now become popular, at least in upscale restaurants. Cheese substitutes, made from soy, rice, almonds, or hemp, bear little resemblance to the real thing; they may substitute for processed cheese slices, but why bother?

Good natural cheeses are available at specialty shops and better grocery stores and, increasingly, on the Internet. Suppliers will usually provide information on their products and help you find ones you like. I encourage you to experiment and to enjoy good cheese without guilt.—**A.W.**

Goat Cheese Toasties with Sun-Dried Tomato and Basil

This spread tastes pretty amazing on a warm, thick piece of French baguette. Sometimes if I don't have a baguette I spread it on bagel chips that I have in the cupboard. Goat cheese definitely has a sharp flavor, but it doesn't fight with the distinct flavors of sun-dried tomato and basil.

13 sun-dried tomatoes (dried in a package, not in oil)
1/2 package of goat cheese (2 ounces), at room temperature
2 tablespoons pesto (page 160)
1/2 French baguette or 1 small baguette
1/4 cup olive oil

1 clove garlic, crushed
Freshly ground black pepper to taste

GARNISH

1 red bell pepper, chopped
1 bunch basil, finely shredded

SERVES 12

PER SERVING:
CALORIES 213.3
FAT 7.7 G
  SATURATED FAT
  2.1 G
(34.7% OF CALORIES FROM FAT)
PROTEIN 11.6 G
CARBOHYDRATE
  29.2 G
CHOLESTEROL 5 MG
FIBER 2.5 G

Preheat broiler.

Soak the sun-dried tomatoes in a bowl of hot water until they become plump and soft, about 20–30 minutes. When they are soft, chop them up. Mix them with the goat cheese and pesto in a bowl until you have a pastelike consistency.

Cut the baguette into 1/2-inch slices. Mix the olive oil and garlic together in a small bowl. Season to taste with black pepper. Using a pastry brush, brush the baguette slices with the oil and garlic mixture. Broil in the oven on the middle rack for less than 1 minute. Remove slices from oven.

Scatter the chopped red pepper and shredded basil on the bottom of a small shallow dish. Scoop up rounded tablespoonsful of goat cheese spread and gently drop the scoops over the peppers and basil. Set the dish in the middle of a large platter and arrange the warm slices of bread on the platter around the dish. Makes 12 slices—1 per person.

Tips from Rosie's Kitchen

If you don't want to use bread, serve this dip surrounded by endive leaves. You can do the same in the Eggplant Dip (page 79). Put the Eggplant Dip or the goat cheese, tomato, and pesto paste on the wide end of the endive leaf and garnish with the chopped red pepper and basil.

Stuffed Mushroom Caps with Couscous

Couscous is a mildly nutty-tasting grain that comes from North Africa. It makes a great stuffing, especially for a small cavity like a mushroom, because it's so moist. When the stuffed mushrooms are baked, the full flavor of the couscous and the mushrooms really come through. These will go fast!

1/4 cup chopped walnuts
2 tablespoons olive oil
2 cloves garlic, minced
3 shallots, chopped
1 1/2 tablespoons natural soy sauce
  (such as tamari)
1 cup white wine
12 medium small-capped mushrooms, washed and stems
  removed

1/2 cup chicken (page 124) or
  vegetable stock (page 122) or
  purified water
1/4 cup couscous
Salt
Freshly ground black pepper
2 tablespoons chopped fresh basil
1 bunch fresh parsley, chopped
1/4 cup freshly grated Parmesan
  cheese

SERVES 6

PER SERVING:

CALORIES 106.9

FAT 5.7 G
  SATURATED FAT
  0.9 G
  (53.4% OF CALO-
  RIES FROM FAT)

PROTEIN 2.6 G

CARBOHYDRATE
  9.6 G

CHOLESTEROL
  1 MG

FIBER 1 G

Preheat the oven to 350°F.

Spread the walnuts on a baking sheet and roast them for 5 minutes, just until they turn slightly more brown. Pour them into a small bowl.

Set a large sauté pan with the olive oil over low heat for less than 1 minute. Drop in the garlic and the shallots. Add the soy sauce, wine, and mushrooms and simmer covered until the mushrooms are tender, about 10 minutes. Use a slotted spoon to shake the mushrooms so that the cooking liquid falls back into the pan, then transfer the drained mushrooms to a baking dish, arranging them hollow side up. Reserve the liquid in the pan.

Cook the couscous by bringing the stock or water to a boil in a separate pot. Pour in the couscous, lower the heat, and simmer covered for 2 minutes. Remove from the heat and let stand, covered, for 10 minutes. All the liquid should be absorbed. Now, dump the couscous into the sauté pan with the reserved liquid, cover, and cook over low heat until all the liquid is absorbed.

Lightly salt and pepper the mushroom caps. Finish the stuffing by mixing the nuts, herbs, and Parmesan cheese into the cooked couscous. Using a tablespoon, pile a small mound of filling inside the cap of each mushroom. Bake for 10 minutes or until the stuffing is lightly browned on top. Makes 12 mushroom caps—2 per person.

SNACKS

Snacks make up more and more of the typical diet, and sales of snack foods have made them very big business for manufacturers. Unfortunately, the kinds of foods we snack on are not terrific for our well-being. They tend to be calorie-dense processed foods that are high in the wrong kinds of fat, the wrong kinds of carbohydrate, salt, and additives while not giving us the nutrients we need. The ultimate snack food is the chip, a morsel of starch, usually with a high glycemic index, that has been fried in partially hydrogenated vegetable oil containing trans-fats and made attractive with salt and other chemicals, including artificial colors. Overconsumption of chips and similar processed snack foods greatly contributes to the epidemics of obesity and type II diabetes in our society, particularly in children.

Americans now commonly eat all day long—on the street, in their cars, in airports, at sporting events. I'm not against snacking. In fact, I think many people need to eat throughout the day rather than eat three defined meals. But I am very concerned about what they eat.

Here are some of the snacks I can recommend:

- a piece of fresh fruit
- some dried fruit
- a small handful of raw, unsalted nuts—pistachios, cashews, or walnuts
- a flavorful piece of natural cheese
- a piece of dark chocolate
- a portion of leftover food.

Most commercial snack foods are simply not very good for you. So, while it is fine to snack, just choose foods to eat between meals with the same care you choose foods to eat at meals. And do your best to encourage kids to do the same.—**A.W.**

Salads

Greek Salad with Mild Red-Chili Dressing

Thai Shrimp and Papaya Salad

Simple Marinated Chicken Salad

Broccoli Salad with Avocado

Tabbouleh Salad

Mixed Greens with Potato Croutons and
Tarragon Dressing

Cobb Salad

Green Bean Salad

Celery, Artichoke, Hearts of Palm, and
Shrimp Salad

Lebanese Salad

Walnut, Apple, and Celery Salad

Warm Chicken and Asparagus Salad

Jicama and Carrot Salad

THE MEDITERRANEAN DIET

Many people talk up the Mediterranean diet these days. I myself am one of its champions, and many of the recipes in this book are consistent with the nutritional philosophy it represents. The Mediterranean diet is a composite of the traditional cuisines of Spain, southern France, Italy, Greece, Crete, and parts of the Middle East. All of them emphasize olive oil, fish above meat, and cheese above milk, and all include an abundance of high-quality fresh fruits and vegetables. People who follow it have low rates of heart disease and cancer and also get to enjoy food that is very flavorful, with enough fat to make it interesting.

Here are the features of the Mediterranean diet that recommend it to health-conscious people as well as food lovers:

- great variety, with tastes that appeal to people of many different cultures
- lots of whole-grain products as opposed to the refined carbohydrates in the typical American diet, hence a reduced glycemic load (see page xx)
- mostly monounsaturated fat and plenty of omega-3 fatty acids from fish, nuts, seeds, and vegetables
- little meat and poultry compared to the American diet; more fish and legumes in place of them
- inclusion of some cheese and yogurt
- a great variety of fruits and vegetables, including low-glycemic-index ones that provide fiber and protective phytochemicals (see page xxvii)
- an emphasis on fresh foods
- little processed food
- use of familiar ingredients and good adaptability to locally available ingredients
- relative ease of preparation compared to other cuisines.

The Mediterranean diet promotes health and is in no way a cuisine of deprivation. I should point out two qualifications about it, however. First of all, the traditional Mediterranean diet, like other traditional diets throughout the world, is changing. In Greece, Italy, and Spain, processed food and American fast food are appearing, as they are everywhere, and affluence is bringing with it greater consumption of calories and meat. We will have to wait to see the effects of these changes on the health of Mediterranean peoples. Also, the traditional Mediterranean diet is part of a whole cultural package that is good for health. People throughout the region get more physical activity than most Americans, and they enjoy strong social and family bonds around meals. Eating together and taking pleasure in food are central to healthy living in Mediterranean cultures. It's not just the olive oil. —A.W.

Greek Salad with Mild Red-Chili Dressing

SERVES 6

PER SERVING:

CALORIES 374.7

FAT 18 G
   SATURATED FAT
   3.9 G
(38.7% OF CALO-
   RIES FROM FAT)

PROTEIN 15.5 G

CARBOHYDRATE
   49.3 G

CHOLESTEROL
   13 MG

FIBER 11.5 G

I love this salad because of all the prominent tastes in the dressing. Here, the dressing is tossed with fresh spinach leaves and topped with crumbly and tangy feta cheese, but you can toss this dressing on any mixed-green combination or vegetables and it would taste excellent!

CITRUS AND MILD RED-CHILI DRESSING

8 sun-dried tomatoes (dried in a
   package, not in oil)
3/4 cup hot purified water
1/4 cup extra virgin olive oil, or
   1/4 cup apple juice
1 teaspoon chili powder
1 clove garlic
2 tablespoons orange juice
   concentrate
1/4 cup apple cider vinegar
1 teaspoon natural soy sauce
   (such as tamari), or low-sodium
   soy sauce

1/4 teaspoon freshly ground
   black pepper

SALAD

11/2 pounds fresh spinach,
   washed and stems removed
   (about 9 cups)
3 ounces feta cheese, finely cubed
Freshly ground black pepper

GARNISH

12 Kalamata olives, pitted
1/8 cup toasted sunflower seeds

Mediterranean olives and olive oil

Soak the sun-dried tomatoes in the bowl of hot water for 20–30 minutes until they become soft and plump. Pour the water and the tomatoes into a food processor and process until blended. Pour in all the remaining dressing ingredients and continue to process until creamy. Cover and refrigerate until you are ready to use it.

Toss the spinach leaves together with the dressing until the leaves are completely coated. Sprinkle in the feta cheese and pepper and serve. Garnish each salad with 2 olives and a dash of sunflower seeds.

Tips from Rosie's Kitchen

Toast your own sunflower seeds by placing them in a medium sauté pan over low heat for 1 minute until browned.

Thai Shrimp and Papaya Salad

The papaya in this salad gives it a subdued, sweet flavor and the shrimp coated in chili oil give it a lively kick.

SHRIMP

12 large raw, cleaned, and
  deveined shrimp
1 tablespoon toasted-sesame oil
1/4 teaspoon prepared chili paste
  (optional)

SALAD

6 cups washed and dried baby
  mixed field greens
1/4 teaspoon salt
1/4 cup freshly squeezed lemon
  juice
1/4 cup olive oil

PAPAYA SALSA

1/2 cup or 1 bunch cilantro
1 cup cubed papaya
1/4 cup cubed red bell pepper
1/4 cup diced red onion

1 small jalapeño pepper, seeded and minced (optional)
2 tablespoons freshly squeezed lime juice

SERVES 6

PER SERVING:

CALORIES 188.2

FAT 14.3 G
  SATURATED FAT
  2 G
(65.1% OF CALO-
  RIES FROM FAT)

PROTEIN 7.8 G

CARBOHYDRATE
  9.4 G

CHOLESTEROL
  40 MG

FIBER 2.3 G

Preheat the broiler for 15 minutes.

Meanwhile, put the shrimp in a medium bowl and add the sesame oil and chili paste. Toss with a spoon to coat the shrimp completely and evenly. Lay the seasoned shrimp on a baking tray and broil them for 1 minute on the middle rack. Turn them over and broil for 1 more minute or until they are cooked through. The shrimp should be pink when they are done.

Toss the mixed greens with the salt, lemon juice, and oil, until all the leaves are thoroughly coated.

Pinch the leaves off the cilantro stems. Put them in a small bowl with the remaining salsa ingredients and mix thoroughly with a spoon. Toss the shrimp into the salsa and stir until they are all coated. Put the mixed greens on a platter and lay the shrimp on top.

ANDY SUGGESTS

Again, I prefer more spice here, so I would add some chili paste to the dressing.

Simple Marinated Chicken Salad

You have a couple of cooking and serving options with this recipe. You can either grill or bake the chicken and serve it as part of an entrée, or serve it as a salad with an entrée.

The marinated chicken is tossed with the greens in a perfectly seasoned dressing with punch from the garlic, lemon, and Worcestershire sauce, mellowed with smooth avocado and cool sour cream. The avocado adds a bit of good fat, too.

SERVES 6

PER SERVING:

CALORIES 263.9

FAT 19.2 G
   SATURATED FAT
   3.4 G
(66.2% OF CALO-
   RIES FROM FAT)

PROTEIN 15.6 G

CARBOHYDRATE
   8.3 G

CHOLESTEROL
   39 MG

FIBER 1.2 G

✻

4 boneless, skinless chicken half-breasts or 1/2 block (8 ounces) Slow-Baked Tofu (page 193)

MARINADE

5 tablespoons freshly squeezed lemon juice
3 tablespoons natural soy sauce (such as tamari)
1/8 teaspoon freshly ground black pepper
1 teaspoon dried basil
2 cloves garlic

DRESSING

1 ripe avocado, pitted
1/2 cup low-fat sour cream
1/3 cup olive oil
1/3 cup freshly squeezed lemon juice
2 large cloves garlic, quartered
2 teaspoons freshly ground black pepper
2 teaspoons Worcestershire sauce

SALAD

2 heads romaine lettuce
2 tablespoons freshly grated Parmesan cheese

Tenderize each chicken piece by laying it down, spaced apart, on a large piece of plastic wrap on a cutting board. Cover it with another piece of plastic wrap. Using a cooking mallet, gently pound the surface of the chicken. Turn the chicken over and repeat. Put the tenderized chicken in a deep pan. Wash your hands, the knife, the cutting board, and anything else that came into contact with the raw chicken.

Mix together all the marinade ingredients. Pour over the chicken, cover, and refrigerate for 30 minutes, or no longer than 2 hours.

Meanwhile get the grill hot.

To grill the marinated chicken: Lay it on the hot grill. You should hear the meat sear (otherwise, the grill may not be hot enough). Grill each side for 4 minutes, basting with the remaining marinade while cooking. Be sure to cook the chicken completely, but don't overcook. You can check it with a knife by cutting it in the center. It should be moist, but not pink on the inside.

To bake the marinated chicken: Preheat the oven to 400°F.

Put the marinated chicken on a baking tray and bake it on the lower shelf for 20 minutes, turning the chicken over after 10–12 minutes and basting the other side to keep it moist. Check the chicken by cutting into the center to make sure there is no sign of pink flesh. Remove from the oven and let cool.

Put all the ingredients for the dressing in a blender and blend until the garlic is puréed and the dressing is smooth.

When the chicken is cool, slice it at an angle. Tear the romaine lettuce leaves into bite-sized pieces and toss them with the chicken in a large bowl. Pour in the dressing and toss until the leaves and the chicken are evenly coated. Garnish with Parmesan cheese and serve.

TOFU VARIATION

PER SERVING:

CALORIES 199.5

FAT 18.5 G
   SATURATED FAT
   3.3 G
   (84.6% OF CALO-
   RIES FROM FAT)

PROTEIN 2 G

CARBOHYDRATE
   8.3 G

CHOLESTEROL
   5 MG

FIBER 1.2 G

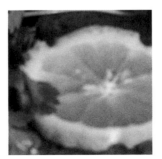

BROCCOLI SALAD WITH AVOCADO

SERVES 4

PER SERVING:

CALORIES 177

FAT 15 G
  SATURATED FAT
  2 G

(76% OF CALORIES
  FROM FAT)

PROTEIN 4.6 G

CHOLESTEROL
  0 MG

FIBER 4.8 G

The contrasting textures of crunchy broccoli and creamy, soft avocado make this quick salad interesting and delicious. It is rich in monounsaturated fat and full of protective phytochemicals and fiber. Don't forget to use the broccoli stems, which, if properly trimmed, are as good to eat as the florets. Cut a slice off the butt end of each large stalk and peel the stalks just below the outer fibrous layer to expose the tender, lighter-colored flesh within.

1 pound broccoli
1 ripe avocado
2 tablespoons extra virgin olive oil

2 tablespoons freshly squeezed lemon juice
1 tablespoon grainy prepared mustard

Trim and wash the broccoli and cut it into bite-sized pieces. Steam or boil the broccoli in a large pot until it is just crunchy-tender and bright green, then drain it well, and cool.

Peel and pit the avocado, then cut it into small cubes. Fold the avocado into the broccoli.

Whisk the olive oil, lemon juice, and mustard together in a small bowl, until well mixed.

Toss the broccoli and avocado with the dressing.

Tabbouleh Salad

Tabbouleh is a moist, light Turkish dish using bulgur, a form of wheat that has had some of the bran removed and then is baked and cracked. Bulgur wheat requires soaking for one hour before adding any seasonings, and at least three additional hours for complete absorption of both liquid and seasonings. So plan ahead—even one day in advance. Tabbouleh makes an excellent alternative to rice or potatoes, and the onions, tomatoes, parsley, and mint tossed into it create a colorful and savory confetti.

1/2 cup dry bulgur wheat
1 cup boiling purified water
1/3 cup freshly squeezed lemon juice
6 tablespoons minced fresh spearmint
1 tablespoon salt

1 teaspoon freshly ground black pepper
1/4 cup extra virgin olive oil
1–2 cups minced fresh parsley
3/4 cup chopped scallions
3 large tomatoes, finely diced
2 cloves garlic, finely minced
1 head red leaf lettuce

SERVES 6

PER SERVING:
CALORIES 154.8
FAT 9.5 G
   SATURATED FAT
   1.3 G
(51.4% OF CALO-
   RIES FROM FAT)
PROTEIN 3.1 G
CARBOHYDRATE
   17.1 G
CHOLESTEROL 0 MG
FIBER 4.9 G

Put the bulgur in a large bowl and pour the boiling water over it. Let soak at room temperature for at least 1 hour.

When the grain has absorbed all the water, mix the lemon juice, mint, salt, and pepper in a separate bowl and slowly stir in the olive oil. Pour the dressing over the bulgur wheat and mix with a large spoon until all the grains are coated. Stir in all remaining ingredients (except the lettuce) until they are thoroughly distributed throughout the grain. The hardest part about making Tabbouleh Salad is waiting for all of the tempting ingredients to set as the grain absorbs all of the liquid. Cover and refrigerate at least 3 hours before serving, or overnight if you are preparing a day in advance. Fluff up with a fork and serve on a bed of red leaf lettuce. Serve as a side dish along with chicken or fish, such as Lemon Grilled Halibut (page 185), or simply scoop up with some warm pita bread.

ABOUT HERBS

Culinary herbs are the delicate green parts of aromatic plants: dill, thyme, marjoram, oregano, basil, parsley, and cilantro among them. Most of us know them as dried ingredients in bottles, but in many parts of the world people have ready access to fresh herbs and make liberal use of them in cooking. Some herbs dry fairly well. I often use dry dill weed, oregano, marjoram, thyme, and bay leaves and am happy with their ability to flavor cooked dishes. But I can't bring myself to use dried parsley, cilantro, or basil when I know how much better the fresh versions look and taste.

I lived for a while in South America (Colombia, Ecuador, Peru) and got in the habit of drinking herb teas there. The reason was that if I ordered peppermint, chamomile, or lemongrass, what I got was a pot full of the fresh herbs steeping in hot water. These infusions had more color, aroma, flavor, and vitality than ones I knew made from tea bags. The experience spoiled me.

Many of these aromatic plants are extremely easy to grow; some, like dill, are truly weeds that can become invasive if you do not keep them in check. And you don't need much space to plant a garden of kitchen herbs that will be ready for clipping whenever you need them. You can even grow some herbs indoors. It is not hard to have a few basil plants, thyme, oregano, tarragon, and chives growing in pots on a kitchen windowsill.

As with other flavorings, learning to use herbs in your cooking takes practice. Become familiar with several, taste them, try them out in cooking, and note the combinations that appeal to you. You may discover that you like dill with cold salmon, cilantro with beans, bay leaf in tomato sauce, parsley with potatoes, chives and basil in salad. Get to know these leaves with their distinctive odors and tastes. They will greatly add to the pleasure you get from both cooking and eating.—**A.W.**

A Corner of Andy's Herb Garden

1. Agave Cactus
2. Italian Large Leaf Basil (herb)
3. Chocolate Mint (herb)
4. Evolvulus 'Blue Daze'
5. 'Red Rubin' Basil (herb)
6. Purple Oregano (herb)
7. Spearmint (herb)
8. Elfin Thyme (herb)
9. Gerbera Daisy
10. Gerbera Daisy
11. Society Garlic
12. Rosemary (herb)
13. Rosemary (herb)
14. 'Purple Ruffles' Basil (herb)
15. Peppermint (herb)
16. 'Sweet Dani' Lemon Basil (herb)
17. Purple Thai Basil (herb)

Rosie's Tips about Growing Herbs

I think you will be surprised by how little effort it takes to grow the fresh herbs that you need to make your cooking taste really good. It is wonderful to have the plants right at your fingertips when you need a sprig of fresh mint for a garnish or a big bunch of basil to make a delicious pesto. Moreover, you'll save a lot of money, because you pay a premium for the fresh herbs that are sold in little packets in supermarkets. And since they don't keep well, you often end up throwing out what you haven't used right away.

My herb garden isn't fancy. I simply chose a sunny space around my patio, planted the seeds in regular garden soil, and let them grow. If you don't have a backyard, you can grow herbs in pots on a sunny windowsill, as Andy suggests. Incidentally, kids love growing things and it helps them to appreciate fresh foods. They feel a pride in something they have nurtured themselves and it is a reminder for them of where things come from—a benefit that we could all share these days.

Basil, mint, and cilantro are the herbs I use most frequently and that really make a difference when they are fresh in pastas, chicken, fish, tofu dishes, soups, and salads. I also use a lot of thyme, rosemary, and oregano, which are perfectly acceptable dried, too.

Just having your own fresh herbs available will encourage you to experiment, to add something special to many tried-and-true recipes, and to create lovely new combinations of flavors on your own. It is the mark of a good cook to know and appreciate the power of fresh herbs.

Mixed Greens with Potato Croutons and Tarragon Dressing

The potato croutons in this salad are so enjoyable that you can eat them alone. They also provide the complex carbohydrates that we sometimes feel are missing when eating a salad by itself. They help curb that feeling of deprivation that often causes us to grab for more bread or pile on more croutons. The red bell pepper, onion, and fennel add great flavor to the croutons and color to the salad.

POTATO CROUTONS

1/4 cup olive oil
1/3 cup very thinly sliced red bell
   pepper
1 small white onion, very thinly
   sliced
1 tablespoon balsamic vinegar
1/2 teaspoon crushed fennel seeds
1/2 teaspoon seasoned salt
Dash ground red pepper
1 pound yellow Finn or Idaho
   potatoes, scrubbed

TARRAGON DRESSING

1/2 cup raspberry vinegar
2 tablespoons minced shallot
1 tablespoon freshly squeezed
   lemon juice
1/2 cup olive oil
1 tablespoon chopped fresh
   tarragon
1 teaspoon honey

9 cups gourmet or mixed salad
   greens (such as romaine,
   arugula, watercress, mâche)
3 teaspoons goat cheese

SERVE 6

PER SERVING:
CALORIES 259.6
FAT 18.8 G
   SATURATED FAT
   2.8 G
(60.7% OF CALO-
   RIES FROM FAT)
PROTEIN 3.6 G
CARBOHYDRATE
   23.8 G
CHOLESTEROL
   2 MG
FIBER 2.5 G

Preheat the oven to 400°F.

Rub 2 cookie sheets with 2 tablespoons of the olive oil. Mix the red pepper, onion, vinegar, remaining olive oil, fennel seeds, salt, and ground red pepper together in a medium bowl. Slice the potatoes very thin by hand, or with an adjustable blade slicer, if you have one, and add them to the red pepper, onion, fennel mixture. Toss well to incorporate all the flavors of the seasonings, onions, and peppers. Spread the mixture of red pepper, onion, fennel, and potato onto the cookie sheets and bake for 15

minutes. Turn them over and bake 5 to 15 minutes more, until the potatoes become crisp and the edges are browned.

Whisk the dressing ingredients in a medium bowl until the honey is dissolved and everything is thoroughly mixed.

Pour 1/3 cup of the dressing over the greens and toss thoroughly. Arrange on 6 salad plates, and then crumble 1/2 teaspoon goat cheese over each salad. Garnish with equal portions of the baked potato crouton, red pepper, onion medley. Pour the remainder of the dressing into a small bowl and pass at the table.

Cobb Salad

Whether you anticipate a summer afternoon running errands or playing on the beach, this is a salad you'll look forward to eating. It's chilled, so you can prepare all the ingredients ahead and then arrange them on plates or in a big bowl, if you prefer, at the last moment. It's especially desirable on a hot day, and has a balance of assorted vegetables plus protein-packed tarragon-flavored chicken. You can personalize this salad to suit your own tastes by eliminating or adding ingredients. For example, if you or your guests are vegetarian, omit the chicken and eggs and replace them with Slow-Baked Tofu (page 193). If artichoke hearts and hearts of palm seem pricey, skip them.

6 skinless, boneless half chicken breasts, or 8 ounces baked tofu
1/4 cup white wine
1 tablespoon chopped fresh tarragon or 1 teaspoon, dried
3 Belgian endives
1 1/2 heads green leaf lettuce or Boston lettuce, shredded
1/2 cup grated carrots

1/2 cup shredded red cabbage
14 ounces canned artichoke hearts or 6 hearts of palm (in water, not marinade or oil), drained and sliced (optional)
6 hard-boiled eggs, sliced
1 small avocado, diced
3 tomatoes, diced

SERVES 6

PER SERVING:

CALORIES 401.1

FAT 21.5 G
SATURATED FAT
4.1 G
(47.4% OF CALORIES FROM FAT)

PROTEIN 32.9 G

CARBOHYDRATE
20.7 G

CHOLESTEROL
267 MG

FIBER 10.1 G

❋

Mixed Greens with Potato Croutons and Tarragon Dressing

DRESSING

3 tablespoons minced shallots

1 teaspoon honey

1/4 cup freshly squeezed lemon
   juice

1 teaspoon salt

1 tablespoon balsamic vinegar

1/4 cup red wine vinegar

1/4 cup olive oil

Freshly ground black pepper to
   taste

Preheat oven to 400°F.

Lay the chicken breasts in a baking pan and pour in the wine. Sprinkle the tarragon over the chicken and bake for 20 minutes. The chicken should be cooked through and not pink inside. Remove from the oven and let cool. When cool, cube the chicken.

Break the endive leaves off the head by trimming the root and separating the leaves. Fan 6 endive leaves on each of 6 plates so that the leaves are pointing outward, creating a "star" look. Mix together the lettuce, carrots, and cabbage and put equal portions around the inside of the endive leaves on each plate. Spoon 1 cup of chicken into the middle. On each plate, create separate piles of equal portions of the artichoke hearts or hearts of palm, hard-boiled eggs, avocado, and tomatoes, around the chicken.

Whisk all the dressing ingredients together in a small bowl. Drizzle some of the dressing over each salad and serve.

Tips from Rosie's Kitchen

If you want to make this a low-fat recipe, use seltzer water instead of olive oil to thin out the dressing.

If you didn't have a chance to make the slow-baked tofu for those who don't eat eggs or chicken, provide a hit of protein using sunflower seeds. Toss 1/4 cup of raw sunflower seeds in a sauté pan over low heat until lightly toasted, about 2 minutes at the most. Serve on the side.

Cobb Salad

GREEN BEAN SALAD

This is one of my favorite vegetable dishes, delightful in its simplic-
ity and perfection of flavors. It is not worth making with the usual
old, tough green beans you find in most supermarkets. Wait until
you can get some beautiful, slender, rich-green filet beans from the
garden, a farmers' market, or a good produce store. Prepare the
salad a few hours ahead so the flavors can develop and blend.

SERVES 4

PER SERVING:

CALORIES 105

FAT 7 G
 SATURATED FAT
 1 G

(60% OF CALORIES
 FROM FAT)

PROTEIN 2.5 G

CARBOHYDRATE
 12 G

CHOLESTEROL
 0 MG

FIBER 4 G

1 pound young tender green beans, preferably French filet-type

2 tablespoons extra virgin olive oil

2 cloves garlic, finely minced

2 bay leaves (Turkish) or 1/2 bay leaf (California)

Salt to taste

1 lemon, preferably organic

Bring 2 quarts of water to a boil.

Trim the ends off the beans and drop beans into rapidly boiling water. Boil them, uncovered, until they are bright green and just crunchy-tender. Taste one after 5 minutes. You do not want them overcooked.

Drain the beans and cover them with cold water to stop their cooking. Drain them again thoroughly, then dry them in a kitchen towel and toss them in a bowl with the olive oil, garlic, bay leaf, and salt to taste.

Use a vegetable peeler to remove 4 strips of yellow zest from the lemon. Add these to the beans, toss well, and let them stand, covered, at room temperature for several hours until the flavors merge.

Remove and discard the bay leaf, toss well, and serve.

WHY "ORGANIC"?

In the recipes in this book we frequently call for ingredients that are "preferably organic." When I use the word "organic," I mean produced without the use of toxic agrichemicals, especially pesticides, and without synthetic fertilizers. My main concern is the toxins. As a physician, I worry that the poisons used in growing conventional fruits and vegetables undermine long-term health, especially when people suffer cumulative exposure to many different agents. I believe that research will eventually link this exposure to increased risk of chronic disease, including cancer and degenerative diseases of the nervous system.

Until recently, the word "organic" might or might not have meant anything depending where you lived. Some states set and enforced standards that gave meaning to the term; others did not. Now we have federal organic standards, and consumers can be more confident that when a package of grapes, for example, carries an organic label, the fruit has been grown without toxic chemicals and with natural fertilizers.

It is still the case that in many parts of the country supplies of organic produce are uncertain, making it hard to get, very expensive, or past its prime by the time it reaches the store. Given a choice between limp, yellow-green organic broccoli in a health-food store and a fresh, bright-green conventional variety in a supermarket, I would take the latter without hesitation.

Because it is often more difficult and more costly to shop organic, it is important to know which crops are most likely to carry significant residues of pesticides. In those cases I would avoid conventional versions or minimize consumption and try to buy organic. As I mentioned earlier, I do not eat conventional strawberries because they contain methyl bromide, a known cancer-causing pesticide, applied to the soil, taken up by the plant, and impossible to wash off the fruit. Other crops to be cautious about are apricots, peaches, winter cantaloupes imported from Mexico, cherries, winter grapes imported from Chile, celery, green beans, potatoes, and spinach. I try to use only organic flour, because conventional wheat is heavily treated with agrichemicals. And I prefer organic soybeans and products made from them, such as tofu. If you use the zest of citrus fruits, as called for in several of our recipes, try to get organic oranges and lemons, because the peel is the most likely part to be contaminated. (If you can't find them, at least scrub the fruit well with a soap-and-water solution.)

As consumer demand grows, the quality and availability of organic produce are improving, and in bigger markets, prices are coming down. There is even some research documenting claims of proponents of organic agriculture that its products are more nutritious and flavorful than conventional ones. Experiment for yourself and see if you can detect differences. In any case, know that by buying organic fruits and vegetables and supporting organic agriculture you are protecting your health and the health of your family.—A.W.

Celery, Artichoke, Hearts of Palm, and Shrimp Salad

SERVES 6

PER SERVING:

CALORIES 279.1

FAT 11.7 G
  SATURATED FAT
  1.7 G
(37.9% OF CALO-
  RIES FROM FAT)

PROTEIN 32.4 G

CARBOHYDRATE
  10.7 G

CHOLESTEROL
  230 MG

FIBER 2.1 G

❉

This salad is a big hit—people are always asking me for the recipe, so here it is. I like to serve this salad all year round.

Hearts of palm, also known as palmetto, come from the stalk of a palm tree that grows in tropical climates. There aren't many salads that have both artichoke hearts and hearts of palm in them, and if it has been a while since you've eaten either, you may find yourself using them more in salads of your own creation. If you have time, steam your own artichokes (see Tips).

2 pounds cooked medium shrimp, cut into bite-sized portions
14 ounces canned artichoke hearts in water, sliced (about 2 cups)
2 cups peeled and chopped celery stalks, including the hearts

14 ounces canned hearts of palm, drained (about 2 cups)
1 cup sliced scallions or green onions

BASIL VINAIGRETTE DRESSING

2 tablespoons pesto (page 160)
2 tablespoons freshly squeezed
    lemon juice
2 teaspoons salt
1/4 cup olive oil
1 teaspoon freshly ground black
    pepper

1 tablespoon chopped fresh basil
3 large shallots, minced
1 teaspoon honey
1/8 teaspoon chili flakes

GARNISH

2 sprigs parsley

Mix all the salad ingredients together in a big bowl.

Mix all the dressing ingredients in a large bowl, and pour over the salad. Toss thoroughly, making sure everything is evenly coated with the dressing. Garnish with the parsley. Cover and refrigerate until ready to serve.

Tips from Rosie's Kitchen

Peel the strings off the celery stalks with a vegetable peeler. Instead of throwing them out, you can refrigerate them in a sealed plastic bag and use them the next time you make vegetable stock.

If you buy raw shrimp, see Spanish Seafood Cocktail, Gazpacho Style (page 64), for cooking instructions.

To Prepare Artichokes: *If you want to cook your own artichokes, buy 3. Cut 2 inches off the top of the artichokes and lay them flat side down in a steamer basket. Lower the steamer basket into a large pot and fill the pot with enough water to reach the bottom of the steamer. Cover and steam the artichokes over medium-high heat for 1 hour, adding more water if necessary. Remove from heat and let cool. When completely cooled, scoop out the furry choke with a spoon and discard. Remove the leaves and set them aside. Chop the artichoke bottoms up. Lay the artichoke leaves out on each of 6 plates to create a base for the salad. Arrange the salad on top of the artichoke leaves and serve.*

LEBANESE SALAD

This dish has a classic Mediterranean look and taste, with its combination of freshly squeezed lemon juice, olive oil, mint, garlic, and onion. Don't even think about using California black olives here; they are a pathetic imitation of the real thing. (Rosie, this means you!) You can add some cubed or crumbled feta cheese and even some broken pieces of toasted whole wheat pita bread at the last minute to make this a main dish and still retain its authenticity. Remember to prepare the salad a few hours ahead so that the flavors can mingle.

SERVES 4

PER SERVING:

CALORIES 287.7

FAT 19.6 G
SATURATED FAT
6.7 G

(58.1% OF CALO-
RIES FROM FAT)

PROTEIN 9.4 G

CARBOHYDRATE
22.4 G

CHOLESTEROL
33 MG

FIBER 5.3 G

2 cucumbers, peeled and diced
4 Roma tomatoes, diced
1 red onion, minced
1/4 cup freshly squeezed lemon juice
2 tablespoons extra virgin olive oil
1 clove garlic, minced
3 tablespoons chopped fresh
spearmint or 1 tablespoon dried
mint leaves

1/4 cup pitted, sliced black olives
(Kalamata or oil-cured)
1 cup cubed or crumbled feta
cheese (optional)
Salt and freshly ground black pepper to taste

Toss all the ingredients together in a salad bowl, adding salt and pepper to taste.

After the ingredients are well mixed, chill the salad for at least 3 hours before serving it.

❄

Walnut, Apple, and Celery Salad

This is a good salad for autumn. It reminds me of a "vegetable ambrosia" salad. Don't limit the dressing to just your salads; you can use it as a mayonnaise on your favorite sandwich.

2 cups cored and cubed apples
Juice from 1 lemon (about 1/4 cup)
2 cups sliced celery
2 cups sliced hearts of palm, drained
1/2 cup chopped walnuts
1 head Boston leaf lettuce or red leaf lettuce

DRESSING

1/2 cup plain low-fat yogurt
1/4 cup apple cider vinegar
1 tablespoon mustard (grainy mustards work well)
1 tablespoon roughly chopped shallots
1 tablespoon pesto (page 160) or 1 clove garlic and 1 tablespoon fresh basil leaves

SERVES 6

PER SERVING:

CALORIES 219.8

FAT 8 G
  SATURATED FAT
  1.3 G
(28.4% OF CALO-
  RIES FROM FAT)

PROTEIN 8 G

CARBOHYDRATE
  37.1 G

CHOLESTEROL
  5 MG

FIBER 4.6 G

Toss the apples (immediately after peeling, seeding, and cubing) with the lemon juice in a small bowl so they don't turn brown. Put the celery, hearts of palm, and walnuts in a big bowl, then mix in the apples and toss.

Put all the dressing ingredients together in a blender and blend until smooth. Pour the dressing over the salad ingredients and toss until everything is thoroughly coated. Tear 6 leaves off the head of lettuce and lay 1 leaf on each of 6 salad plates. Spoon equal amounts of the salad on the lettuce leaves and serve.

Tips from Rosie's Kitchen

If you'd like to use the dressing as a mayonnaise alternative in tuna salad or on sandwiches, just double the dressing ingredients and store half in a covered plastic container. This dressing also goes well with Scrambled Tofu (page 10) to make an egg-salad style sandwich.

NUTS

Nuts are totally taboo in spa cuisine, relegated to the list of off-limits ingredients, along with olives and avocados, because of their fat content. It is true that most nuts are high in fat, but in most cases it's the kind of monounsaturated fat that's best for our bodies and comes along with a number of key micronutrients, including vitamin E, trace minerals, fiber, and, in the case of walnuts, vital omega-3 fatty acids. I love nuts, eat them frequently, and also use them in my cooking. But there is information about them you need to know.

Except for chestnuts, which are best considered a starchy vegetable, and coconuts, which contain a lot of saturated fat, nuts are rich in protein as well as the best kinds of fat. (Remember that peanuts are legumes, not nuts, and have a less desirable fatty-acid profile.) The oil in nuts is good for health and often delicious in food, as long as you do not heat them. For example, both walnut and hazelnut oils are wonderful in salad dressings.

I use mostly raw, unsalted nuts, and I store them in the refrigerator until I need them. Unsaturated nut oils oxidize quickly on exposure to heat, light, and air, creating rancidity that should immediately offend your senses of smell and taste. Roasted chopped or ground nuts go rancid much more quickly than whole raw ones. In any case, smell nuts before eating them or adding them to recipes, and discard any that smell rancid. It is easy enough to toast nuts yourself as you need them by stirring them about in a dry skillet over medium-high heat or putting them in a 350°F oven on a baking sheet and tossing them occasionally until they are done to your liking.

I use freshly ground nuts—walnuts especially—as a base for spreads and dips and often use nut milk (recipe on pages 34–5) in place of cream—in soups and desserts, for example.

If you have avoided nuts because you thought they were fattening, please renew your acquaintance with them. In moderation, nuts of good quality are a delightful component of the optimum diet.—**A.W.**

Warm Chicken and Asparagus Salad

There will be days when you'll just want to serve a light meal, and salads are the answer. Tossing together various herbs and greens gives you the confidence to be creative and experiment with other ingredients. Eating salads helps you get some of your greens in for the day, and eating a really, really good salad is a simple joy. If you're not convinced, this salad may change your mind.

12 baby red potatoes, cut in half
6 boneless, skinless half chicken
   breasts or Slow-Baked Tofu
   (page 193)
1/2 teaspoon freshly ground black
   pepper
1/2 teaspoon salt or to taste
1/4 cup white wine
1 tablespoon minced fresh basil
1 tablespoon minced fresh parsley
1 bunch fresh asparagus
2 cups mixed greens

LEMON DILL VINAIGRETTE

1 large shallot, minced
2 cloves garlic, minced
2 tablespoons freshly squeezed
   lemon juice
3 tablespoons balsamic vinegar
3 tablespoons rice vinegar
1/4 cup olive oil
2 tablespoons white wine
2 tablespoons chopped fresh dill
   weed
1/4 teaspoon salt or to taste

GARNISH

6 radishes, cut into rosettes

SERVES 6

PER SERVING:
CALORIES 405.6
FAT 10.8 G
   SATURATED FAT
   1.7 G
   (25.4% OF CALO-
   RIES FROM FAT)
PROTEIN 26.3 G
CARBOHYDRATE
   45.1 G
CHOLESTEROL
   51 MG
FIBER 4.5 G

Preheat oven to 325°F.

Steam the potatoes by putting them in a large pot filled with about 2 inches of boiling water. Cover the pot and steam the potatoes until tender, approximately 30 minutes. Drain and transfer the potatoes to a large bowl.

Put the chicken into a baking dish, season with salt and pepper, and add the wine, basil, and parsley. Bake for 30 minutes. Make 2 diagonal slices across each chicken breast, creating 3 pieces of chicken per breast.

Meanwhile, cut 2 inches off the bottom of each asparagus

stalk and blanch stalks in a pot of boiling water, just until they are tender, about 2 minutes. Lay the asparagus on a platter and let them cool at room temperature. When they are cool, cut lengthwise down the center of each stalk.

Whisk together thoroughly all the dressing ingredients in a large bowl.

Arrange some mixed greens (about 1/3 cup) on each of 6 plates and lay 6 or 7 of the cut asparagus stalks on top of the lettuce, spaced apart, with the tips pointing outward, creating a "fan." Lay 3 pieces of chicken between the "fanned" asparagus stalks.

Pour half of the dressing over the potatoes and mix gently with a spoon so they are completely coated with the dressing. Place 4 potatoes in the center of each asparagus arrangement and drizzle 1 tablespoon of the remaining dressing over the top. Garnish each plate with a radish rosette.

Tips from Rosie's Kitchen

When choosing asparagus, I always look for bright green, thin stalks. Sometimes a bundle of thin stalks will yield more asparagus than thicker spears. If you can't find good-looking asparagus, steamed green beans are a perfectly fitting alternative.

Transforming simple radishes into blooming roses sounds tough, but is in fact very simple. It's a garnish idea that you can steal for other recipes. Your guests will certainly notice them. Once they are cut, the radishes must sit in ice water for 2 hours to achieve the look of blooming flowers, so make them before you prepare the rest of the dish.

First, wash the radishes well. Using a small paring knife, cut the tops and bottoms off the radishes so both ends are flat. Following the illustrations on page 209, start at the top of the radish and make a small cut into the bulb, going in only about 1/4 inch. Make another cut, spaced a little bit apart from the first cut. Picture these cuts as "flaps" that will spring out from the bulb when iced, to create the look of open flower petals. Continue to cut all the way around the radish, then start another row of small cuts below this first one.

Warm Chicken and Asparagus Salad

Jicama and Carrot Salad

Jicama comes from Mexico and it doesn't really taste like any other vegetable. Its white, crunchy meat has a texture similar to an apple and it tastes somewhat like a mixture of apple and potato. Like carrots, jicama can be easily munched on alone. Bok choy is similar to celery and, like the other vegetables in this salad, has a lot of flavor and crunch. It takes no time at all to cut up some carrots, jicama, and tomatoes and mix up the dressing, so you'll probably rely on this salad a lot when you need a quick solution to a light meal.

SERVES 6

PER SERVING:

CALORIES 98.8

FAT 6.7 G
  SATURATED FAT
  0.8 G
(56.1% OF CALO-
  RIES FROM FAT)

PROTEIN 2.9 G

CARBOHYDRATE
  8.8 G

CHOLESTEROL
  0 MG

FIBER 2.6 G

1/2 cup sunflower sprouts
  (optional)
2 tomatoes, diced
1/2 large jicama, peeled and
  grated, or sliced "matchstick"
  style
2 carrots, grated or sliced "matchstick" style
2 stalks bok choy, chopped
1 head Boston lettuce

DRESSING

1/3 cup freshly squeezed lime juice
1/4 cup apple juice
1 teaspoon chili powder
1 teaspoon salt
2 minced shallots
2 minced cloves garlic
2 tablespoons Dijon mustard
1/3 cup olive oil

GARNISH (OPTIONAL)

Radish rosettes (page 209) or
  edible flowers (page 303)

Toss the salad ingredients together, except the Boston lettuce, in a large bowl. In a separate bowl, whisk together the dressing ingredients thoroughly. Pour the dressing over the salad ingredients and toss well. Arrange the Boston lettuce on plates and scoop the salad onto the lettuce. If you wish garnish with radish rosettes or edible flowers.

Tips from Rosie's Kitchen

Cutting vegetables "matchstick" style, known as "julienne," adds a bit of flair to the traditional look of cut-up vegetables. Following the illustrations, first, cut the peeled jicama and carrots on the diagonal or at a slant to make thin slices. Note how you should hold your bent fingers on the vegetable so you don't risk cutting the fingertips. Now make a stack of the thin slices and cut them into thin sticks. Again note the way the hand holding the stack of vegetables has the fingers tucked under and is moved back a little after each slice.

Holding the carrot with the bent fingers of one hand so that the knuckles are flush with the blade of the knife, Rosie slices at an angle, moving her fingers back a little with each slice.

To julienne, she makes a stack of slices and cuts down at about 1/8-inch intervals to make matchstick slices.

Soups

THE PROS AND CONS
OF SALT

Salt brings out the flavors of food and is indispensable in cooking. How much to use is an important question, because taste varies from person to person, and medical authorities continue to try to convince us that salt is not good for our health.

Sodium in sodium chloride is an essential mineral, used by the body to regulate water content of tissues and normal functioning of nerves and muscles. Yet the amount we need each day is probably no more than that in a gram of table salt—about a quarter-teaspoon. Most people eat much more than that, not only by way of the salt shaker but especially as a result of consuming processed foods, many of which are very high in sodium.

What happens if you eat more salt than you need? Most people probably do not have to worry. Their bodies eliminate the excess in sweat and urine. But a minority of people are salt-sensitive: too much makes them retain water, increasing blood volume and blood pressure and the workload on the heart. African-Americans and people with family histories of hypertension are more likely to be in this category.

I use salt in cooking but never add it at the table. I have learned to avoid foods with visible salt on them, preferring unsalted nuts, for example, and unsalted chips if I eat them. I like olives and capers and Parmesan cheese and often use them in food or cooking in place of added salt. I have found it easy to change my taste away from liking very salty foods; as a result, I often find restaurant food to be oversalted.

In cooking I prefer to use high-quality sea salt or earth salt, meaning brands that are free of chemical additives. I add salt until a dish tastes right to me. Some of my guests may find my cooking undersalted; they are free to add salt at the table. No one ever complains that my cooking is oversalted.

Rosie and I both feel that most Americans eat too much salt, and we tend to add it to our recipes with a light hand. We specify an amount of salt to use in some. More often we tell you to put in "salt to taste." You can learn to like less salt by cooking as we do—using as many fresh foods and as few processed ones as possible. —A.W.

Rosie's Vegetable Stock

I think of stock as the gold in my refrigerator. Many of my recipes, and Andy's too, call for vegetable stock, and you'll find that your refrigerator probably holds most of what is needed to make this versatile and essential ingredient. When vegetables become wilted, don't throw them away—throw them in the cooking pot. When you are pinching leaves off cilantro, basil, or parsley, keep the stems and use them too. This is one of the most undemanding and useful recipes you will make.

10 cups purified water
2 cups coarsely chopped carrots (about 4 carrots)
2 medium potatoes
1/2 cup chopped parsnips
1/2 cup chopped turnip or rutabaga
1 cup chopped celery (about 4 stalks)
2 medium onions with skin, quartered

4 cloves garlic
2–3 sprigs parsley
2 tablespoons salt
1–2 bay leaves
1/2 teaspoon thyme
1/4 teaspoon freshly ground black pepper
Pinch cayenne pepper

MAKES ABOUT 8 CUPS

PER SERVING:
CALORIES 91.8
FAT 0.6 G
  SATURATED FAT 0.1 G
(5.3% OF CALORIES FROM FAT)
PROTEIN 3.7 G
CARBOHYDRATE 20.2 G
CHOLESTEROL 0 MG
FIBER 5.4 G

Put all the ingredients in a large pot filled with water. Bring it to a boil, then reduce the heat and simmer for 3 hours. Strain the stock through a fine sieve or colander. Store in an airtight container and refrigerate 3 to 5 days or cool and freeze.

Tips from Rosie's Kitchen

Parsnips, rutabaga, and turnips are winter root vegetables and may not be as readily available in the warmer seasons. So use mushroom stems, zucchini, and an extra potato in the summertime. Whatever the season, you're in for a treat!

ANDY'S VEGETABLE STOCK

Vegetable dishes and soups will be much better if you make them with a vegetable stock instead of water. It is convenient to produce a quantity of stock and freeze it in batches for later use. If you have none on hand or do not have time to make your own stock, use instant vegetable broth powder (preferably low-sodium) from a natural food store.

1 tablespoon extra virgin olive oil
2 leeks, white and light green parts
  only, well washed and chopped
4 medium onions, chopped
6 large carrots, peeled and chopped
3 stalks celery, chopped
1 small bunch parsley stems

2 teaspoons dried whole marjoram
1/2 teaspoon dried whole thyme
3 Turkish bay leaves or 1/2 California
  bay leaf
1 1/2 gallons cold purified water

Heat the olive oil over medium heat in a large pot. Add the vegetables and stir-fry to brown lightly. Add the marjoram, thyme, bay leaves, and cold water. Bring the pot to a boil, reduce the heat, cover, and simmer for 1 hour.

Strain the stock through a fine sieve or a cheesecloth-lined colander. Press or squeeze the vegetables to extract their liquid. Discard the vegetables.

Use the stock as called for in recipes or chill and freeze it for later use.

MAKES ABOUT
20 CUPS

PER SERVING:

CALORIES 36

FAT LESS THAN 1 G
  SATURATED FAT
  0 G

(LESS THAN 30%
  OF CALORIES
  FROM FAT)

PROTEIN LESS
  THAN 1 G

CARBOHYDRATE
  7 G

CHOLESTEROL 0 G

FIBER 2 G

❄

Chicken Stock

Stocks are an excellent base for soups, sauces, and gravies. They are rich in flavor but not in extra calories or sodium. Any vegetables can be added to stock except cabbage, broccoli, or cauliflower, because these have a tendency to turn the stock bitter. When you make a big batch of stock, don't worry that you won't use it fast enough; it will keep for up to 2 days covered in the refrigerator. After 2 days, freeze it. It will keep for up to 3 months. Use it to punch up the flavor of soups or pour it over warm rice or grains, vegetables, or meat.

MAKES 12 CUPS

PER SERVING:

CALORIES 52.1

FAT 0.6 G
    SATURATED FAT
    0.1 G

(9.8% OF CALO-
    RIES FROM FAT)

PROTEIN 5.2 G

CARBOHYDRATE
    7.9 G

CHOLESTEROL
    7 MG

FIBER 3.6 G

2 pounds chicken bones
1 pound skinless chicken parts, cubed
2 medium onions with skin, quartered
2 carrots, coarsely chopped
2 stalks celery, coarsely chopped
4 cloves garlic, unpeeled
6 sprigs parsley
1 teaspoon thyme
1–2 bay leaves
14–16 cups purified water

Put all the ingredients in a large pot and bring to a boil. Reduce the heat to low and cook for 4 hours. Strain the stock through a fine sieve and skim off any fat. Store in a covered, airtight container and refrigerate or cool and freeze.

Fish Stock

Like Vegetable Stock or Chicken Stock you can use Fish Stock as a base for soups, sauces, or a flavoring over cooked grains or rice. It's likely that most of the ingredients called for are already in your refrigerator.

MAKES 4 CUPS

PER SERVING:

CALORIES 53.3

FAT 0.2 G
    SATURATED FAT
    0 G

(5.4% OF CALO-
    RIES FROM FAT)

PROTEIN 0.8 G

CARBOHYDRATE
    6.7 G

CHOLESTEROL
    0 MG

FIBER 1.3 G

1 pound bones and trimmings of any white fish, chopped
1 cup sliced onion
1/2 cup dry white wine
2 tablespoons freshly squeezed lemon juice
3–4 cups purified water
1–2 bay leaves

Put all the ingredients in a heavy saucepan and bring to a boil. Skim the froth that collects at the surface and discard. Reduce the heat and simmer for 30 minutes. Strain the stock through a fine sieve. Pour it into an airtight container and store in the refrigerator for up to 2 days, or in the freezer for up to 3 months.

Miso Soup

This is a light yet fortifying soup made with miso, a highly nutritious food made from soybeans. Miso is rich in protein and vitamin B. Miso's color variations are due to the amount of soybean and salt that are used. I always use light yellow because it has the right amount of texture and flavor.

2 cups vegetable stock (page 122)
41/2 cups purified water
1/2 cup chopped wakame seaweed
1/4 package silken tofu, finely
   cubed
1/4 cup light yellow miso (bean
   paste)

GARNISH

3/4 cup chopped tofu
3 scallions or green onions,
   chopped (about 1/4 cup)

Bring the vegetable stock and 4 cups of the water to a boil in a soup pot. Reduce the heat and simmer. Add the wakame and the tofu and continue to simmer for 5 minutes.

   Mix the miso with the remaining 1/4 cup of water in a large bowl and stir it with a spoon to make a paste. Add a ladleful of soup to the miso paste and mix, then return it to the soup pot.

   Ladle soup into small bowls and sprinkle 2 tablespoons of tofu and 1 tablespoon of scallions or green onions into each bowl.

SERVES 6

PER SERVING:
CALORIES 43.4
FAT 0.9 G
  SATURATED FAT
  0.1 G
(6.1% OF CALO-
  RIES FROM FAT)
PROTEIN 2.9 G
CARBOHYDRATE
  7.7 G
CHOLESTEROL
  0 MG
FIBER 2.1 G

BEANS, BEANS

Beans are a superlative food—nutritious, satisfying, versatile, and inexpensive. They are full of fiber, protein, and the kind of carbohydrate you want to eat and, except for soybeans and peanuts, contain almost no fat. They provide folic acid, a B vitamin that most people do not get enough of, as well as iron for people on plant-based diets.

I much prefer to start with dried beans than to use canned ones (except for canned baked beans, which I find convenient). It is not that difficult to soak them overnight and boil them. Adding baking soda to the water softens the skins and shortens the cooking time of larger varieties like garbanzos and kidney beans. It does not signficantly lower the nutritional value. People often make the mistake of cooking beans insufficiently. They have the best flavor and texture when they are quite tender and begin to melt into the liquid. Lower the heat and keep an eye on them in the final stages, stirring frequently to avoid burning the bottom layer.

Some people object to the gas-forming properties of beans. The solution to the problem is to select varieties that contain lower amounts of the indigestible sugars that cause it. Black beans and Anasazi beans are relatively innocuous, for example, whereas pink beans and soybeans can be problematical.

Cooked beans can be turned into hearty soups, dips and spreads, salads, main-dish combinations with grains, and even desserts. (The most common Japanese sweets contain a paste of red beans mixed with sugar.) —**A.W.**

Mixed-Bean Minestrone Stew

This Italian vegetable soup with pasta and beans is a great way to warm and fill you up during the cold winter months. You can always exchange other vegetables for the ones listed or leave a few out and give your minestrone your own accent. After all, the greatest soups are simply medleys of whatever's on hand in your kitchen! This Mixed-Bean Minestrone Stew is an ample lunch or supper entrée with slices of Whole Wheat Baguette with Sun-Dried Tomatoes and Herbs (page 255).

2 cups mixed dry beans (navy, garbanzo, kidney are all good)
1 teaspoon baking soda
1 bay leaf

1 cup chopped onion
3 carrots, peeled and sliced (about 1 cup)
1 cup chopped celery
3 garlic cloves, sliced
1/4 cup olive oil
1 tablespoon Italian seasoning
1/8 teaspoon chili flakes
1 teaspoon dried rosemary
1 teaspoon salt
1 cup peeled and cubed eggplant (or cabbage, squash, broccoli)

4 cups chopped fresh tomatoes (or 32 ounces canned)
1 large Idaho or baking potato, cubed (about 1 cup)
6 cups purified water (or vegetable stock for added flavor—and see Tips)
1 cup chopped fresh green beans or frozen peas
1 1/2 cups alphabet pasta or prepared barley (see Tips)

GARNISH

Fresh cracked pepper (optional)
3/4 cup freshly grated Parmesan cheese
1/4 cup pesto

MAKES 24 CUPS
SERVES 6

STEW WITH
GARNISH

PER SERVING:
CALORIES 571
FAT 21.1 G
  SATURATED FAT
  5.3 G
(33.2% OF CALO-
  RIES FROM FAT)
PROTEIN 24.6 G
CARBOHYDRATE
  75.4 G
CHOLESTEROL
  11.8 MG
FIBER 17.5 G

Soak the beans in a large pot with 6 cups of water and the baking soda overnight. Add the bay leaf to the pot, place over medium-high heat, and boil the beans for 45 minutes until tender (they should pierce easily with a fork). Meanwhile, you can prepare the vegetables.

In a separate large pot, sweat the onions, carrots, celery, and garlic in the olive oil on low heat for about 10 to 15 minutes, stirring occasionally to bring out the natural vegetable juices as a base for the soup. Stir in the Italian seasoning, chili flakes, rosemary, and salt, along with the eggplant, tomatoes, potatoes, and any other vegetables you'd like to use, then pour in the water or stock and continue to cook for 20 minutes. Add the cooked beans, green beans or peas, and pasta or cooked barley to the soup and cook on medium heat for another 15 minutes.

Serve in a large soup bowl and sprinkle with fresh cracked pepper (optional) and 1 tablespoon Parmesan cheese. Or you could add a small dollop of pesto, if you have some on hand.

Tips from Rosie's Kitchen

This recipe uses a cooking technique known as sweating, which means cooking something over low heat in a little oil in a covered pot or the oven in order to bring out the juices without browning.

You can use the already cooked barley remaining from the Cranberry Barley Tonic (page 38) along with the pasta in this recipe. For additional flavor you can use vegetable stock, if you have it on hand, instead of water. If you really want to add some flair, add 1/4 cup pesto to the soup right before you're ready to serve.

Cooled leftover soup should be stored in small airtight containers or zip-lock bags in the freezer to make it easy to take to work. It will keep for up to 3 weeks.

GREEN SQUASH SOUP

This is another easy, flavorful soup that can either be a first course or a main course in a meal with salad, bread, and cheese. Eat it right away; the fresh taste of the vegetables is what makes it appealing.

1 medium leek, preferably organic
1 pound summer squash, such as
    zucchini, preferably organic
2 tablespoons extra virgin olive oil
Salt and freshly ground black pep-
    per to taste
4 cups vegetable stock

1 tablespoon chopped fresh
    marjoram or 1 teaspoon dried
    marjoram
2 tablespoons artichoke purée
    (see *Note*)

GARNISH
Freshly grated Parmesan cheese

SERVES 6

PER SERVING:

CALORIES 24

FAT 0.2 G
    SATURATED FAT
    0 G

(5.8% OF CALO-
    RIES FROM FAT)

PROTEIN 1.2 G

CARBOHYDRATE
    5.3 G

CHOLESTEROL
    0 MG

FIBER 1.3 G

Remove the root end and green top part of the leek. Wash the white part of the leek well to remove any dirt, then chop it into fine pieces.

Wash and trim the squash and chop it into medium-sized pieces.

Heat the olive oil in a skillet over medium heat. Add the chopped leek and sauté it until it is translucent. Add the squash and sauté, stirring, until the squash softens, about 10 minutes. Season with salt and pepper.

Add the stock and marjoram, heat to boiling, cover, reduce heat, and boil gently for 30 minutes. Add the artichoke purée and mix well.

Pour the soup into a food processor and process into a coarse purée. Serve the soup in warm bowls with freshly grated Parmesan cheese to garnish.

Note: Artichoke purée is available in specialty grocery stores. You can also make your own simply by draining a jar of water-packed baby artichokes and grinding them in a blender or food processor. Store any leftover purée in the refrigerator and use it as a base for a pasta sauce or a dip for raw vegetables.

Clam Chowder

The two types of clam chowder are Manhattan clam chowder, using tomatoes, and New England, using milk and cream. It is simply a matter of taste as to which one you choose to make. Ideally, clam chowder should be made with fresh clams, but you also can make it with canned clams.

1 cup chopped onion
2 cloves garlic, chopped
1 tablespoon clarified butter or olive oil
1/2 cup chopped celery
1 teaspoon dried thyme
1/4 cup unbleached white flour
3 cups purified water
11/2 cups peeled, cubed potatoes
2 cups half-and-half *or* 2 cups chopped fresh tomatoes

2 pounds fresh clams or mussels or 16 ounces canned minced clams
11/2 cups white wine
1 teaspoon Worcestershire sauce
1/8 teaspoon Tabasco sauce (optional)
1/4 teaspoon freshly ground black pepper

GARNISH

2 tablespoons chopped fresh parsley

Put the onions, garlic, and clarified butter or olive oil in a big, heavy pot. Sauté on low heat for 2 minutes. Add the celery and thyme and cook for 3 minutes, stirring occasionally. Sprinkle the flour on top of the vegetables. Pour the water in slowly and use a whisk to break up the clumps of flour. Add the potatoes and then turn up the heat to medium-high until mixture comes to a boil. Boil for 10 minutes, then turn down the heat.

Add the half-and-half or tomatoes, depending on which style chowder you are making. Simmer, covered, for 20 minutes or until the potatoes are cooked completely.

Meanwhile, if you are using fresh shellfish, soak the clams or mussels in a large pot full of cold water for 5 minutes. Scrub the shells with a vegetable scrubber or the abrasive side of a clean

Manhattan Clam Chowder

SERVES 6

MANHATTAN CLAM CHOWDER

PER SERVING:

CALORIES 268.3

FAT 4.2 G
   SATURATED FAT 0.5 G

(16.4% OF CALORIESFROM FAT)

PROTEIN 22.4 G

CARBOHYDRATE 25.9 G

CHOLESTEROL 51 MG

FIBER 2.7 G

❄

NEW ENGLAND CLAM CHOWDER

PER SERVING:

CALORIES 449.9

FAT 23.9 G
   SATURATED FAT 12.9 G

(52% OF CALORIES FROM FAT)

PROTEIN 23.8 G

CARBOHYDRATE 25.9 G

CHOLESTEROL 121 MG

FIBER 21 G

sponge to remove any seaweed or mud. Put the clams or mussels and the wine in a large, lidded pot with enough space to hold them without them being cramped. Steam until the shellfish open up, about 10 minutes. Discard any shellfish that remain closed. Take the shellfish out of the pot and reserve the cooking liquid. Remove the clams from their shells, setting aside a few to garnish each bowl, if you wish, and add the clam meat and the reserved liquid to the rest of the soup. Cook the soup for an additional 5 minutes. Season with the Worcestershire sauce, Tabasco sauce, and black pepper. Garnish with fresh parsley and (optional) clams in their shells.

Tips from Rosie's Kitchen

In almost every fishing town, local restaurants serve a fish stew special. It usually is a chowder-based soup with a fresh, white fish, such as halibut, cooked in. The addition of fresh fish to clam chowder is optional, though it adds a mild, yet richer, fish taste. With or without the fresh fish, this is a full-bodied soup.

BLACK BEAN SOUP

Black bean soup is a staple of Mexican and Caribbean cuisines. It turns up in many different versions that vary in texture and spicing. With cilantro and chilies, this recipe has an authentic Latin American character. If you wish, you can garnish it with low-fat sour cream, finely chopped sweet onions, or a bit of grated cheese, such as a sharp cheddar.

2 cups dry black beans
12 cups cold purified water
2–4 large cloves garlic, peeled and mashed
Salt to taste
2 tablespoons extra virgin olive oil
1 medium onion, chopped

2 large green chili peppers, such as anchos or Anaheims, stemmed, seeded, and chopped
2 hot green chili peppers, such as jalapeños or serranos, stemmed, seeded, and chopped
1 cup chopped cilantro leaves

SERVES 8

PER SERVING:
CALORIES 287
FAT 5.5 G
   SATURATED FAT
   1 G
(17% OF CALO-
   RIES FROM FAT)
PROTEIN 15 G
CARBOHYDRATE
   46.5 G
CHOLESTEROL
   0 G
FIBER 11 G

Pick over the beans to remove any foreign objects. Wash and drain the beans and place them in a large pot with the cold water. Bring to a boil, and continue boiling for 3 minutes. Stir well, cover, remove from the heat, and let beans sit for 1 hour.

Return the beans to a boil, reduce the heat, cover, and simmer them gently, stirring occasionally, until they are tender, about 2 hours. Add the garlic and let them cool for 30 minutes.

Transfer the beans, in batches, to a food processor and process them into a coarse purée—don't overdo. The mixture should still have texture. Return the purée to the pot and add salt to taste. If the soup seems too thick, add water until the consistency is to your liking.

Heat the olive oil in a skillet over medium-high heat, add the onions and peppers, and sauté, stirring frequently, until the vegetables are softened and the onions are beginning to color, about 10 minutes.

Add the sautéed onions and peppers to the beans and heat the soup to the simmer. Simmer for 15 minutes. Add the chopped cilantro, cook for a few minutes more, and serve in warm bowls.

Cold Cucumber Soup

Early summer, when cucumbers are cheap and plentiful, is the best time to make this soup. It is so easy that you'll be making it a lot on warm afternoons or when you feel you want to eat something less than a complete meal. When I have guests for a late-evening meal, I serve this soup, along with Steamed Alaskan Crab Legs (page 65), and mixed field greens, because it is so light. The crab legs and the salad round out the meal.

You can make this soup ahead of time and chill it, covered, in the refrigerator until ready to use.

SERVES 6

PER SERVING:

CALORIES 168.3

FAT 3.7 G
  SATURATED FAT
  1.9 G
(18.1% OF CALO-
  RIES FROM FAT)

PROTEIN 7.9 G

CARBOHYDRATE
  29.8 G

CHOLESTEROL
  11 MG

FIBER 6.1 G

3 leeks, washed and sliced in
  rounds
2 cups vegetable stock (page 122)
2 cups milk
6 cucumbers, peeled, sliced, and
  seeded
3 tablespoons minced fresh dill
1 tablespoon freshly squeezed
  lemon juice
2 tablespoons chopped green
  onion or chive

1 teaspoon salt
1 teaspoon freshly ground black
  pepper

GARNISH

Mock Sour Cream (page 62) or
  low-fat sour cream
2 tablespoons capers

Cook the leeks in the stock in a large soup pot for 10 minutes. Add the milk and cucumbers. Pour small batches at a time into a blender and purée until smooth. Add the dill, lemon juice, green onions or chives, salt, and pepper. Stir once or twice. Chill covered in the refrigerator for 3 hours. Pour 1-cup servings into each of 6 bowls, garnish with a dollop of Mock Sour Cream or low-fat sour cream, and sprinkle a few capers on top.

Tips from Rosie's Kitchen

If you want to cut down on the fat from the milk, use 2 cups of skim milk instead.

ESCAROLE SOUP

This almost-instant soup couldn't be easier. The Parmesan cheese is indispensable for giving the soup body and flavor. I use a good-quality powdered vegetable broth if I do not have any stock on hand. The soup should be served and eaten as soon as it is made; it does not keep.

1 head escarole
4 cups vegetable stock (page 123)
1 tablespoon extra virgin olive oil
Salt and freshly ground black pepper to taste

GARNISH

1 cup freshly grated Parmesan cheese

SERVES 4

PER SERVING:

CALORIES 173

FAT 9.4 G
    SATURATED FAT
    4 G
    (48% OF CALO-
    RIES FROM FAT)

PROTEIN 20 G

CARBOHYDRATE
    3 G

CHOLESTEROL
    16 MG

FIBER 3.5 G

Trim the escarole, removing and discarding the outer leaves. Wash it, shake it dry, and chop it coarsely.

Bring the stock to a boil in a large saucepan. Stir in the olive oil and season to taste with salt and black pepper. Add the escarole to the stock. Mix well, and remove from the heat.

Serve immediately in warm bowls with freshly ground pepper and the grated Parmesan cheese.

Mexican Chicken Soup

SERVES 6

PER SERVING:

CALORIES 486

FAT 15.2 G
SATURATED FAT
2.7 G

(28.2% OF CALO-
RIES FROM FAT)

PROTEIN 8.9 G

CARBOHYDRATE
25.2 G

CHOLESTEROL
24.4 MG

FIBER 7.1 G

❁

I find the smell of this soup alone soothing. I love the scent and flavor of thyme, and it is prominent here. I also love to taste the Spanish rice with every bite. Nurture yourself with this soup when you've come down with a cold. It makes you feel nourished, and it's just the right amount of food.

SPANISH RICE

1 tablespoon olive oil
1/4 cup chopped white onion
1/4 cup chopped celery
1/4 cup chopped carrots
1 cup chopped tomatoes
1/8 teaspoon cayenne pepper
1 tablespoon paprika
11/2 cups brown rice
3 cups chicken stock (page 124) or
    vegetable stock (page 122)
1/2 teaspoon salt

SOUP

1 cup coarsely chopped onions

1 cup peeled, cubed carrots
1 cup coarsely chopped celery
3 tablespoons olive oil
8 cups chicken stock
1 cup cubed potatoes
1/4 teaspoon thyme
1 bay leaf
1 tablespoon salt
1 whole boneless chicken breast,
    cubed
3 ears of corn, cut in half

GARNISH

3/4 cup fresh Salsa (page 8 or 217)
1 ripe avocado, cubed

To make the rice: Heat the olive oil in a big soup pot over low heat, add the onions, celery, carrots, tomatoes, and sauté, stirring, for 3 minutes. Add the spices, rice, stock, and salt. Cover and bring to a boil, then reduce heat and simmer, covered, for 45 minutes.

To make the soup: Put the onions, carrots, and celery in the olive oil in a large sauté pan. Cook over low heat until they become limp. Add the stock, potatoes, thyme, bay leaf, and salt and bring to a boil. Reduce heat and simmer, covered, for 30 minutes. Add the chicken. Cook for 15 more minutes and add the corn. Continue to cook for 5 more minutes.

Put 2 tablespoons of rice into each of 6 soup bowls. Ladle 11/2 cups of soup into each bowl along with 1/2 ear of corn. Garnish with 2 tablespoons of salsa and 1 tablespoon of avocado.

BARLEY AND VEGETABLE SOUP

Barley is a grain that is unfamiliar to most of us. The round, chewy kernels are delightful in soup, especially in a well-flavored vegetable broth. Barley and mushrooms are used together in many dishes from central and eastern Europe.

3/4 cup medium pearl barley
11 cups vegetable stock (page 123)
3 tablespoons extra virgin olive oil
1 1/2 cups chopped onion
1 cup chopped carrot
1 cup mushrooms (shiitake, crimini, or regular button), thinly sliced
1/2 cup chopped celery

Salt and freshly ground black pepper to taste
1/2 cup dry sherry or vermouth

GARNISH
1/4 cup chopped fresh parsley

SERVES 8

PER SERVING:
CALORIES 331
FAT 7 G
   SATURATED FAT
   1 G
(19% OF CALORIES FROM FAT)
PROTEIN 25 G
CARBOHYDRATE
   39 G
CHOLESTEROL
   0 MG
FIBER 13 G

Rinse the barley and place it in a saucepan with 3 cups of the stock and a pinch of salt. Bring to a boil, reduce heat, cover, and simmer until the liquid is absorbed, about 1 hour. Remove from the heat and fluff the barley with a fork.

Meanwhile, heat the olive oil over medium heat in a large pot and add the onions, carrots, mushrooms, and celery. Cook the vegetables for 5 minutes, stirring constantly, until they begin to soften.

Add the remaining stock and salt and pepper to taste, and bring to a boil. Reduce heat, cover, and simmer for 30 minutes.

Add the cooked barley and sherry or vermouth, mix well, and simmer for 5 minutes more. Correct the seasoning. Garnish with the chopped parsley.

Brown Rice Soup with Asparagus

This soup is chunky and thick with vegetables and rice so it can stand on its own with no real need for a side dish. And it's healthy. I serve soups with a warm baguette.

3/4 cup brown rice
1/4 cup wild rice
2 teaspoons salt or to taste
1 bunch asparagus
1 tablespoon olive oil
2 celery stalks, chopped fine
  (about 2/3 cup)
1/2 onion, chopped fine (about 1/3
  cup)
1 small carrot, chopped fine
  (about 1/3 cup)
1/2 teaspoon dried thyme
6 cups vegetable stock (page 122)

2 tablespoons minced scallions or
  green onions
1 tablespoon chopped fresh
  parsley
1 tablespoon natural soy sauce
  (such as tamari)
1/2 teaspoon hot pepper sauce
Freshly ground black pepper (to
  taste)

GARNISH

Parsley sprigs

Put the rice with the salt in 3 cups of water in a medium saucepan. Bring it to a boil, reduce the heat, cover, and simmer until the rice is tender and the water is absorbed, about 45 minutes.

Trim the tough ends off the asparagus stalks and discard. Steam the asparagus until tender yet crisp, about 2 minutes. Drain it in a colander, then rinse under cold water. Let the asparagus cool for a few minutes. When completely cooled, cut into 1-inch pieces, reserving 1/4 cup of tips for garnish.

Coat the bottom of a large pot with the olive oil. Add the celery, onion, carrot, and thyme. Cover and cook over low heat for 4 minutes, stirring occasionally, until tender. Add the vegetable stock and cooked rice and bring to a boil. Reduce the heat, cover, and simmer for 10 minutes. Remove from the heat and let cool a bit.

Carefully transfer small batches to a blender and blend until smooth. Return all the blended mixture to a pot. Stir in the asparagus, scallions, parsley, soy sauce, pepper sauce, and ground pepper. Return to a simmer for 2 minutes. Ladle into bowls and garnish with reserved asparagus tips and parsley sprigs.

Tips from Rosie's Kitchen

I usually use a combination of wild rice and brown rice for this soup. It is sold together and you can find it at any grocery store, or mix your own. You may discover that you have some rice on the shelf that you haven't cooked yet and making this soup gives you an opportunity to use it up.

To Cook Brown Rice: *If you want to use plain brown rice, cook 1 cup rice in 2 cups of water with 1 tablespoon of salt and olive oil, for 45 minutes. Or you can use leftover cooked rice (you'll need about 2 cups; just skip the first step of the recipe in that case).*

If asparagus is out of season, or if you don't want to use it, you can use broccoli and make this soup a year-round favorite.

TOMATO, CORN, AND BASIL SOUP

Normally, I would have thought of this as a soup for summer, when you can get wonderful fresh corn and tomatoes. But I am very impressed with the quality of the new frozen supersweet corn, both yellow and white, and I find canned, organic tomatoes (the Muir Glen brand especially) to be very flavorful and convenient. So as long as you can get fresh basil, you can make this satisfying soup any time of year. It is very easy to make.

SERVES 4

PER SERVING:

CALORIES 191

FAT 8 G
   SATURATED FAT
   1 G
(38% OF CALO-
   RIES FROM FAT)

PROTEIN 5 G

CARBOHYDRATE
   31 G

CHOLESTEROL
   0 MG

FIBER 4 G

1 cup finely chopped onion
2 tablespoons extra virgin olive oil
3–4 cloves garlic, minced
28 ounces canned ground tomatoes, preferably organic
1 cup purified water

3 cups fresh corn kernels cut from the cob or 1 pound frozen sweet corn, preferably organic
Salt and freshly ground black pepper to taste
1 cup finely chopped fresh basil

Sauté the onions in the olive oil in a saucepan over medium-high heat until they just begin to brown. Add the garlic and sauté for a minute, stirring constantly. Pour in the tomatoes and cook, stirring occasionally, until they give up their juice. Cover and continue cooking about 5 minutes more.

Add the water and corn to the soup and cook until the corn is soft and the kernels lose their raw taste, about 5 minutes. Season to taste with salt and pepper. Stir in the basil, mix well, remove from heat, and serve immediately.

CHICKPEA SOUP

This is a hearty soup that could be the centerpiece of a meal when combined with a salad and some good, grainy bread. It provides protein, healthful carbohydrate, fiber, and other micronutrients associated with legumes. The crispy onions provide a great flavor and texture complement to the smooth richness of the soup.

1 pound dry chickpeas
8 cups cold purified water
2 teaspoons baking soda
Salt and freshly ground pepper to
    taste
1 large onion, coarsely chopped
2 tablespoons extra virgin olive oil
4 cloves garlic, minced
1$\frac{1}{2}$ tablespoons ground cumin
1$\frac{1}{2}$ tablespoons ground coriander
1$\frac{1}{2}$ teaspoons ground allspice

GARNISH

1 medium onion, sliced
1 teaspoon extra virgin olive oil
$\frac{1}{4}$ cup chopped fresh parsley

SERVES 8

PER SERVING:
CALORIES 265.7
FAT 7.9 G
  SATURATED FAT
  0.9 G
(25.7% OF CALO-
  RIES FROM FAT)
PROTEIN 11.8 G
CARBOHYDRATE
  39.4 G
CHOLESTEROL
  0 MG
FIBER 10.6 G

Wash and drain the chickpeas and put them in a large pot with the cold water. Stir the baking soda into the water. Let soak at room temperature for 8 hours or overnight.

Bring the chickpeas in their soaking water to a boil over high heat. Skim off the first batch of foam that accumulates, stir the pot, reduce heat, cover, and boil gently until the chickpeas are tender, about 45 minutes.

Preheat oven to 250°F.

Meanwhile, prepare the garnish: Toss the sliced onion rounds with the 1 teaspoon of olive oil and season them with salt and pepper. Place the onion slices on a nonstick baking sheet, making sure they are separated as much as possible and bake until lightly browned, about 45 minutes. Remove and set aside.

Sauté the chopped onions in the 2 tablespoons of olive oil on medium heat, stirring frequently, until the onions are translucent. Add the garlic and sauté, stirring, for another minute. Add the cumin, coriander, allspice, and black pepper to taste. Stir-fry the mixture for another minute, then add it to the chickpeas, mixing well.

Simmer the chickpeas, covered, for 20 minutes. Working in batches, ladle out the chickpeas with their cooking liquid into a food processor and process into a smooth purée. Return the purée to a pot and add salt to taste. Bring it to a simmer. Correct the seasoning and serve the soup in warm bowls. Garnish with the crisp onions and chopped parsley.

ROASTED WINTER SQUASH AND APPLE SOUP

I think this rich soup is a showstopper. See if conversation doesn't come to a halt when people taste it at your table. Roasting brings out a striking depth of flavor in the squash, and the combination with apples and onions is irresistible. The Cilantro Walnut Pesto puts it over the top. I dream about this soup. And you will be delighted to find how easy it is to make. You get all sorts of goodies here: antioxidant carotenes from the squash, omega-3 fatty acids from the walnuts, and plenty of vitamins, minerals, and fiber.

SERVES 4

PER SERVING:

CALORIES 274

FAT 8 G
  SATURATED FAT
  1 G
(26% OF CALORIES
  FROM FAT)

PROTEIN 17 G

CARBOHYDRATE
  40 G

CHOLESTEROL
  0 MG

FIBER 11G

❀

1 large winter squash (about 2½ pounds), such as butternut, buttercup, or kabocha, peeled, seeded, and cut into 2-inch pieces
2 medium onions, peeled and quartered
3 cloves garlic, peeled
2 tart, firm apples, peeled, cored, and quartered
2 tablespoons extra virgin olive oil
Salt and red chili powder to taste
4–5 cups vegetable stock (page 123)

Preheat oven to 400°F.

In a large roasting pan, toss the squash, onions, garlic, and apples with the oil to coat. Season well with the salt and chili powder. Roast, stirring every 10 minutes, until the vegetables are fork-tender and lightly browned, about 40 minutes.

Put half of the vegetables with 2 cups of the stock in a food processor and purée until smooth. Repeat with the remaining vegetables and broth. Return puréed mixture to the pot. If the soup is too thick, add more broth. Correct the seasoning and heat to a simmer.

Serve in warm bowls with dollops of Cilantro Walnut Pesto (page 144).

Roasted Winter Squash and Apple Soup

Cilantro Walnut Pesto

1 cup walnut pieces
2 cups cilantro leaves, stems
  removed
1 jalapeño pepper, seeded and
  chopped

1/2 teaspoon salt, or to taste
1 tablespoon cider vinegar
1/4 cup purified water (approximate)

SERVES 16

PER SERVING:

CALORIES 50

FAT 4.7 G
  SATURATED FAT
  0.4 G

(84.2% OF CALO-
  RIES FROM FAT)

PROTEIN 1.2 G

CARBOHYDRATE
  1.7 G

CHOLESTEROL
  0 MG

FIBER LESS THAN
  1 G

Put the walnuts in a food processor and grind them fine. Add the cilantro, jalapeño pepper, salt, vinegar, and 2–3 tablespoons of water and blend. Blend in a little more water if necessary to make a thick sauce. Taste and correct the seasoning, adding more salt if necessary.

    Keep any leftover pesto in the refrigerator in a tightly covered container and use as a dip or spread.

DIETARY SUPPLEMENTS

Millions of people take dietary supplements. Sales of vitamins, minerals, and related products are in the billions of dollars. Is it really necessary to take them? Shouldn't your diet provide you with everything your body needs?

Ideally, yes. If we all ate high-quality fresh foods prepared in healthful ways and, especially, got a variety of fruits and vegetables at every meal, our nutritional needs would be satisfied and there would be no need to supplement. But that's not the case for most of us. I'm not always in control of my diet. When I travel, for example, I am rarely able to eat optimally. Furthermore, some dietary supplements may offer specific preventive or therapeutic benefits that are worth considering.

A common mistake is to think that supplements are substitutes for whole foods, that taking a multivitamin makes up for not eating fruits and vegetables, for example. That is not the case. Whole foods contain large arrays of compounds beneficial to health; pills provide a limited selection of them. For example, we know that foods containing beta-carotene, the principal member of the carotenoid family of pigments that give color to yellow and orange fruits and vegetables and also occur (less visibly) in dark, leafy greens, are highly cancer-protective. Many people assume that taking isolated beta-carotene in pill form gives the same protection. It does not. In fact, evidence suggests that supplemental beta-carotene may actually raise cancer risks in some people (smokers, for example). It is the whole family of carotenoids, taken together, that does the trick. Some supplements now contain mixed carotenoids; still, they do not provide the whole spectrum of these pigments in the same balance that nature does, and I would not count on them as substitutes for the natural sources.

A better way to think of supplementation is as insurance against gaps in the diet, to compensate on those occasions when your intake of micronutrients is less than ideal, or to provide for increased needs that result from stress or exposure to environmental toxins.

I take a multivitamin and multimineral supplement every day because I want to be sure I'm getting enough folic acid and vitamin E. Folic acid, a B vitamin that occurs in beans, leafy greens, and orange juice, regulates many metabolic reactions and many of us do not get enough of it—deficiency of it can raise risks of many chronic diseases, including heart disease and cancer. There is also some evidence that the body can use supplemental folic acid even better than some of the food sources of it. I recommend taking 400 micrograms a day in addition to whatever you may be getting from your diet. As for vitamin E, studies indicate that 400 to 800 international units a day gives maximum antioxidant protection. To get that amount from food, you would have to eat a pound or so of nuts and seeds, taking in much too much fat in the bargain. My multivitamin provides 400 IU of the natural form of vitamin E, which I prefer.

My bottom line is this: I make an effort to eat an optimum diet, and for the most part I eat the kinds of food described in this book. I do not go overboard on supplements, but I use some of them judiciously to cover those days when I may not be getting all the micronutrients I need to maintain optimum health.

—A.W.

Entrées

Savory Roasted Cornish Hens with
   Roasted Garlic

Cold Vegetable Pasta Primavera

Linguine with Steamed Clams and
   Mussels

White Beans and Fusilli

Eggplant Rollatini with Spinach and
   Cheese Filling

Vegetable Lasagna

Roasted Pepper Turkey with Orange
   Liqueur

Savory Lobster-Mushroom Crepe

Fish with Spinach *en Papillote*

Grilled Fresh Sardines

Seared Salmon with Orange Glaze

Grilled Ahi Tuna with Cilantro Ginger
   Sauce

Duxelles-Stuffed Sole

Grilled Salmon with Mustard Sauce

Lemon Grilled Halibut

Grilled Fish with Tropical Relish

Baked Curried Sea Bass with Lentils

Vegetarian Shepherd's Pie

Slow-Baked Tofu with Stir-Fry

Baked Pressed Tofu with Greens

Baked Spicy Tofu with Bean Thread
    Noodles, Corn, and Mango

Teriyaki Sampler Plate

Turkey Burgers

Hummus Pinwheels with Raw Veggie
    Crudités

Orange Chicken Pita with Vegetables and
    Tahini Dressing

Santa Fe Chicken

Grilled Fish Tacos

Chicken Quesadillas

Tofu Fajitas

Baked Bean and Rice Cheese Burrito

Gallo Pinto (Costa Rican Rice and Beans)

Tostadas with Salsa and Guacamole

Steamed Broccoli with Gluten

Cauliflower with Curried Gluten

MEAT AND MEAT SUBSTITUTES

This book does not have any recipes for red meat but does have several that call for tofu and gluten, which some people think of as meat substitutes. Rosie and I avoid red meat for a number of reasons, primarily because of concerns for our health and the health of the planet. Meat certainly provides protein that the body can easily use, but it also gives us a great deal of saturated fat and toxins. The toxins represent pollutants in the environment that large animals tend to concentrate in their tissues as well as residues of drugs and hormones used in the commercial raising of animals for food. If you do eat meat, we recommend that you try to use drug-and-hormone-free, organically raised products. Even so, we worry that the large-scale raising of animals for food is terribly wasteful of resources—the grain they consume would be much better used to feed people directly. And our methods of raising them cause serious pollution of groundwater, soil, and the atmosphere.

Epidemiological studies consistently reveal that populations that eat more meat have decreased longevity and poorer health than populations that eat less. The impact of meat eating on cardiovascular health may account for much of the difference. People who eat less meat also tend to eat more fish and vegetables, which have beneficial effects on health. Neither Rosie nor I am a militant vegetarian. I eat fish, and Rosie likes to cook with chicken. But we both want to demonstrate the possibilities for creating satisfying main dishes without using meat.

Many American vegetarians eat less-than-optimum diets. They eat a lot of macaroni and cheese, or meatless lasagna, for example, which are high in fat and low in many of the nutrients we need. They would do better to explore the range of vegetarian dishes from ethnic cuisines, such as those of India, China, Southeast Asia, and the Middle East.

Some vegetarians—to the puzzlement of others—gravitate toward imitations of familiar dishes: veggie burgers and veggie sausages, for example, or even "tofurkeys," holiday tofu roasts complete with stuffing and gravy. Actually, the tradition of "facsimile food" has a long history in the Buddhist temple cuisine of China and Japan, where monks developed meat substitutes that enabled them to copy classic dishes without violating their religious beliefs. There are

Chinese restaurants today that serve these creations: everything from sweet-and-sour "pork" to Peking "duck," all made without animal products.

The meatlike proteins used in these dishes are ingenious derivatives of soybeans and wheat. For example, the skin that forms on the surface of a pan of soymilk can be dried, soaked, and deep-fried to produce a tasty facsimile of the crisp skin of a roasted duck or chicken. A flour-and-water dough can be kneaded under water until all the starch washes out, leaving the pure wheat protein—gluten. Gluten is a rubbery, neutral-tasting product that can be flavored, then braised, baked, or fried to yield a remarkable range of tasty, chewy morsels that closely reproduce the qualities of meat in stir-fries and stews.

We have given some examples of this kind of cooking in these pages—recipes using baked tofu and prepared gluten. Try them to see if you like these meat substitutes as much as we do. I prefer to think of them not as substitutes but rather as delicious foods in their own right that extend the range of creative possibilities in the kitchen. Whether you come to use them or not, it is worth knowing how to turn out meatless dishes that are good enough not to leave guests wondering when the main course is coming. —**A.W.**

Savory Roasted Cornish Hens with Roasted Garlic

Small, free-range chickens can be substituted for the Cornish game hens. Cornish hens are small, hybrid chickens. Free-range chickens are raised with room to move about both indoors and outdoors as opposed to being raised in a cage. They are free of growth hormones and antibiotics, and because of this some people believe they have a richer flavor.

The roasted garlic head tastes wonderful squeezed onto slices of crusty French bread, making a good accompaniment to the poultry. Or you could squeeze the bulbs over Mashed Potatoes and Parsnips (page 231).

Savory Roasted Cornish Hens
with Roasted Garlic

MAKES 8 HALF-HEN
SERVINGS

PER SERVING:

CALORIES 376.1

FAT 14.4 G
  SATURATED FAT
  4.2 G
  (35.4% OF CALO-
  RIES FROM FAT)

PROTEIN 30.8 G

CARBOHYDRATE
  28.2 G

CHOLESTEROL
  153 MG

FIBER 2.5 G

4 Cornish hens or 2 free-range
  chickens
1/2 cup freshly squeezed lemon
  juice
4 teaspoons lemon pepper
Salt
4 cups quartered plum tomatoes,
  or whole cherry tomatoes
  (about 2 pints)
8 large shallots
4 large cloves garlic
2 cups chopped fennel (1 small
  bulb)
1/2 teaspoon salt
1/2 cup lightly packed chopped
  fresh basil
1 cup red wine
4 bay leaves
4 lemon slices
4 sprigs fresh rosemary

ROASTED GARLIC

8 whole garlic bulbs
1 teaspoon olive oil
3 tablespoons water

GARNISH

8 sprigs fresh rosemary
1 lemon, cut into 8 slices

Rinse the Cornish hens thoroughly, letting the water gush inside each cavity and drain back out. Rub the lemon juice, lemon pepper, and a little salt over the birds and let marinate for 1 hour or overnight. Put the tomatoes, shallots, garlic, fennel, a pinch of salt, basil, and red wine together in a medium bowl and stir until everything is thoroughly mixed.

Preheat oven to 375°F.

Place 1 bay leaf, 1 lemon slice, 1 rosemary sprig, and equal portions of the tossed tomato filling inside each hen. Each cavity should be full. Spoon the remaining filling over the bottom of a roasting pan. Set the birds on top, spacing them evenly apart, spoon the lemon marinating juice over them, then sprinkle a little salt over them. Roast for 1 1/4 hours. (For chicken, roast 1 1/2 hours.) The skins will be golden brown, and the juices will run clear when they are done.

Meanwhile, prepare the roasted garlic: Cut 1/2 inch off the top of each garlic bulb so that the cloves can be easily squeezed out after roasting. Put the olive oil and water in the bottom of a 9-inch baking pan. Arrange the garlic bulbs in the pan, cut side on top. Cover the pan with a lid or foil. After the hens have been roasting for 30 minutes, place the garlic dish in the same oven and bake for 45 minutes.

Remove the hens from the oven to a platter or board and let them rest at room temperature for 15 minutes. When all the hens are cool, scoop the filling out from each hen and put it into the roasting pan with the remaining filling. Remove all the bay leaves and discard. Set the pan over low heat and simmer, stirring and scraping up the browned bits, for 3–4 minutes.

Split each hen in half by cutting directly down the middle of the spine, slicing completely through to the other side. If you wish, remove and discard the skins. Place all the hens on a serving dish or half a hen on each of 8 plates, with the breasts lying flat, and spoon the warm filling on top. You may put everything in the oven for a couple of minutes to keep warm until ready to serve. Garnish with a sprig of rosemary and a slice of lemon. Serve with slices of warm crusty bread to squeeze the roasted garlic onto.

Tips from Rosie's Kitchen

If you have time, marinate the hens or chickens in the lemon juice, pepper, and salt overnight. It is worth it, because the flavors of the marinade are sealed into the meat, and then baked in it, along with the meat's own juices. What you get is juicier and more flavorful meat. Just stuff the birds as directed, marinate them in a large pot, cover, and refrigerate.

If you want to remove the bones of the hens before serving, open the cavity slightly and pull them out gently. Discard the bones and repeat this process for the remaining 3 hens. I usually pull the bones out, but if you find this to be a hassle, leave them in.

Polenta (page 76) is also a great accompaniment to this dish. Spoon the hot polenta on individual serving plates, top with a Cornish hen, and serve immediately.

GARLIC

For centuries, people have esteemed garlic as a remedy as well as a powerful flavoring agent; some even claim it's an aphrodisiac. Chinese cooks add garlic to dishes as much for its health benefits as for its taste; doctors in the West are just starting to learn about those benefits. Garlic not only lowers blood pressure and cholesterol, it also thins the blood (reducing risk of heart attack) and counteracts the growth of yeast and many kinds of bacteria. It's hard for me to imagine cooking without garlic. If I smell it in a kitchen, I feel right at home.

When you buy garlic, look for heads that are plump and firm, not dry or shrunken. Big cloves are easier to deal with than little ones. There are many ways of preparing the cloves, from smashing them with the broad side of a knife to putting them through a garlic press. However you do it, be aware that the medicinal virtues of garlic develop only when the flesh is exposed to air and dissipate under the influence of heat. When garlic is cut or crushed, an oxidation reaction quickly turns an inactive precursor into allicin, the main compound responsible for the medicinal properties. Allicin also creates much of garlic's pungency. Cooking tames that quality and also destroys much of the therapeutic effect. Therefore, to get the maximum benefit, let minced or crushed garlic stand for a few minutes before adding it to food, use some raw (as in salad dressings), and add it near the end of cooking when possible to preserve allicin content. (Baked garlic, recently popular as an appetizer to be eaten with bread or with bread and cheese, is not the best way to get real garlic flavor and power.)

Some people are afraid of garlic because they think it will make them smell bad to others. I have never minded that smell, and I have also found that by starting with small amounts of garlic, eating it regularly, and gradually working up, most people can learn to digest it without problems of breath or body odor. If you are timid about garlic, I urge you to make friends with it. For me, food without it is so drab. **—A.W.**

ABOUT SHELLFISH

Shellfish are of two types: crustaceans and mollusks. Crustaceans include crabs, crayfish, lobsters, and shrimp. Their flesh contains cholesterol but little fat and provides high-quality protein. I eat shrimp occasionally, the others very rarely. My concerns about them have to do with their feeding habits. Crustaceans are scavengers and bottom feeders; they live in places where toxic pollutants accumulate. These creatures can be farmed, and if farmers take care to give them clean water, their value as protein foods is much higher. Shrimp farming, however, is a major contributor to environmental pollution, and most of it goes on in developing countries. If you eat shrimp, look for trap-caught spot prawns as an alternative to the farmed varieties.

Be aware that crustaceans spoil quickly once they die. Pay attention to freshness and quality of any that you cook. Also, you should know that crustacean allergies are not uncommon and that the reactions can be severe.

Mollusks include clams, mussels, oysters, and scallops—all "filter feeders" that actually clean the water they live in. It is especially important to get them from unpolluted waters because of the risk of toxic contamination. Eating raw mollusks is additionally risky because of the possibility of viral and bacterial infection. Serious diseases like hepatitis and cholera can be acquired from these foods, and other shellfish-borne infections that would not bother most of us can be life-threatening for those with compromised immune systems (patients on immunosuppressive drugs and people with AIDS).

Bottom line: Exercise caution with shellfish. Find out where they come from and pay particular attention to freshness and quality. —**A.W.**

Cold Vegetable Pasta Primavera

Cold pasta dishes are often overlooked, perhaps because we are used to seeing them looking tired in a deli counter. When the noodles are made fresh and tossed with seasoned, grilled vegetables and home-made sauce, it makes all the difference.

Serves 6

Per serving:

Calories 696.5

Fat 28.1 g
  Saturated fat
  6.8 g
(34.9% of calo-
  ries from fat)

Protein 19.9 g

Carbohydrate
  97.8 g

Cholesterol
  22 mg

Fiber 14.6 g

SEASONING

1/4 cup olive oil
1 tablespoon Italian seasoning
1/8 teaspoon cayenne pepper
  (optional)
1/4 teaspoon salt
1/8 teaspoon coarsely cracked
  black pepper

GRILLED VEGETABLES

1 zucchini, cut lengthwise into
  slices 1/2-inch thick
2 summer squash, cut lengthwise
  into slices 1/2-inch thick
4 Japanese eggplants, cut lengthwise into slices 1/2-inch thick
1 onion, cut into 1/2-inch slices
1 red bell pepper, stem and seeds
  removed, cut lengthwise into
  3/4-inch slices

PASTA SAUCE

1 tablespoon minced garlic
3 tablespoons finely minced shallots or white onions
Juice from 1 lemon (about 1/4
  cup)
1/4 cup balsamic or red wine
  vinegar
4 tablespoons olive oil
6 cups peeled, seeded, and diced
  tomatoes
1 teaspoon salt
1 pound fusilli
1 teaspoon grated lemon zest
1/2 teaspoon freshly ground black
  pepper
20 fresh basil leaves, shredded
1 cup sliced green or black olives
1/4 cup capers
1 cup cubed feta cheese

Mix all the seasoning ingredients together in a large bowl, then put in the sliced vegetables and toss until all the vegetables are completely coated. Spread out the vegetables on the grill and cook over medium-low heat for 1 1/2 minutes on each side.

Make the sauce: Mix the garlic, minced shallots, lemon juice, vinegar, and 3 tablespoons of the olive oil together in a bowl. Place the tomatoes in a blender or food processor to purée, then add them to the bowl. Cover and refrigerate.

Bring a large pot of water and 1/2 teaspoon of the salt to a boil and cook the pasta until it is done. Drain through a colander. Transfer the pasta to a large bowl and toss with the remaining 1 tablespoon of olive oil. Add the grated lemon zest, pepper, the remaining 1/2 teaspoon salt, and the grilled vegetables and toss again.

Remove the sauce from the refrigerator just before you are ready to serve, and mix in the shredded basil leaves until they are evenly distributed throughout the sauce. Pour the sauce over the pasta and grilled vegetables, add the olives and capers, and toss until all the strands of pasta and the vegetables are evenly coated. Top with sprinkles of feta cheese and serve.

Tips from Rosie's Kitchen

Be sure to start the grill ahead of time so that you have embers to grill over. You can also broil the vegetables if you prefer.

The grilled vegetables alone make a wonderful first course if you don't want to make the pasta. Or if you don't want to bother to grill, just make the pasta and serve it with the sauce, hot or cold.

I always find it handy to know how to mix my own seasonings. If you don't have Italian seasoning on hand and wish to mix it yourself, follow the recipe for Rosie's Italian Seasoning: 1/4 teaspoon sage, 1 teaspoon thyme, 1 teaspoon basil, and 1 teaspoon oregano.

Linguine with Steamed Clams and Mussels

SERVES 6

PER SERVING:

CALORIES 494.1

FAT 8.3 G
  SATURATED FAT
  1.2 G

(16.1% OF CALO-
  RIES FROM FAT)

PROTEIN 29.3 G

CARBOHYDRATE
  67.9 G

CHOLESTEROL
  47 MG

FIBER 2.5 G

❋

Although this pasta dish consists of fairly basic and quick cooking ingredients, you can give it a formal presentation. I steam just the clams or mussels if I'm serving this dish as an appetizer, or I pair the entrée with a mixed-green salad and warm slices of Whole Wheat Baguettes with Sun-Dried Tomatoes and Herbs (page 255) for a full meal.

2 pounds mussels or clams, or 1 pound each
1 pound linguine
1 teaspoon salt
1 cup white wine
1/2 cup purified water
3 cloves garlic, sliced
3 shallots, chopped
2 tomatoes, chopped (about 2 cups)
2 tablespoons chopped fresh basil

1/4 teaspoon salt
1/2 teaspoon freshly ground black pepper
1/8 teaspoon chili flakes (optional)
2 tablespoons olive oil
Juice of 1 lemon (about 1/4 cup)
1 teaspoon grated lemon zest

GARNISH

2 tablespoons chopped fresh parsley

Soak the clams or mussels in a pan full of cold water for 5 minutes. Scrub the shells to remove any seaweed or mud using a vegetable scrubber or the abrasive side of a clean sponge.

Bring a large pot of water to a boil. Drop the linguine into it, add the salt, and cook until it is al dente.

Meanwhile put the clams or mussels in a large, lidded pot with enough space to hold them without them being cramped. Add the white wine, water, garlic, and shallots. Cover and cook over high heat, shaking the pot occasionally, until the shellfish open, about 10 minutes.

Drain the pasta in a colander, then toss it with the shellfish. Add the tomatoes, basil, salt, pepper, chili flakes, and olive oil, and toss again. Squeeze the lemon over everything, toss in the zest, and garnish with parsley. Serve immediately.

ANDY SUGGESTS

In order to get a more intense flavor, I would increase both the garlic and red pepper flakes.

PASTA

Who does not like pasta? People all over the world love noodles, but some of us shun them because we fear they will make us fat. There is no question that many pasta dishes are fattening, fettucine Alfredo being a case in point—with all the butterfat in it, it is not good for the cardiovascular system, either. But pasta remains a nourishing and satisfying food that can be very good for you if you follow a few suggestions.

First of all, buy high-quality pasta made exclusively with hard (durum) wheat. It has more protein and less starch. Experiment with pasta that contains some whole wheat. To my taste most whole wheat pastas are terrible: gritty and lacking in the elastic quality I like. Japanese udon noodles are wonderful, however, as are some Italian shaped pastas made with a mixture of whole wheat and semolina. I'm also fond of Japanese soba noodles, prepared from a mixture of buckwheat and wheat flours. I like them in low-fat hot soups and also cold, dipped into a richly flavored, non-fat sauce. Get to know Southeast Asian rice stick noodles and Chinese cellophane noodles, made from mung beans rather than grain and therefore much higher in protein and lower in starch.

Next, learn to cook pasta properly. One of the best pieces of news to come out of research on carbohydrate foods is that pasta has a significantly lower glycemic index than bread and so has less of an impact on blood sugar. The reason is that digestive enzymes take longer to get to the starch in pasta because it is more compact than that in bread, which offers much greater surface area for enzymatic action. For the many of us who are carbohydrate sensitive, that means we can enjoy pasta in moderation, even if we ought to minimize consumption of bread (especially the fluffy white sort). You should know that the glycemic index of pasta is still lower when it is cooked al dente, and so even more resistant to quick digestion. Many Americans find the pasta of Italy underdone on first meeting it, but if, like so many of us, you can learn to prefer it this way, you will be eating more healthily as a result.

Another obvious suggestion is to find ways of eating pasta without drowning it in fat, especially butter, cream, and cheese. I recommend looking to the cuisines of Asia for inspiration here rather than to Italy. Asians eat noodles in flavorful, low-fat soups or stir-fry them with vegetables and protein foods in small amounts of unsaturated oils. If you want an Italian preparation, pasta is delicious with a fresh tomato sauce made with a small amount of olive oil and topped with a modest amount of freshly grated Parmesan cheese. Not only will you get the health benefits of olive oil in this dish, you will get a good helping of lycopene, the red pigment from tomatoes with anticancer properties. Lycopene is available from cooked tomatoes, not raw, and needs fat to be absorbed, so this is a perfect way to include it in your diet. **—A.W.**

White Beans and Fusilli

This makes a great lunch as well as an entrée for dinner. I make this pasta dish with beans because they provide a bit of protein. Serve with a green salad and a sliced French baguette brushed with olive oil and toasted.

SERVES 6

PER SERVING:

CALORIES 538.3

FAT 4.1 G
  SATURATED FAT
  0.6 G
(6.9% OF CALORIES
  FROM FAT)

PROTEIN 26 G

CARBOHYDRATE
  100.1 G

CHOLESTEROL 0 MG

FIBER 12.8 G

❋

WHITE BEANS

1 cup Great Northern or cannellini beans, soaked overnight in 3 cups of water to cover and 1/2 teaspoon baking soda
1 bay leaf
3 cups vegetable stock (page 122)

PESTO

1/2 cup walnuts
5 cups fresh basil
5 large cloves garlic, peeled or smashed
1/4 cup freshly grated Parmesan cheese
2 tablespoons olive oil

PASTA

1 pound fusilli or pasta shells
1/2 teaspoon salt
1 small onion, chopped (about 1/2 cup)
2 cloves garlic, chopped
1 bunch escarole, chopped
1/3 teaspoon dried rosemary
1 tablespoon olive oil
Salt to taste

GARNISH

1 lemon, sliced

Drop the bay leaf into the pot of water that the beans have been soaking in overnight. Bring the water to a boil, pour in the vegetable stock, and cook for 45 minutes or longer. The beans should be able to be easily pierced with a fork.

Make the pesto: Put all the pesto ingredients, except the oil, in a food processor and blend. Slowly add the oil and continue to process until it becomes a smooth paste. Set aside.

Bring a large pot of water with the salt to a boil. Add the pasta and cook until it is al dente.

Meanwhile, sauté the onions, garlic, escarole, and rosemary in 1 tablespoon of olive oil until limp. Add salt to taste and mix in with the beans.

Drain the pasta in a colander and pour it into a large bowl. Add about 1/3 cup of the pesto or more to taste and toss well until it is distributed evenly and the strands of pasta are coated.

Serve the pasta in 6 individual pasta bowls and ladle white beans on top. Garnish each with a slice of lemon.

Tips from Rosie's Kitchen

Store any leftover pesto in ice cube trays, then cover and freeze. Pesto is wonderful tossed with warm noodles or mixed with béchamel or white sauce and tossed with pasta. Check the index for other recipes that include pesto.

Eggplant Rollatini with Spinach and Cheese Filling

The tomato sauce is always best when it's fresh, but it can be made up to one day in advance if necessary.

Finish this dish off with a side of freshly steamed broccoli, a crunchy green salad, and a warm slice of whole grain baguette.

SERVES 6

PER SERVING:

CALORIES 309.9

FAT 18.2 G
 SATURATED FAT
 4.1 G

(53.1% OF CALO-
 RIES FROM FAT)

PROTEIN 14.5 G

CARBOHYDRATE
 26.4 G

CHOLESTEROL
 11.7 MG

FIBER 8.1 G

Tomato Mushroom Sauce (page 256)
2 bunches spinach (about 1 pound), stems removed
2 large onions, finely chopped
2 large cloves garlic, minced
5 tablespoons olive oil
2 ounces feta cheese
1 cup low-fat cottage cheese or skim ricotta
1/8 cup finely chopped walnuts
2 egg whites
1/2 cup whole wheat bread crumbs
2 tablespoons minced parsley
1 teaspoon salt
1 teaspoon freshly ground black pepper
1/4 teaspoon nutmeg or mace
1/2 teaspoon ground fennel or cumin
2 medium eggplants, washed

GARNISH

6 Kalamata olives, pitted and sliced
2 tablespoons freshly grated Parmesan cheese
1/4 cup chopped fresh parsley

Prepare the Tomato Mushroom Sauce so it will be ready when you put together the dish.

Preheat oven to 375°F.

To cook the spinach, set a steamer basket inside a large pot and fill it with enough water so that it barely touches the bottom of the basket. Put the spinach leaves in the basket, cover the pot, and steam for 2 minutes, maximum. Drain the spinach in a colander and let it cool. When it is completely cooled, squeeze the excess water from the leaves by wrapping the spinach in cheesecloth and squeezing gently. If you don't have cheesecloth, put a bowl or plate directly on top of the spinach, inside the colander, and press down gently.

Sauté the onions and garlic in a sauté pan in 2 tablespoons of the olive oil until soft. Add the cooked spinach, feta and cottage cheese, walnuts, egg whites, bread crumbs, parsley, and spices. Stir with a wooden spoon until all the ingredients are thoroughly blended.

Slice the eggplants lengthwise into thin slices and lightly brush them with the remaining olive oil, using a pastry brush. Broil them on a cookie sheet on the middle rack, just until lightly browned, about 3 minutes. Remove the eggplants from the oven and cover the cookie sheet with plastic wrap to allow them to steam, then cool. Once they are cool, arrange 2–3 tablespoons of the spinach filling at the narrow end of each slice and roll it up. Arrange the rolls in a baking dish with the seam facing down. Pour the tomato sauce over the top of each rollatini and bake until the sauce is bubbling, about 20–25 minutes. Garnish with the olive slices and a sprinkling of Parmesan cheese and parsley.

Vegetable Lasagna

What I love about this lasagna is that most of it can be made ahead of time and the noodles that I use are pre-boiled, which saves a lot of time.

This lasagna has two sauces in it, but you have the option of making it with just one of them. The white sauce should be made fresh, but the red sauce and the filling can be made a day in advance and refrigerated.

When children want to participate in the kitchen, it usually involves making a dessert, but this is an entrée that children can help

make. I think laying the noodles down, pouring sauce or spreading the filling on top can be fun for kids and will make them feel that a substantial meal was successfully completed due to their efforts.

MARINARA SAUCE

1 cup chopped onion

3 cloves garlic

1/2 cup chopped, peeled carrots

3 tablespoons olive oil

1/2 cup red wine

1/2 teaspoon dried oregano

1 teaspoon dried basil

16 blanched plum tomatoes, peeled and seeded (or 28 ounces canned peeled whole tomatoes)

1/2 cup chopped mushrooms

1 tablespoon honey or sugar

1/2 teaspoon salt or to taste

1 tablespoon Italian seasoning

EGGPLANT

1 medium eggplant, sliced lengthwise 1/2 inch thick

Salt to taste

Less than 1/8 teaspoon cayenne pepper

2 tablespoons olive oil

SPINACH

2 bunches (about 1 pound) washed, stems removed

5 ounces goat cheese or ricotta cheese

1 tablespoon olive oil

1/2 cup chopped onion

2 cloves garlic, sliced

1/8 teaspoon freshly ground black pepper

2 tablespoons chopped fresh basil

BASIC WHITE SAUCE

(page 169)

LASAGNA

12 sheets oven-ready lasagna noodles

1 cup purified water

1 1/2 cups mozzarella, shredded

10 Kalamata olives, pitted and halved

SERVES 12

PER SERVING:

CALORIES 583.6

FAT 18.9 G

  SATURATED FAT 5.9 G

(29.1% OF CALORIES FROM FAT)

PROTEIN 20.5 G

CARBOHYDRATE 83.1 G

CHOLESTEROL 25 MG

FIBER 6.3 G

Make the marinara sauce: Sauté the onion, garlic, and carrots in the olive oil in a medium saucepan over low heat for 3 minutes. Add the red wine, oregano, and basil, and cook for an additional 5 minutes until the wine is reduced by half. Add the tomatoes, mushrooms, honey or sugar, salt, and Italian seasoning, and continue to cook until the mushrooms become limp, about 15 minutes.

Vegetable Lasagna

Tips from Rosie's Kitchen

If you want to cook your own lasagna instead of buying oven-ready ones, don't add the cup of water when you are laying the cooked lasagna in the pan. The water is poured over the oven-ready lasagna before baking only to add some moisture.

Preheat the broiler.

Broil the eggplant: Brush both sides of the eggplant with olive oil, salt lightly, sprinkle on a little cayenne, and lay on a baking tray. Broil for 3 minutes on the middle rack under the broiler until it turns brown. Remove from the oven and let cool.

Prepare the spinach: Steam the spinach for 1 minute in a pot filled with 1/2 cup purified water. Remove from the heat and let cool. Squeeze the spinach, using clean hands, to remove excess water.

Put the softened goat cheese or ricotta in a medium bowl. Add the spinach and mix together thoroughly with a fork.

Put the olive oil, onions, and sliced garlic in a small sauté pan over low heat. Sauté for 2 minutes until the onions turn

light golden brown. Remove from the heat and cool. Add it to the softened cheese and spinach and mix. Add the pepper and the fresh basil and mix again until all the ingredients are thoroughly blended in.

Make the white sauce.

Preheat oven to 375°F.

To assemble the lasagna: Cover the bottom of a deep baking dish with 1/2 cup marinara sauce. Lay 4 sheets of the oven-ready noodles on top. Spoon the spinach filling over the noodles and spread it around until all of them are covered. Pour the white sauce on top, covering all the noodles. Lay 4 more sheets of noodles on top of the white sauce. Lay the eggplant slices lengthwise over the noodles. Sprinkle the mozzarella cheese on top. Pour 1 cup of marinara sauce over the cheese. Lay another 4 sheets of noodles over the sauce. Slowly pour the water over the lasagna stack. Pour the remaining marinara sauce on top of the noodles. Sprinkle the top with remaining mozzarella cheese and the olives. Cover with foil and cook for 11/2 hours in the oven. When it is completely cooked, remove from the oven and let cool for 5 minutes. Cut into squares.

A serving of the
Vegetable Lasagna

Getting kids to help with the lasagna—making a layer of
eggplant and sprinkling on the cheese

Roasted Pepper Turkey with Orange Liqueur

I make this for a holiday dinner or when I'm planning to have a large group of friends and family over.

The outside of the turkey is encrusted with a baked-on pepper rub. Inside, the meat is juicy and tender. This is great served with the Serrano Chili and Cilantro Cornbread Muffins (page 253), a side of Pear Relish (page 252) or Fresh Applesauce (page 249), and/or Steamed and Roasted Baby Red Potatoes (page 242).

SERVES 12,
WITH LEFTOVERS

PER SERVING:

CALORIES 185.9

FAT 6.9 G
   SATURATED FAT
   2.1 G
   (7.4% OF CALORIES
   FROM FAT)

PROTEIN 182.8 G

CARBOHYDRATE
   11.1 G

CHOLESTEROL
   58 MG

FIBER 1.8 G

❄

One 10–12-pound turkey
1/2 cup white wine

PEPPER RUB

11/2 teaspoons dried basil
11/2 teaspoons dried oregano
1 teaspoon cayenne pepper
1 tablespoon paprika
11/2 teaspoons salt

3 tablespoons Grand Marnier

SEASONING

5 cloves garlic
2 small onions, sliced
2 carrots, cut in rounds
1 bay leaf
2 orange slices

Preheat oven to 350°F.

Remove the neck and other organs from the turkey cavity and reserve to make stock at a later time. Rinse the turkey in the sink and let the water gush inside the cavity.

Mix all the ingredients for the rub together with the Grand Marnier. Spread it over the outside of the turkey, reserving 1 tablespoon. Spoon the 1 tablespoon into the cavity of the turkey. Stuff the cavity with all of the seasoning ingredients.

Set the turkey in a roasting pan and pour in the wine. Cover the turkey with foil and roast. After 2 hours, uncover the turkey and baste with the cooking juices. Continue to baste the turkey with the juices every 20 minutes for the next 11/2 hours, until it is done. Total roasting time should be 31/2 hours.

Let the turkey cool for at least 15 minutes before carving.

Tips from Rosie's Kitchen

Save the turkey bones to make stock!

Invariably with a good-sized turkey, there are leftovers, and that's part of the pleasure.

Turkey Sandwiches: *This is the time to make sandwiches spread with an impressive mayonnaise made by combining the Mock Sour Cream recipe (page 62) and the Pesto recipe (page 160). Serve the sandwiches on dense whole wheat bread, topped with crunchy lettuce and cold tomato slices. If you can't eat up all the leftovers within a few days, store the meat in airtight zip-lock bags or plastic containers in the freezer for up to 3 weeks. When you are ready to eat it, defrost the meat slowly in the refrigerator.*

Savory Lobster-Mushroom Crepe

The powerful flavors of lobster or crab, saffron, and mushrooms all wrapped together in a freshly made, tarragon-flavored crepe create a very elegant dish. Even though it is rich, it doesn't overwhelm the taste buds. I like to serve this entrée with a salad and the Lemon Dill Vinaigrette (page 113).

BASIC WHITE SAUCE OR BÉCHAMEL

2 tablespoons olive oil

2 cups warm milk

2 tablespoons unbleached white flour

1/4 cup freshly grated Parmesan cheese

1/4 cup thinly sliced scallions or green onions

1/8 teaspoon nutmeg, preferably freshly grated

1/8 teaspoon cayenne pepper

3/4 teaspoon salt

CREPE BATTER

1 cup unbleached white flour
1 egg
2 cups milk
1/8 teaspoon lemon zest
3/4 teaspoon salt
5 tablespoons melted butter
1 tablespoon chopped fresh tarragon, or 1 teaspoon dried

LOBSTER FILLING

3 large lobster tails, defrosted (about 3 cups uncooked, shelled lobster) (see Tips), or 5 Alaskan king crab legs, fresh or frozen (page 65 for preparation)

1/4 cup white wine
1/2 teaspoon saffron threads (optional)
2 tablespoons olive oil
1/2 cup chopped button mushrooms, or 2 cups chopped shiitake or oyster mushrooms (see Tips)
1/2 cup white wine
1 cup peeled and minced shallots
1/8 teaspoon chili flakes

GARNISH

1/4 cup chopped fresh parsley

MAKES 12 CREPES
TO SERVE 6

PER SERVING:

CALORIES 552.4

FAT 27.5 G
  SATURATED FAT
  11.7 G
  (46.5% OF CALO-
  RIES FROM FAT)

PROTEIN 38.4 G

CARBOHYDRATE
  32.9 G

CHOLESTEROL
  220 MG

FIBER 1.1 G

Make the white sauce: Pour the olive oil into a medium saucepan over low heat. Put the milk in a separate saucepan over low heat only until it becomes warm; do not let it boil. Gradually stir the flour into the warm oil, stirring constantly. Let cook for about 1 minute to make a brownish roux. Slowly add 1/4 cup of the warm milk and whisk it to blend it in. Pour in the remaining milk, continuing to whisk. Allow the sauce to simmer about 2 minutes just to thicken slightly, then turn off the heat. Mix in the cheese, spices, and salt. Cover the sauce with plastic wrap until ready to use.

Make the crepes: Put the flour in a large bowl and in the middle make a small well big enough to hold the egg. Crack the egg into the well. Pour the milk around the flour. Add the zest, salt, butter, and tarragon. Whisk everything together until the batter is smooth. Let the batter set, covered, for 1 hour.

Set a medium (about 6-inch-bottom) nonstick pan over medium-high heat for a few seconds until it starts to get hot. Pull the pan away from the heat, and pour 3 tablespoons of batter into the pan. With the pan still away from the heat, roll the pan around so that the batter spreads evenly across the bottom. Set the pan back on the heat until the edges of the batter curl up and bubbles appear on the surface, then flip the crepe over and cook on the other side for about 1 minute. Remove each crepe when done and continue with the rest of the batter. Let the crepes cool before you stack them, or they will become mushy. When completely cooled, stack them individually with wax paper between each crepe until ready to use.

Make the lobster filling: Using kitchen scissors, cut the lobster tails lengthwise through the cartilage to remove the lobster meat. Cut down the center of the lobster tail to remove the pink digestive tract and discard. Cut the lobster meat into fairly large cubes. If you are using crab legs, steam them (page 65), cut them in half using clean kitchen scissors, then cut down the leg for easy access to the meat. Pull out the long pieces with a fork, remove the cartilage; some pieces will flake off, while the larger pieces should be cubed.

Heat the white wine in a small saucepan until it comes to a low boil. Turn off the heat and, if using, add the saffron threads. Let them steep for a few minutes.

Meanwhile, pour the olive oil into a large sauté pan, and set over medium-high heat. Add the raw lobster meat and stir with a fork a few times. Turn the lobster, slowly browning it, about 2 minutes. Add the mushrooms, the white wine, shallots, chili flakes, and, if you are using it, the saffron and its soaking liquid. Cook until the

Tips from Rosie's Kitchen

Lobster tails vary in size depending on where they're from, so if the lobster tails you find are on the smaller side, you might want to add an extra one to yield 3 cups shelled.

For a low-fat version of the béchamel, or white sauce, use evaporated skim milk instead of the whole milk.

The key to making the béchamel sauce or white sauce is proper preparation of the olive-oil-and-flour mixture, which is a form of roux. Roux is a thickener or base for white sauce that usually involves butter and flour. Here, I am using olive oil because it gives the roux a good flavor. It is important to add the milk slowly to the oil-and-flour mixture. It will thicken right after the initial 1/4 cup of milk is poured in, but if you keep an eye on it and stir constantly, you will have excellent white sauce.

With the lobster, white sauce, and mushrooms, this recipe is quite full-bodied. You have the option of making it with or without the lobster. If you don't use the lobster, try the more exotic, flavorful mushrooms, such as shiitake, Portobello, or oyster. If you are using the lobster, the button mushrooms will be fine to balance the intensity of the lobster and the white sauce.

wine reduces by half and the vegetables are tender (if using crab, add it along with the vegetables rather than before, since it is already cooked).

Add 1 1/4 cups of the white sauce and stir once or twice. Place 1/3 cup of filling on each crepe. Fold over. Drizzle 1 tablespoon of the white sauce on top of each crepe, and sprinkle with 1/2 teaspoon chopped parsley.

MAKES 6
PAPILLOTES

PER SERVING:

CALORIES 248.3

FAT 1.8 G
  SATURATED FAT
  0.4 G

(7.7% OF CALO-
  RIES FROM FAT)

PROTEIN 40.1 G

CARBOHYDRATE
  13.4 G

CHOLESTEROL
  149 MG

FIBER 1.5 G

❉

Fish with Spinach *En Papillote*

In cooking terms, papillote *is the French word for a paper bauble that is used to adorn the bones on chops or ribs.* En papillote *means food that is wrapped and baked inside parchment paper, not only for the presentation but to seal in and heighten the flavor of the food. In this recipe, tuna is the fish of choice, but mahimahi or ono would work just as well. It is best to use thin slices so butterfly each thick fillet (see Tips).*

Make the marinade first, because the fish will need to sit in the liquid for 30 minutes before it can be sealed in the parchment paper. You can marinate it for up to one day, if you want to.

This recipe is fun to make—the cutting of the heart-shaped parchment paper is reminiscent of cutting shapes out of construction paper that we did in grammar school, only here the end product is edible, savory, and elegant. Papillotes *offer cooks a unique way of presenting food, and the cleanup is easy.*

The heart-shaped parchment paper

MARINADE

1 cup low-sodium soy sauce

1 small, fresh jalapeño pepper, seeded and chopped

2 tablespoons peeled, grated ginger

Juice from 3 limes (1/4 cup)

1 bunch cilantro, leaves only, reserving 6 sprigs for garnish

Six 5 1/2-ounce fresh tuna steaks, butterflied

FILLING

6 cups fresh, washed, and chopped spinach leaves with tough stems removed (page 75)

1/2 cup sliced oyster mushrooms or red bell pepper strips

1/4 teaspoon orange zest

3 tablespoons grated fresh ginger

3/4 cup thinly sliced red onion

1 egg white, slightly beaten

GARNISH

1 lemon

6 sprigs cilantro (reserved from above)

Tips from Rosie's Kitchen

To butterfly a fish steak, cut each steak lengthwise until just before you get to the very end, then open the steaks up like a book and lay them down on each of 6 beds of spinach. Cutting the fish steaks this way will help you to close the parchment over the filling.

Whisk all the ingredients for the marinade together. Coat the fish steaks with the marinade by turning them over in the juice a couple of times to completely wet both sides. Cover and refrigerate for 30 minutes or up to 1 day.

Cut the parchment paper into 6 squares that measure approximately 13 × 18 inches. Fold each square in half and cut the shape of 1 half of a heart. When you open up the parchment paper, you will have 1 complete heart-shaped piece.

Preheat oven to 350°F.

Remove the fish from the refrigerator after 30 minutes, when the fish has soaked up the flavors of the marinade. Toss the chopped spinach, mushrooms or peppers, orange zest, ginger, and onions together in a bowl. Open up the heart-shaped parchment and lay 1/6 of the spinach mixture a little off-center on the heart. Arrange the fish on top of the spinach. Drizzle

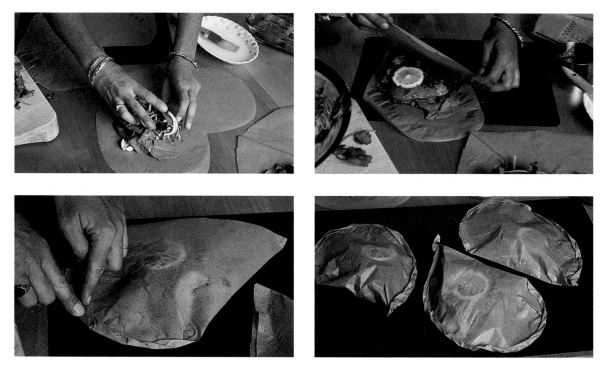

Top left: filling the *papillote* on one side of the heart-shaped paper; top right: folding the paper over the filling; bottom left: pleating the edge all around; bottom right: the *papillotes* ready for the oven

1 tablespoon of the leftover marinade over the fish. Repeat for each heart-shaped parchment paper.

Brush the outer edges of each parchment paper with the egg white, using a pastry brush. Fold one edge of the parchment paper over to meet the other edge. Seal the contents inside by making small folds starting at the top, all around the outer edge of the paper, twisting the paper at the end. Put the *papillotes* on a baking sheet and bake for 15 minutes. When completely cooked, the parchment will puff up with steam.

Using a zester, make 6 grooves in the side of the lemon from top to bottom, then cut the lemon into 6 slices.

Before serving, let the *papillotes* deflate a bit. If you try to open them immediately after cooking, you will get burned by the steam that has accumulated inside. Unseal the *papillote* along the outer edge to reveal the food inside. Garnish with cilantro sprigs and lemon slices.

Fish with Spinach *En Papillote*

FISH

In 1970 I changed from an omnivore to a lacto vegetarian. I gave up eating all foods of animal origin except dairy products, mostly yogurt and cheese. That diet agreed with me, kept me healthy and strong, and gave me pleasure and variety. But after fifteen years of it, I decided I needed a change. As an experiment I cut back on dairy products and started to eat fish. Not only did I enjoy the change, it gave me greater freedom when traveling (to Japan, for example, where being a lacto vegetarian is a challenge) and dining out. Furthermore, my nutritional research convinced me of the health benefits of fish.

Populations that eat fish regularly live longer and have less chronic disease than populations that do not. Whether this is because fish displaces meat or because it has positive attributes of its own is not clear. Certainly, fish provides high-quality protein without the saturated fat present in meat and poultry. And some kinds of fish—specifically, fatty fish from cold northern waters—also provide omega-3 fatty acids, the special, unsaturated fats our bodies need for optimum health. Salmon, mackerel, herring, sardines, and bluefish are rich in them, as is, to a lesser extent, albacore tuna. Omega-3 sources other than fish are few: walnuts, flax seeds, hemp seeds, and the oils extracted from them, and, to a lesser extent, soy and canola oils and specially fortified eggs.

Most Americans are deficient in omega-3s and as a result are more likely to develop cardiovascular disease, cancer, inflammatory disorders, and mental and emotional problems. Recent research suggests that supplementing the diet with omega-3 fatty acids not only can reduce these risks but can also help treat depression, bipolar disorder, autism, and attention deficit hyperactivity disorder. Fish is, indeed, a brain food.

The healthful qualities of fish can be neutralized by unhealthful ways of cooking it. Fish that is battered and fried, slathered with butter, or blanketed in creamy sauces becomes just another vehicle for putting saturated fat and excess calories into the body. I prefer fish that is raw (sashimi and sushi), marinated (ceviche), steamed, grilled, broiled, or smoked (as in salmon and trout). I much prefer fresh fish to frozen, and I often eat it in restaurants, where the quality is usually better than I can get to cook at home. (That may not be the case for all readers.)

Despite my enthusiasm for fish, I have two serious concerns about recommending that people eat more of it. The first is its content of environmental toxins, the result of pollution of lakes, rivers, and oceans. The second is the possibility of losing fish as a natural resource by overfishing those same bodies of water.

Take salmon as an example. Almost all of the salmon served today is farmed ("Atlantic salmon"). Farmed salmon has less flavor, less protein, and more fat than wild salmon, and its content of omega-3 fatty acids may not be as high. It may also contain residues of antibiotics and other drugs used to control diseases that occur when fish are crowded together in the pens of fish farms. Those diseases may escape and decimate wild populations of salmon. Most people assume that fish farming is a way of protecting an endangered resource. Few know that it takes several pounds of feed fish to produce one pound of salmon. The net result of salmon farming is greatly accelerated depletion of the numbers of fish in the oceans. If you can get wild Alaskan salmon, use it for the salmon recipes in this book. It tastes better and is more nutritious, and eating it does not have the environmental impact of eating farmed salmon.

As for other fish, be aware that larger, more carnivorous fish are more likely to contain dangerous levels of toxins. I avoid swordfish, marlin, shark, and bluefish for that reason. The safest and best fish for omega-3 fatty acids is probably the sardine. I love fresh sardines, grilled with nothing but salt and lemon juice, and I'm happy to see them increasingly available. (I used to be able to get them only in better Greek and Italian restaurants.) I also buy water-packed canned sardines and mash them up with mustard and onion as a spread. Give that a try; it's an easy way to get some safe fatty fish into your diet.

I avoid grouper, black sea bass, rockfish, and most snapper because those species are endangered from overfishing. Cod, pollock, flounder, halibut, sole, and plaice are still relatively abundant in the Pacific but seriously depleted in the Atlantic. Finally, skate, Chilean sea bass, and orange roughy are threatened, because they do not spawn until they are old—thirty years in the case of orange roughy—and unless they are managed well, they will be overfished to depletion. Species that are still abundant and well managed include striped bass, Alaskan salmon, herring, sardines, anchovies, mackerel, mahimahi, Alaskan halibut, and Pacific albacore. Try to keep these distinctions in mind if you want to continue enjoying fish. —**A.W.**

Grilled Fresh Sardines

SERVES 4
(1 LB. SARDINES)

PER SERVING:

CALORIES 116

FAT 13.8 G
  SATURATED FAT
  1.4 G

(64.9% OF CALO-
  RIES FROM FAT)

PROTEIN 13.8 G

CARBOHYDRATE
  2.9 G

CHOLESTEROL
  0 MG

FIBER 0.3 G

Fresh sardines are becoming more widely available. They taste completely different from any canned sardines you have ever tried. Cut the heads off if you wish and rinse them under cold water. Brush the sardines with olive oil and sprinkle lightly with salt. Place them on a grill or under a hot broiler. Cook them about 2 minutes per side until the flesh is just firm and the skin lightly browned. Serve immediately with fresh lemon wedges.

Tips from Rosie's Kitchen

Searing meat or fish is a way to lock in the juices by exposing it to very high temperature. The correct way to sear is in a hot skillet or on a grill, for a very short amount of time, then slowly finish cooking in the oven. Be careful not to get the skillet too hot too fast or the oil will burn.

If you want to serve this dish for lunch, serve half of a fillet with a side of salad.

Ono or opah works beautifully with this recipe as an alternative to salmon.

Seared Salmon with Orange Glaze

Not an ounce of flavor escapes this dish! The salmon is seared, trapping its rich flavor, briefly baked, and then drizzled with a thick, lightly fragranced orange ginger glaze—a balanced companion for a fish as flavorful as salmon. Salmon provides ample amounts of protein, B vitamins, vitamin A, and omega-3 oils.

Six 6-ounce salmon fillets
1 tablespoon sesame oil
3 teaspoons low-sodium soy sauce
1/4 cup white wine
1 cup freshly squeezed orange
   juice
1 teaspoon orange zest
3 tablespoons sherry
1/2 teaspoon grated fresh ginger
2 slices orange

Preheat oven to 400°F.

Sear the fish fillets in the sesame oil in a large, very hot skillet for 1 minute on each side. You should hear the fish sizzle. Remove fillets from the heat and transfer them to a glass baking dish or baking pan. Drizzle the soy sauce and the wine over them and bake them for 10 minutes. Remove them from the oven.

Meanwhile, heat the orange juice, zest, sherry, and ginger together in a small saucepan over medium-high heat until reduced by half. Add the orange slices, and stir once or twice, until the sauce becomes thick. Remove from heat, drizzle the sauce over the fish, and serve.

SERVES 6

PER SERVING:
CALORIES 271.8
FAT 8.2 G
   SATURATED FAT
   1.3 G
(29.8% OF CALORIES FROM FAT)
PROTEIN 34.3 G
CARBOHYDRATE
   9.7 G
CHOLESTEROL
   88 MG
FIBER 0.2 G

GRILLED AHI TUNA WITH CILANTRO GINGER SAUCE

Grilled ahi satisfies all of my remaining carnivorous cravings. I like it cooked rare to medium-rare, and while I understand that some people prefer it well done, ahi that is cooked through is as uninteresting to me as a well-done steak must be to most beef lovers. The cilantro ginger sauce is a snap to make and provides a depth of flavor that easily stands up to the taste and texture of the tuna.

Two 4- to 6-ounce ahi tuna steaks, about 1 inch thick
2 teaspoons extra virgin olive oil
Salt and freshly ground black pepper to taste

SAUCE

1 tablespoon canola or grapeseed oil
2 tablespoons peeled and finely chopped fresh ginger
1 cup chopped fresh cilantro
2 tablespoons shoyu or other natural soy sauce
1 tablespoon light brown or raw sugar
1/4 cup purified water

SERVES 2

PER SERVING:

CALORIES 349.9

FAT 16.6 G
    SATURATED FAT 3 G

(43.4% OF CALORIES FROM FAT)

PROTEIN 41.3 G

CARBOHYDRATE 7.6 G

CHOLESTEROL 65 MG

FIBER LESS THAN 0.8 G

Rinse the tuna steaks under cold running water and pat them dry. Rub them with the olive oil and season them with salt and pepper.

Preheat grill or broiler.

While the grill is heating, prepare the sauce: Heat the canola or grapeseed oil in a small skillet over medium-high heat and add the ginger. Stir-fry for 1 minute, then add the cilantro and stir-fry for another minute, until the cilantro is bright green. Mix in the soy sauce, sugar, and water and cook for 1 minute over high heat. Remove the skillet from heat.

Grill the tuna steaks on high heat or broil them until desired doneness; for medium-rare, about 2–3 minutes per side. Spoon the sauce over the fish and serve immediately.

Andy seasoning his Grilled Ahi Tuna

Duxelles-Stuffed Sole

*Duxelles is a mixture of finely chopped mushrooms and shallots some-
times cooked with a little brandy; it is used primarily in stuffings or
sauces. Here, thin fish fillets are stuffed with it and rolled up. The
strong flavor of the duxelles coupled with the delicate and choice taste
of sole makes it a complete meal. Serve this dish with steamed broccoli
and a warm baguette.*

SERVES 6

PER SERVING:

CALORIES 167

FAT 3.8 G
  SATURATED FAT
  0.3 G

(22% OF CALO-
  RIES FROM FAT)

PROTEIN 21.1 G

CARBOHYDRATE
  9.5 G

CHOLESTEROL 0 MG

FIBER 1.6 G

1 tablespoon olive oil
3/4 cup finely chopped shallots
1 tablespoon brandy
3 cups minced mushrooms
1 teaspoon salt
1/8 teaspoon white pepper
1 tablespoon chopped fresh
  parsley
Six 2 1/2-ounce sole fillets
1/4 teaspoon paprika

Pinch cayenne pepper
1/4 cup wine
1 tablespoon tangerine or orange
  zest
1/2 cup freshly squeezed tangerine
  or orange juice
1 tablespoon capers

GARNISH

1 sprig parsley

Preheat oven to 350°F.

To make the duxelles, heat the olive oil in an 8-inch sauté
pan. Slowly add the shallots and sauté them over medium heat
for 2 minutes. Add the brandy and minced mushrooms and
sauté until the mushrooms have released their liquid and start to
brown, about 4 minutes. Season with salt, pepper, and parsley
and remove from the heat to
cool.

Lay the sole fillets on a
sheet of wax paper and sprinkle them with the paprika and
cayenne pepper. Drop 2 tablespoons of the duxelles at the
end of each fillet and roll them
up. Insert a wooden skewer
or toothpick through each to
hold them together. Arrange
the rolled fillets in a layer in a

ANDY SUGGESTS

*As a change from fruit top-
pings on fish, prepare this dish
with a Dijon mustard sauce,
such as the one for my grilled
salmon (see the next recipe).*

glass or ceramic baking pan and then pour in the wine. Cover and bake for 15 minutes or until fish has visibly steamed through. Fish should be firm and white.

Pour off the baking juices into a small pan. Add the tangerine zest and the juice and simmer for 3 minutes. Drop in the capers. Pour the sauce over the hot fish, garnish with parsley, and serve.

Tips from Rosie's Kitchen

The secret to making this dish successfully is in using thin fillets; they roll up more easily. Sole is usually sold as a fillet and tends to be thin. If you'd like larger portions, serve 2 per person.

Make extra duxelles while you're at it and store it in the freezer either in a covered container or packed into ice cube trays. It is a home cook's treasure. Use a little to invigorate the flavor of a sauce. For example, add 1 tablespoon of duxelles to 1/2 cup of any cream-based pasta sauce, or pop out a few cubes from the ice tray and toss them in with chicken soup while it's cooking. Duxelles also makes a wonderful coating for vegetables, such as string beans or asparagus, or as a stuffing for zucchini boats.

Zucchini Boats

Buy three 6-inch zucchini and cut them lengthwise, only going in about 1/4-inch deep. Scoop out the seeds to create a cavity and pack about 1/4 cup of duxelles into each cavity. Bake covered in the oven at 350°F for 15 minutes. Allow them to cool and then cut them in half. Serves 6.

GRILLED SALMON WITH MUSTARD SAUCE

SERVES 4

PER SERVING:

CALORIES 236

FAT 8.5 G
   SATURATED FAT
   1 G
(32% OF CALORIES
   FROM FAT)

PROTEIN 36 G

CARBOHYDRATE
   3 G

CHOLESTEROL
   88 MG

FIBER 1 G

Here is simple grilled salmon dressed up with a strongly flavored sauce that complements the natural oiliness of the fish. And unlike many sauces recommended for fish, this one is very low in fat. (Salmon is full of healthful omega-3 fatty acids and certainly does not need to be cooked with butter or served with any additional fat.) I much prefer salmon fillets to bony salmon steaks, and I like them to be moist when cooked, never dry.

4 salmon fillets (about 6 ounces each)
1 lemon, cut in half
Salt and freshly ground black pepper to taste

SAUCE

1/2 cup Dijon mustard
1 teaspoon extra virgin olive oil
3 tablespoons chopped fresh dill, or 1 tablespoon dried dill
1 handful chopped fresh basil

Rinse the fillets under cold running water and pat them dry. Squeeze the juice from 1/2 lemon over the fillets, then season them with salt and pepper.

Preheat grill or broiler.

Meanwhile, prepare the sauce: Whisk together the mustard, olive oil, and dill in a small bowl. Add the basil and the juice from the other 1/2 lemon, mixing well.

Grill the fish on high heat or broil until desired doneness, but do not overcook. Spoon the sauce over the fish and serve immediately.

Lemon Grilled Halibut

The mellow flavor of this low-fat fish comes from marinating it in vigorous spices. After cooking, it is topped with homemade salsa rich with the flavor of tangy onions, fiery jalapeño peppers, and cool papaya.

Make the salsa first, before you start preparing the fish. It is also best to make the marinade far enough in advance so that the flavors can blend together for at least 2 hours before you actually marinate the fish in it for 30 minutes. Keep this in mind when deciding what time you want to serve this dish.

I couple this entrée with a side of Steamed and Roasted Potatoes (page 242).

PAPAYA SALSA

1/2 cup cilantro leaves
1 cup cubed papaya
1/4 cup cubed red bell pepper
1/4 cup diced red onion
1 small jalapeño pepper, seeded and minced
2 tablespoons freshly squeezed lime juice

MARINADE

3 tablespoons freshly squeezed lemon juice

1 tablespoon grated lemon zest
1 tablespoon olive oil
1 tablespoon grated fresh ginger
3/4 teaspoon freshly ground black pepper
1/2 cup minced fresh cilantro

Six 6-ounce halibut steaks, sliced in half lengthwise
3 medium bulbs fennel, trimmed and sliced
2/3 cup purified water
9 black or white peppercorns

Make the salsa: Put the salsa ingredients in a small bowl, mixing with a spoon until everything is thoroughly melded in. Cover and refrigerate until you are ready to use.

Make the marinade: Stir together the lemon juice, zest, oil, ginger, pepper, and cilantro in a bowl. Let the flavors mingle together for at least 2 hours, covered, in the refrigerator.

After the 2 hours, put the fish in a baking pan, pour the marinade evenly over it, and let it sit for 20–30 minutes, covered, in the refrigerator.

SERVES 6

PER SERVING:
CALORIES 322
FAT 7.1 G
   SATURATED FAT
   1 G
(20.2% OF CALO-
   RIES FROM FAT)
PROTEIN 39.6 G
CARBOHYDRATE
   24.4 G
CHOLESTEROL
   54 MG
FIBER 7.9 G

❋

Preheat oven to 400°F.

Meanwhile, cook the fennel in the water with the peppercorns in a large, flameproof sauté pan, covered, over high heat for about 6–8 minutes, until just tender, adding liquid if necessary. Remove from the heat.

Remove the halibut steaks from the refrigerator and bake them for 5 minutes on each side. The halibut should be flaky and white.

Arrange equal portions of the fennel on each of 6 plates, put the halibut on top, and spoon 1 tablespoon of Papaya Salsa on the fish.

Tips from Rosie's Kitchen

Zest is the aromatic, colored top skin of the citrus. The oils in the zest are what intensifies the flavors of food. The zest can be peeled off with a zester or a sharp paring knife.

Red snapper and sea bass are excellent alternatives to halibut. Buy the same amount of these fish fillets if you are substituting, but because these fillets are thinner, you don't need to slice them in half.

GRILLED FISH WITH TROPICAL RELISH

The tropical relish in this recipe is more to my liking than a pure fruit topping because the sweetness of the mango is offset by the robust tartness of the capers, vinegar, and salsa, and the basil provides an unexpected, spicy note.

4 fish fillets, such as cod or halibut, about 6 ounces each
1 teaspoon extra virgin olive oil
Salt and freshly ground black pepper to taste

RELISH

1 ripe mango, peeled, pitted, and finely chopped

1 sweet onion, finely chopped
1 red bell pepper, seeded and finely chopped
1 bunch fresh basil, chopped
1 tablespoon capers, drained
1 teaspoon balsamic vinegar
1 tablespoon salsa

SERVES 4

PER SERVING:

CALORIES 227

FAT 9 G
   SATURATED FAT
   1 G
(35% OF CALO-
   RIES FROM FAT)

PROTEIN 36.5 G

CARBOHYDRATE
   13 G

CHOLESTEROL
   54 MG

FIBER 2 G

❇

Rinse the fish fillets under cold running water and pat them dry. Brush them with the olive oil and season them with salt and pepper.

Preheat grill or broiler.

Meanwhile, prepare the relish: Stir together the mango, onions, peppers, basil, capers, vinegar, and salsa in a bowl. Grill the fish on high heat or broil, about 2–3 minutes per side or until desired doneness. Spoon the relish over the grilled or broiled fish.

Baked Curried Sea Bass with Lentils

SERVES 8

PER SERVING:

CALORIES 187.6

FAT 3.9 G
SATURATED FAT
0.5 G

(17.6% OF CALORIES
FROM FAT)

PROTEIN 12.3 G

CARBOHYDRATE
28.3 G

CHOLESTEROL
0 MG

FIBER 12.7 G

Sea bass is a firm white fish with a buttery taste. Here it is lightly breaded with ground almonds and spices, quickly sautéed, then baked. I would serve this with the Warm Quinoa-and-Zucchini-Stuffed Tomatoes (page 236).

CURRIED LENTILS WITH VEGETABLES

31/4 cups purified water
1 bay leaf
1 cup lentils
1 tablespoon Cajun seasoning
1 cup sliced onion
2 cloves garlic, thinly sliced
1 cup sliced shiitake or button
  mushrooms
1/2 cup broccoli florets
1/2 cup yellow or red bell pepper
2 tablespoons olive oil
2/3 cup nutritional yeast
1 teaspoon salt
1/8 teaspoon curry powder
1 tablespoon cornstarch
1/4 cup purified water

SEA BASS SAUTÉ

1/2 cup almond meal (or 1/2 cup
  blanched, ground almonds)
1 teaspoon salt
Pinch cayenne pepper
1 tablespoon curry powder
Four 6-ounce sea bass steaks, cut
  in half
2 tablespoons olive oil
3 tablespoons freshly squeezed
  lemon juice (from 1 lemon)

Bring 3 cups of water to a boil in a large saucepan. Add the bay leaf and the lentils and cook for 40–45 minutes. Remove from heat when completely cooked and let cool briefly. Drain off any liquid and stir in the Cajun seasoning.

Sauté the onions, garlic, mushrooms, broccoli, and bell peppers in the olive oil until the onions are transparent and limp, about 4 minutes. Add the yeast, salt, and curry powder and stir until everything is blended in. Add to the cooked lentils. Dissolve the cornstarch in the water and stir it into the lentils and vegetables. Continue to cook for 3 minutes, until the mixture thickens. Remove from the heat.

Preheat oven to 400°F.

Mix the almond meal, salt, cayenne pepper, and curry powder on a plate and flip both sides of the fish steaks on it until they are coated with the mixture. Heat the olive oil in a large sauté pan and lay the fish in. Sauté over medium heat, turning once, for 5 minutes on each side. Drizzle the lemon juice over the fish. If you aren't using an ovenproof Dutch oven or pan, transfer the fish to a baking dish. Put the lentil and vegetable mixture around the fish, cover with foil, and bake for 10 minutes to cook the steaks through; when you cut into one, the flesh should be a pale white color, not translucent.

Vegetarian Shepherd's Pie

Traditional shepherd's pie is usually made with ground meat and white potatoes. I like this one because it has sweet potatoes mixed in. The curried lentil filling is sandwiched between two layers of creamy potato filling sitting on a crouton crust baked on top of sweet zucchini. I serve this as an entrée with a simple chopped tomato salad.

SERVES 6 AS A SUPPER ENTRÉE OR 12 AS A SIDE DISH

PER SERVING:

CALORIES 503.1

FAT 6.8 G
  SATURATED FAT
  1.1 G
(11.8% OF CALO-
  RIES FROM FAT)

PROTEIN 22.8 G

CARBOHYDRATE
  92.2 G

CHOLESTEROL
  0 MG

FIBER 22.3 G

2 medium or large sweet potatoes, peeled and cubed
6 medium or large white potatoes, peeled and cubed
1 tablespoon olive oil
1 tablespoon Italian seasoning
1 tablespoon Cajun seasoning

CURRIED LENTIL FILLING

31/4 cups purified water
1 bay leaf
1 cup lentils
2 teaspoons Cajun seasoning
1 cup sliced onions
2 cloves garlic
1 cup sliced shiitake or button mushrooms

1/2 cup broccoli florets
1/2 cup yellow or red bell pepper
1 tablespoon olive oil
2/3 cup nutritional yeast
1 teaspoon salt
1 teaspoon curry powder
1 tablespoon cornstarch
1 zucchini, cut in rounds (about 2 cups)
1 cup bread crumbs or premade croutons

GARNISH

1/2 cup thinly sliced scallions or green onion

Preheat oven to 350°F.

Bring a large pot of water to a boil. Drop the cubed sweet and white potatoes into the water and simmer for 45 minutes. They should be easily pierced with a fork. Strain the potatoes, reserving 2 cups of the water. Pour 1 cup of the water back into the pot and mash the potatoes using a potato masher or a large fork. Add the olive oil, Italian seasoning, and Cajun seasoning and mash again until seasonings are completely blended into the potatoes.

Meanwhile, cook the lentils: Bring 3 cups of the water to a boil. Add the bay leaf, lentils, and Cajun seasoning and cook for 45 minutes. Remove from heat when completely cooked and let cool briefly. Drain off any liquid.

Sauté the onions, garlic, mushrooms, broccoli, and bell peppers in the olive oil in a large sauté pan until the onions are transparent and limp, about 4 minutes. Add the reserved cup of potato water, nutritional yeast, salt, and curry powder and stir until everything is blended in. Add to the cooked lentils. Dissolve the cornstarch in the remaining 1/4 cup water and stir it into the lentil and vegetable mixture. Continue to cook for 3 more minutes, until the sauce thickens. Remove from heat.

Line the bottom of a casserole dish with the zucchini rounds. Sprinkle half of the bread crumbs or croutons on top of the zucchini. Spoon out 4 cups of the mashed potatoes and spread across the zucchini rounds. Spoon out 2 cups of the curried lentils and spread on top of the potatoes. Spoon the remainder of the mashed potatoes and smooth them out on top. Sprinkle the rest of the bread crumbs and the scallions or green onion on top. Bake for 50 minutes. Let cool for 15 minutes before cutting and serving.

Tips from Rosie's Kitchen

Nutritional yeast is high in B vitamins, and it is often sprinkled over various foods for added flavor. You can find it in health-food stores.

ABOUT TOFU

Tofu is a traditional food of China, Japan, and Korea, now eaten in other countries of Asia and, increasingly, in the West. Sometimes called "soy cheese," it is made from soy milk in much the same way that fresh farmer's cheese is made from cow's milk—that is, a coagulant is added to heated milk, causing the protein to form curds that are then drained and pressed. (Soy milk is easily obtained from dried soybeans by soaking, cooking, grinding, and squeezing them.) Depending on how the curds are handled and how much liquid is pressed out of them, the finished tofu can be soft and silken or firm and "meaty." The former can be used as the base for puddings, pie fillings, and other Western desserts; the latter can serve as a substitute for meat or chicken.

You can now buy many varieties of tofu in supermarkets as well as health-food stores and Asian groceries, usually packed in water in plastic tubs and kept in refrigerated cases. Always check the dates on these packages and use up the tofu sooner rather than later. Tofu should have a very mild, pleasant taste and smell. It should never appear discolored or smell sour.

Tofu is a bit scary to Westerners, who don't know all of the ways Chinese and Japanese cooks get it to absorb the flavors of sauces and take on exactly the right textures for particular dishes. You can't just dump raw tofu into a salad and expect your family and guests to like it. But you can drain firm tofu well, crumble it, and sauté it in olive oil until it becomes golden, then add it to a tomato sauce instead of beef, and most people will never know.

There are a number of advantages to learning how to cook with tofu. Not only is it extremely versatile, it is a healthful alternative to protein foods of animal origin, because it has hardly any saturated fat, and the fat it does contain is relatively good for us. In addition, tofu provides isoflavones, compounds that reduce risks of heart disease and cancer (especially breast and prostate cancer). And tofu is quite inexpensive compared with meat and poultry.

One kind of tofu I use often is the baked variety. This comes in vacuum packs and can be found in the refrigerated cases of natural-food stores. Baked tofu looks brown and firm. It has been pressed to a very meaty consistency and simmered in a flavored broth. I can eat it right out of the package and make sandwiches with it, but I also put cubes and slices of it into stir-fries. —**A.W.**

Slow-Baked Tofu
with Stir-Fry

It is really worth the time to experiment with recipes that call for tofu. You can always marinate and bake it ahead of time to make it easier to incorporate in your favorite recipes. Once you've learned how to work with it, you can substitute it in recipes that call for chicken or meat. As we have all experienced, eating the same source of protein all the time can get boring. This dish is great because you get your helping of vegetables in and they are all tossed and cooked in a delicious marinade.

This stir-fry is great over Brown Rice Pilaf (page 246) topped with Peanut Dipping Sauce (page 52) to add more flair, protein, and flavor.

3 cups Spanish Rice (page 136) or steamed rice

MARINADE

1 teaspoon toasted-sesame oil
3 cloves garlic, sliced
1/4 cup of natural soy sauce (such as tamari)
2 tablespoons peeled, sliced fresh ginger
1 tablespoon Dijon-type mustard
1 tablespoon ground cumin

16 ounces packaged firm tofu

STIR-FRY

1/2 head broccoli
1 large onion, sliced and peeled
2 garlic cloves, sliced
2 carrots, peeled and cut match-stick style (page 117)
2 tablespoons olive oil
1/4 pound snow peas, strings removed
1/2 cup sliced mushrooms
2 tablespoons natural soy sauce (such as tamari)
1/4 cup purified water or vegetable stock (page 122)

GARNISH

11/2 cups Peanut Dipping Sauce (page 52) or 2 tablespoons sesame seeds

SERVES 6

PER SERVING:

CALORIES 371.2

FAT 26 G
    SATURATED FAT
    4.2 G
(58.7% OF CALO-
    RIES FROM FAT)

PROTEIN 13.3 G

CARBOHYDRATE
    24 G

CHOLESTEROL
    0 MG

FIBER 6.3 G

Prepare the Peanut Dipping Sauce, if using.

Preheat oven to 300°F.

Whisk all the marinade ingredients together in a baking dish. Drain the tofu and slice it vertically into nine 1/2-inch segments.

Lay the tofu slices in the marinade and turn them gently, using a spoon, to completely coat each one. Bake on the top rack of the oven for 30 minutes.

To cook brown rice takes about 45 minutes, so unless you are using leftover prepared rice start preparing it now.

Turn the tofu over and baste the tops with the marinade in the baking dish. Continue to bake for another 30 minutes, until the tofu slices puff up, turn light brown, and become slightly hard. Remove from the oven and let cool for 15 minutes. When completely cooled, cut into cubes.

Cut the florets off the head of the broccoli, slicing the large ones in half so they are all more or less the same size. You should have about 2 cups. Discard the stalks or save them for another stir-fry or for soups.

Sauté the onion, garlic, and carrots for 3 minutes in the olive oil in a wok or sauté pan over medium-high heat, being careful not to burn the oil. It should not smoke. Toss in the broccoli, snow peas, and mushrooms. Stir with a wooden spoon to keep the vegetables moving for another 2 minutes.

Stir the soy sauce into the vegetables, then add the water or vegetable stock. Drop in the cubed tofu, toss a few times, cook for 2 more minutes, then turn off the heat. Cover the pan with a lid and let the vegetables steam for about 6 minutes.

Place 1/2 cup prepared rice on each of 6 plates, cover with equal portions of the stir-fry, and top with some peanut sauce or 1 teaspoon sesame seeds.

Tips from Rosie's Kitchen

Although using a wok is ideal for stir-fry dishes, you can use a sauté pan and achieve excellent results.

The marinated and slowly baked tofu is another item that is very useful to have on hand in the fridge a few days in advance to cube up and use in this or other stir-fries, or to toss in your favorite salad as a meat alternative.

BAKED PRESSED TOFU WITH GREENS

The addition of baked tofu transforms this simple recipe into a satisfying main dish with none of the saturated fat that would be present if meat or poultry were in it. Be careful not to overcook the greens. They should have a rich green color and be just tender. You could have some balsamic vinegar and red pepper flakes on the table in case people want to add more seasoning.

4 cups greens (kale, chard, collards, or a mixture of these)
2 tablespoons extra virgin olive oil
1 large onion, chopped

1 cup baked pressed tofu, cut into cubes or slices (see *Note*)
Salt to taste

Wash the greens. Remove any coarse stems and midribs and discard, then chop the greens coarsely.

Heat the olive oil in a large skillet over medium-high heat and add the onions. Sauté, stirring, until the onions just begin to brown. Add the greens, tossing them until they wilt. Reduce the heat to medium and add the tofu. Stir-fry the tofu and greens for 2–3 more minutes. Season the dish to taste with salt and serve.

Note: Baked pressed tofu that has been simmered in a flavored broth comes in 8-ounce vacuum-sealed packs and can be found in the refrigerated cases of natural-food stores and supermarkets that sell tofu products. There is a choice of flavors—savory, five-spice, and hickory-smoked, for example—all of which work in this dish, although the hickory-smoked variety is my favorite. A good brand is Soy Deli.

SERVES 4

PER SERVING:
CALORIES 93
FAT 6 G
    SATURATED FAT
    LESS THAN 1 G
    (57% OF CALO-
    RIES FROM FAT)
PROTEIN 1.8 G
CARBOHYDRATE
    7.3 G
CHOLESTEROL
    0 MG
FIBER 1 G

Baked Spicy Tofu with Bean Thread Noodles, Corn, and Mango

Tofu surprises everybody who has never had it well prepared. The real bonus of eating tofu, besides the taste, is that it's high in protein, low in both sodium and calories, and is virtually cholesterol free. See Andy's comments on the subject (page 192).

This is an uncomplicated dish, yet the flavors and textures that mingle together—sweet corn, mango, fennel, cilantro, and sweet onions—are intense. I believe that you'll develop a real taste for tofu and begin to enjoy cooking and serving this wonderful food. Tofu is really nature's gift to all of us.

SERVES 6

PER SERVING:

CALORIES 343.2

FAT 9.7 G
  SATURATED FAT
  1.4 G

(42.6% OF CALO-
  RIES FROM FAT)

PROTEIN 2.3 G

CARBOHYDRATE
  31.9 G

CHOLESTEROL
  0 MG

FIBER 4.9 G

MARINADE

1/4 cup toasted-sesame oil
1 teaspoon ground fennel seed
1/2 teaspoon salt
1 teaspoon red chili paste, or more to taste
2 tablespoons honey
1/4 cup freshly squeezed lime juice

One 16-ounce block tofu, soft or firm

1 package (3 1/2 ounces) bean thread noodles

2 sweet onions, thinly sliced
2 ears of corn, kernels cut off the cob (about 2 cups)
1/2 cup vegetable stock (page 122) or purified water
2 tablespoons natural soy sauce (such as tamari)
2 mangoes, peeled, pitted and cubed
1 bunch cilantro, washed

GARNISH

1 bunch mint

Whisk all the marinade ingredients together in a small baking dish.

Preheat the oven to 450°F.

Drain the tofu and chop it into 1/2-inch cubes. Drop the tofu cubes into the marinade and turn them gently, using a spoon to completely coat each one. Make sure that the tofu cubes are close together and sitting in the marinade. Bake in the hot oven for 15 minutes.

Meanwhile, soak the bean thread noodles in a pot of hot water for 20 minutes, and then strain through a colander to remove excess water.

Simmer the onions and the corn in the vegetable stock in a large sauté pan until the onions are tender and the corn is bright yellow (about 3 minutes). Add the soy sauce, mangoes, tofu, and the juices from the marinade. Pinch the leaves off the cilantro and sprinkle them in. Add the bean thread noodles and toss until everything is thoroughly coated. Cook for 2 more minutes. For a handsome presentation, you can make a bed of the cellophane noodles and nestle the tofu, corn, and mango mixture on top. Then toss it all at the table. Garnish with mint.

Tips from Rosie's Kitchen

Bean thread noodles, also called cellophane noodles, can be found in the ethnic section of any supermarket, or in Asian grocery stores. You will want to cut them into 6-inch lengths with a pair of clean kitchen scissors after they have soaked in water, as this will make them more manageable to work with.

The key to well-flavored tofu is the baking dish. It must be small enough, so the tofu squares are touching and sitting in the marinade. Tofu is porous, and baking the pieces this way allows all the juices to be soaked up and locked in.

Teriyaki Sampler Plate

This recipe was inspired by an evening spent with guests, some of whom were vegetarian and others who weren't. When the tofu is marinated and baked, it actually takes on an uncanny resemblance to chicken in both texture and taste.

You can marinate both the chicken and the tofu for as little as fifteen minutes or up to one full day, if you plan ahead. If you don't have that kind of time, the chicken and the tofu will still have enough teriyaki flavor if they marinate for just 15 minutes. The teriyaki looks pretty served on a bed of buckwheat noodles (see Tips).

TERIYAKI MARINADE

1/4 cup orange marmalade or
   apricot jam
1/2 cup natural soy sauce (such as
   tamari)
1/4 cup freshly squeezed orange
   juice
3 tablespoons grated fresh ginger
1/4 cup dry sherry

One 16-ounce block firm tofu
1 whole boneless, skinless chicken
   breast

1/2 pound asparagus, ends cut off,
   cut into 4-inch pieces

GARNISH

1 tablespoon sesame seeds

SERVES 6

PER SERVING:

CALORIES 297.3

FAT 13 G
   SATURATED FAT
   2.7 G
   (42% OF CALO-
   RIES FROM FAT)

PROTEIN 25.4 G

CARBOHYDRATE
   17.6 G

CHOLESTEROL
   39 MG

FIBER 2 G

Preheat the oven to 400°F.

Mix the ingredients for the marinade together and pour 1/2 cup of it into each of 3 different baking dishes for the chicken, tofu, and asparagus.

Slice the tofu block into three 11/2-inch-thick pieces. Cut each of the 3 pieces at an angle from corner to corner. Lay them in a baking tray in the teriyaki marinade.

Put the chicken in a plastic bag or wrap it in plastic wrap and gently tap it with a tenderizing hammer for a few minutes,

Baked Spicy Tofu with Bean Thread
Noodles, Corn, and Mango

concentrating on the thicker parts of the chicken. Make 4 diagonal slices across the chicken to create 5 pieces. Lay the chicken in its own baking dish in the marinade.

Put the chopped asparagus in the last baking dish and cover with foil.

Put all 3 baking dishes in the oven and bake for 30 minutes. Sprinkle the sesame seeds on top of the chicken and tofu and serve.

Tips from Rosie's Kitchen

Tenderizing the meat not only helps it absorb the marinade, but also helps it to cook more evenly.

I like to serve this dish with buckwheat noodles. They are easy to make and can be bought at any health-food store. Boil the noodles for 5 minutes, then strain and rinse them in cold water. Put them in a bowl, pour the cooking juices over them, and toss. Lay 1 1/2 cups of noodles on each of 6 plates and lay the tofu, or chicken, and asparagus on top.

If asparagus is out of season, broccoli is another great accompaniment. Salmon can be substituted for the chicken.

SPROUTS

In Asia, mung bean sprouts have long been used as a vegetable, usually lightly stir-fried. In the West, sprouts became popular only with the rise of interest in health food in the 1970s, and people mostly eat them raw. Alfalfa sprouts, especially, are a New Age staple, replacing lettuce in sandwiches, filling salad bowls, and forming great mounds of garnish on platters. Sunflower sprouts are a more recent novelty. Now I see lentil, chickpea, and radish sprouts at salad bars, and I know people who like to drink wheatgrass juice, pressed from the sprouts of our staple grain.

The idea that sprouts are good for health has little basis in fact. As the youngest forms of green plants, they are probably full of enzymes associated with new growth, but those compounds are destroyed in our stomachs. Actually, some sprouts might not be good for us at all. Raw legume sprouts, in particular, contain natural toxins. For example, alfalfa, a legume, makes a toxin called canavanine that is present in the sprouts and can harm the immune system. It is broken down by simple cooking, but cooking turns delicate alfalfa sprouts into an unappetizing mush. So I remove raw alfalfa sprouts from any foods that I am served and recommend that you do, too. I also avoid raw clover, mung bean, lentil, chickpea, and other bean sprouts (which don't taste very good anyway). I have no problem with cooked bean sprouts and no objection to raw sprouts of nonleguminous seeds.

If you like sunflower, radish, and buckwheat sprouts, eat them. But don't try to tell me that they are any better for me than other fresh vegetables or fruits. —**A.W.**

Turkey Burgers

Turkey meat can be a bit dry, but the addition of mushrooms in this recipe transforms the meat into a succulent and tender consistency. Barbecuing burgers made of well-seasoned turkey instead of traditional beef is a healthy alternative, and I think you'll really be surprised at how delicious they are.

SERVES 4

PER SERVING:

CALORIES 431.9

FAT 13.3 G
SATURATED FAT
2.8 G
(26.8% OF CALORIES FROM FAT)

PROTEIN 33.7 G

CARBOHYDRATE
47.8 G

CHOLESTEROL
90 MG

FIBER 10.8 G

❁

1 pound ground turkey
4 ounces button mushrooms, minced or chopped
1 small onion, minced or chopped
1 teaspoon prepared BBQ sauce
1 tablespoon chili powder
1 teaspoon Cajun seasoning
Cracked black pepper to taste

1 tablespoon Worcestershire sauce
Cooking oil spray
4 whole wheat hamburger buns

GARNISH

1 beefsteak tomato, sliced
1 red onion, sliced
1 head butter leaf lettuce

Put the ground turkey, mushrooms, and onions along with the seasonings, spices, and Worcestershire sauce in a medium bowl. With a big wooden spoon or clean hands, blend everything together, making sure that the mushrooms and onions are distributed throughout the meat. Make 4 patties of equal size.

Heat the grill or a sauté pan over medium-high heat. Spray patties lightly with cooking oil spray and cook each patty approximately 7 minutes on each side, until completely cooked through. Warm the buns on a cookie sheet on the lower level under the broiler. Put the patties on the buns and garnish each with 1 tomato slice, 1 slice red onion, and butter leaf lettuce.

Tips from Rosie's Kitchen

If you want to make your own Cajun spice blend, use 1 teaspoon paprika, 1/2 teaspoon cayenne pepper, 1 teaspoon salt, 1/2 teaspoon oregano, and 1/2 teaspoon basil.

Turkey Burger with trimmings

Hummus Pinwheels with Raw Veggie Crudités

I love tortillas, especially when they are wrapped around something good. Here they are topped with a thick garbanzo bean spread alive with the taste of orange, paprika, cayenne pepper, garlic, and lemon, then layered with fresh spinach, carrots, cucumbers, or sunflower sprouts.

These are great to take to work or for a packed lunch if you're on the run. Wrap them in parchment paper and seal them closed with a fancy toothpick.

SERVES 12

PER SERVING:

CALORIES 157.3

FAT 4.9 G
    SATURATED FAT
    0.7 G
(27.9% OF CALO-
RIES FROM FAT)

PROTEIN 5.9 G

CARBOHYDRATE
    23 G

CHOLESTEROL
    0 MG

FIBER 3.9 G

❈

2 cups garbanzo beans, soaked overnight in 6 cups of water to cover and 1 teaspoon baking soda
1 tablespoon miso paste
2 tablespoons natural soy sauce (such as tamari)
1 teaspoon paprika
1/2 cup freshly squeezed orange juice
1 tablespoon lemon zest
1/4 cup tahini
Pinch cayenne pepper
2 cloves garlic
1/2 teaspoon salt
1/4 cup freshly squeezed lemon juice
1/4 cup roasted bell pepper purée (optional) (page 76)
1 teaspoon chopped fresh tarragon or 1/2 teaspoon dried
6 tortillas, flavored or whole wheat

FILLING

3 cups spinach (about 1/2 pound), washed with tough stems removed
1 1/2 cups peeled and grated carrots
1 1/2 cups sunflower sprouts or 1/2 cucumber, peeled and sliced lengthwise

Do not drain the water that the beans have been soaking in overnight. Bring the water to a boil and cook the beans, covered, for 45 minutes. The beans should be easily pierced with a fork.

After the beans are cooked, drain them in a colander, reserving 1/4 cup of the water. Mix the water with the miso in a bowl. Put all the remaining ingredients including the red pepper purée if you are using it, but not the tarragon, in a food processor and process until smooth. Pour in the miso and process again. Fold in the tarragon.

Trim the round sides off the tortillas to make a square and spread 1/4 cup hummus over each of the 6 tortillas. Starting 1/2 inch up from one side of the tortilla, lay 1/4 cup of each of the filling ingredients on top of each other, in thin layers. Roll the tortillas up. When you get to the end of the roll, use the hummus on the inside edge of the tortillas to act as a sealer to keep the tortilla closed. When you are ready to serve, cut the rolled tortillas in half at an angle.

Tips from Rosie's Kitchen

After you've made hummus once, you won't underestimate the number of ways it can be enjoyed.

Hummus Dip: *I like to serve hummus as a dip with raw vegetables. All you need is 2 carrots, 1/2 jicama, 2 celery stalks, 1 medium cucumber, and 1 zucchini or yellow squash, cut into thin sticks. You can also cut the florets off a 1/2 head of broccoli or use cherry tomatoes, radishes, or any of your favorite vegetables. Serve the hummus in a bowl in the center of a platter and arrange the cut vegetables around it.*

Orange Chicken Pita with Vegetables and Tahini Dressing

This recipe might inspire you to have an afternoon picnic with good friends. You'll need to plan ahead, because the garbanzo beans will have to soak overnight, but that takes virtually no effort (you can also used canned beans). You may also want to consider marinating the chicken overnight, because it makes a big difference in the way it tastes. The extra soaking time tenderizes the meat and maximizes the taste so you end up with rich, full flavor, not a weak hint of distant spices.

If you're preparing for an outdoor lunch, wrap the stuffed pitas in wax paper and seal the wrap with deli toothpicks that have colored cellophane ends, or buy wax paper bags at the grocery store. Also, when taking along stuffed pitas to go, store the dressing in a separate container with a lid until ready to use.

MAKES 6 PITAS

PER SERVING:

CALORIES 605

FAT 20.6 G
  SATURATED FAT
  5 G

(31.3% OF CALO-
  RIES FROM FAT)

PROTEIN 40.1 G

CARBOHYDRATE
  62 G

CHOLESTEROL
  82 MG

FIBER 6.4 G

❖

1 tablespoon Italian seasoning
1 cup garbanzo beans, soaked overnight in water to cover and 1/2 teaspoon baking soda, or 16 ounces canned garbanzo beans

MARINADE

1 cup freshly squeezed orange juice
1 tablespoon paprika
1 teaspoon turmeric
1 1/2 teaspoons ground cumin

2 whole skinless, boneless chicken breasts

TAHINI DRESSING

1/4 cup tahini
1/2 cup low-fat sour cream or plain low-fat yogurt
1/2 cup freshly squeezed orange juice, or 1/4 cup frozen concentrate
1 tablespoon natural soy sauce (such as tamari)
1 whole shallot, peeled and chopped
2 cloves garlic, peeled and chopped
1 tablespoon chopped fresh parsley
1 teaspoon chopped fresh chives
1 tablespoon mirin (sweet rice wine)

PITA FILLING

2 whole tomatoes, cut into wedges

1/2 cup shredded cabbage

1/2 cup grated carrots

1 tablespoon pitted and sliced Kalamata olives

1/4 cup thinly sliced radishes

1/2 cucumber, peeled if waxed and thinly sliced

1/2 cup sliced red or yellow bell peppers

1/2 cup thinly sliced scallions or green onions

1/2 cup grated low-fat cheddar cheese

6 whole wheat pita breads

Sprinkle the Italian seasoning into the pot of water that the beans have been soaking in overnight. Drain the beans well. Bring to a boil and cook for 45 minutes to 1 hour. The beans should be soft and be easily pierced with a fork.

Mix the orange juice, paprika, turmeric, and cumin together. Lay the chicken breasts in a rimmed baking pan and pour the marinade over them. Cover and refrigerate overnight. If you're making the chicken the same day, let it sit in the marinade for as much time as you can give it. Preheat the broiler, then broil the chicken breasts in their marinade on the top rack for 8–10 minutes on each side, basting with the marinade to keep them moist. Or you can bake the chicken in a preheated 400°F oven for 12 minutes on each side until they are completely cooked through. Remove from the oven and cool for 15 minutes. When completely cooled, cut into thin slices.

Mix all the dressing ingredients in a bowl and whisk together for 1 minute.

Mix the vegetable filling ingredients together with the garbanzo beans. Cut 1 inch off the top of the pita bread to make an opening. Stuff each of the 6 pitas with an equal amount of chicken and vegetable filling and garnish with a dollop of dressing.

Tips from Rosie's Kitchen

You can reserve the leftover marinade juices in a covered container to use as a flavoring for rice or any other grain. Or if you have leftover chicken, store it with the juices to keep it moist.

Santa Fe Chicken

The marinade in this dish is what gives the chicken such a smooth flavor. Although it is ideal if the meat can soak in the marinade for at least 1 hour before cooking to absorb the intricate flavors of the marinade, if you don't have time, don't be discouraged, because the chicken will still be flavorful. If you are really planning ahead, you can soak the meat in the marinade for up to two days.

Serve this dish with a side of Spanish Rice (page 136) and the Jicama and Carrot Salad (page 116). The flavors together are very complementary.

SERVES 4

PER SERVING:

CALORIES 212.3

FAT 4.4 G
  SATURATED FAT
  0.8 G

(46.8% OF CALO-
  RIES FROM FAT)

PROTEIN 30.1 G

CARBOHYDRATE
  13 G

CHOLESTEROL
  72 MG

FIBER 0.9 G

MARINADE

Juice from 3 limes
1/4 cup low-sodium soy sauce
11/2 teaspoons olive oil
11/2 teaspoons chili powder
11/2 teaspoons cumin seed
11/2 teaspoons ground coriander
6 cloves garlic, minced
11/2 teaspoons honey

2 whole breasts boneless, skinless
  chicken

1/4 cup white wine
3 tablespoons chopped cilantro
  leaves

GARNISH

Mock Sour Cream (page 62) or
  low-fat sour cream
1 lime, sliced into 6 thin slices
6 scallion firecrackers (see Tips)
1/4 cup fresh Salsa (page 8) or
  Papaya Salsa (page 185)

Mix together marinade ingredients in a bowl, stirring thoroughly. Pour into a shallow baking pan and lay the chicken breasts in. Cover and refrigerate for 1 hour.

Preheat the broiler.

After 1 hour, when the chicken has absorbed all the flavors of the marinade, pour in the white wine. Broil the chicken under a medium flame for 8–10 minutes, basting it with the juices to keep it moist.

Transfer the chicken to a platter and slice it at an angle. Garnish each piece with a little of the pan juices, a dollop of Mock Sour Cream or low-fat sour cream, slices of lime, and a scallion firecracker, as well as a dollop of salsa.

Tips from Rosie's Kitchen

The scallion "firecracker" is a lively garnish that gets its name from the way the leaves of the onion curl away from the body of the onion, creating a "firecracker" appearance. Cut 2 inches off the green leafy side of the scallion. Trim the roots at the white, bulbous end. Then, following the top illustration, cut 3 slits about 1/2 inch down through the white, bulbous end of the scallion. Fill a bowl with ice water and drop in the freshly cut scallions.

It is never too much trouble to cook extra chicken breasts. They hold the flavor of the marinade and are wonderful for chicken salad or sandwiches for work or school.

Rosie cutting three slits in the white, bulbous end of a scallion

After trimming the top off the radish, she makes small cuts into the bulb all around.

Soaking the radish rosettes and the scallion firecrackers in ice water

ANDY SUGGESTS

I'd like more salsa with this, either a good commercial one or a quick salsa fresca like the one that Rosie uses (page 8).

Grilled Fish Tacos

MAKES 12 TACOS

PER SERVING:

CALORIES 184.9

FAT 7.4 G

SATURATED FAT
3.7 G

(33.3% OF CALO-
RIES FROM FAT)

PROTEIN 14.9 G

CARBOHYDRATE
15.9 G

CHOLESTEROL
3.7 MG

FIBER 2.1 G

Fresh grilled fish tacos are just right for summertime. You have a couple of options of white fish to choose from, but before you buy it, look at it to make sure it's fresh. It should glisten, giving off a sort of rainbow effect.

Juice from 1 lemon or 2 limes
  (about 1/4 cup)
Three 6-ounce mahimahi fillets or
  3 halibut steaks
1 tablespoon chili powder
1 tablespoon paprika
1/2 teaspoon dried oregano
1/2 teaspoon salt
12 corn tortillas
11/2 cups grated cheddar cheese
11/2 cups fresh Guacamole (page
  211)
1/2 cup Mock Sour Cream (page
  62) or low-fat sour cream
3 cups shredded cabbage

1/2 cup fresh Salsa (page 8) or
  Pace Louisiana's Hot Sauce, or 1
  tomato, chopped, mixed with 2
  teaspoons Tabasco sauce
2 limes, cut in 6 wedges

GARNISH

1 lime, cut in 6 wedges

Tips from Rosie's Kitchen

You can either grill or broil the fish. I like to grill it because I like the way the fish tastes that way, and it sets the mood for a summertime meal. If you broil the fish, cook it 4 minutes on each side, for a total of 8 minutes.

If you grill the fish, make sure that the grill is hot and that the fish fillets aren't too close to the coals.

It's worth grilling extra fish so you have some left over. You can use it to make Clam Chowder (page 131) or cold fish sandwiches for the next day's lunch. Put about 2 ounces of fish between 2 slices of toasted wheat bread. Spread some Mock Sour Cream on the bread and top with lettuce and cold tomato slices.

Drizzle the lemon or lime juice over the fish and sprinkle the chili powder, paprika, oregano, and salt on both sides. Grill for approximately 3–5 minutes on each side for a total cooking time of approximately 6–10 minutes. Transfer to a platter and slice the fish into 1-inch-thick strips.

Wrap 3 stacks of 4 tortillas in foil and place them on the grill for a couple of minutes to warm them up. Or if you prefer, warm directly on the grill. Fill each tortilla with 1 1/2 ounces of fish, 1 tablespoon each of cheese and guacamole, 1 teaspoon of sour cream, 1/4 cup of shredded cabbage, and 1 teaspoon of fresh salsa. Garnish each plate with 1 lime wedge.

Serve the leftover lime wedges, salsa, and sour cream on the side in small bowls.

Chicken Quesadillas

This is a popular dish because of everything you can taste—the marinated chicken, a little bit of cheese, salsa, garlic, onions, cilantro, and guacamole, all wrapped in a warm corn tortilla. It would save you some time to prepare the salsa ahead of time if you are making it fresh, but be sure to make the guacamole fresh, just before you are ready to serve.

2 skinless, boneless half chicken
   breasts
1/4 cup white wine
2 tablespoons chili powder
1 red bell pepper
8 corn tortillas
10 Kalamata olives, pitted and
   sliced
5 mushrooms, sliced
2 cups low-fat cheese
1/2 cup fresh salsa (page 8) or 1
   tomato, chopped and seasoned
   with Tabasco sauce to taste

GUACAMOLE

2 pinches salt
2 small cloves garlic
1 avocado
1 sprig cilantro
1 tablespoon plain yogurt
1 1/2 teaspoons freshly squeezed
   lime juice (1/2 lime)
2 tablespoons minced onion
1 small jalapeño pepper, diced
   (optional)

SERVES 8

PER SERVING:
CALORIES 210.5
FAT 10.7 G
  SATURATED FAT
  4.2 G
(46% OF CALO-
  RIES FROM FAT)
PROTEIN 14.2 G
CARBOHYDRATE
  14.2 G
CHOLESTEROL
  38 MG
FIBER 2.3 G

Preheat oven to 400°F.

Put the chicken breasts in a shallow glass baking dish. Pour the wine over them and sprinkle them with some of the chili powder. Bake for 10 minutes, then turn the chicken over and sprinkle with the remaining chili powder. Bake for 10 more minutes. The chicken breasts should be tender but not pink. Let them cool and then slice into strips. Pour the leftover baking juices into a covered plastic dish and refrigerate.

Broil the red bell pepper on a shallow baking pan, turning it so that all sides become brown and blistered. Remove from the oven and drop it into a small brown bag and twist closed. When completely cooled, peel the skin off, scrape out the seeds, and slice the pepper into strips.

Arrange the tortillas on the baking pan and evenly distribute the chicken, pepper strips, olives, and mushrooms on top. Sprinkle 4 tablespoons of cheese on top of each tortilla and bake until the cheese melts, usually 5–10 minutes. Bake longer for crispy tortillas.

Meanwhile, make the guacamole: Sprinkle some salt into a bowl and mash the garlic against it with a fork. The grains of the salt will help to mash it up. Using the same fork, mash the avocado in the same bowl. Add the cilantro, yogurt, lime, onions, and pepper. Serve immediately. Serve the quesadillas hot with the guacamole and the salsa alongside.

GUACAMOLE
SERVES 8

PER SERVING:
CALORIES 59.9
FAT 4 G
SATURATED FAT
0.7 G
(55.3% OF CALO-
RIES FROM FAT)
PROTEIN 1.1 G
CARBOHYDRATE
6.1 G
CHOLESTEROL
0 MG
FIBER 1.3 G

Tips from Rosie's Kitchen

Baking juices can be stored in a covered container and used later to flavor soups or rice.

TOFU FAJITAS

For a quick and exciting meal, this healthful version of a popular Mexican dish is hard to beat. The baked tofu neatly replaces beef and, along with olive oil, provides good fat. Nonfat whole wheat tortillas make very good fajitas. They have none of the hydrogenated fat of conventional white flour tortillas and give you some fiber. The freshness of the ingredients makes these fajitas both visually appealing and delicious.

2 tablespoons extra virgin olive oil
1 large onion, sliced
1 red bell pepper, seeded and
   julienned
1 green pepper, such as ancho, Ana-
   heim, or bell, seeded and julienned
1 hot pepper, such as jalapeño or
   serrano, seeded and minced
1 cup sliced mushrooms, such as
   crimini or portobello

2 cups sliced, baked pressed tofu
   (preferably savory or hickory-
   smoked flavor)
Salt to taste
6 nonfat whole wheat tortillas,
   warmed

GARNISH

Low-fat sour cream, salsa, chopped
   fresh tomatoes, avocado, and
   scallions

SERVES 6

PER SERVING:
CALORIES 303
FAT 10.5 G
   SATURATED FAT
   1 G
(31% OF CALO-
   RIES FROM FAT)
PROTEIN 23 G
CARBOHYDRATE
   32 G
CHOLESTEROL
   0 MG
FIBER 8 G

Heat the olive oil in a large skillet over medium-high heat, then add the onions. Sauté, stirring, until the onions are translucent. Stir in the peppers and mushrooms and sauté until the vegetables begin to soften, about 5 minutes. Add the tofu and stir-fry for 5 minutes more. Season with salt to taste and serve in the tortillas.

Top the fajitas with low-fat sour cream, salsa, chopped fresh tomatoes, avocado, scallions, or a combination of these.

Baked Bean and Rice Cheese Burrito

You will find that you can make a better burrito right at home than some of the ones you eat in restaurants. An additional benefit of this dish besides the fact that it's simple to make is that it's fairly nutritionally balanced. The beans provide some protein, and the rice and the tortilla provide carbohydrates. I make my burritos with black beans, but you can use the traditional pinto beans if you prefer them.

MAKES 8

PER SERVING:

CALORIES 662.6

FAT 35.6 G
  SATURATED FAT
  6.8 G
(47.5% OF CALO-
  RIES FROM FAT)

PROTEIN 17.4 G

CARBOHYDRATE
  71.1 G

CHOLESTEROL
  15 MG

FIBER 9.1 G

❄

FILLING

1 1/2 cups black beans, soaked overnight in water to cover with 1 teaspoon of baking soda, or 24 ounces canned black beans
1 bay leaf
2 garlic cloves, peeled
1 tablespoon oregano
1/2 teaspoon chili flakes

1 1/2 cups brown rice

ENCHILADA SAUCE

6 large fresh tomatoes or 8 ounces canned tomato purée
1 onion, diced
2 carrots, peeled, thinly sliced
Cayenne pepper to taste
1 teaspoon salt
3 tablespoons chili powder
1 tablespoon olive oil
1/4 cup vegetable stock (page 122) or purified water
8 large, burrito-sized tortillas, flavored or whole wheat
1/2 cup sliced scallions or green onions
1/2 cup fresh Salsa (page 8) or Pace Louisiana's Hot Sauce
1 cup grated chili jack cheese or plain jack cheese
3 tablespoons low-fat sour cream

GARNISH

6 black olives

Prepare the beans. Drop the bay leaf, garlic cloves, oregano, and chili flakes into the pot of water that the beans have been soaking in overnight. Bring it to a boil and cook for 45 minutes. The beans should be soft and easily pierced with a fork. When they are ready, remove them from the heat, drain any remaining liquid, and remove the bay leaf. If using canned beans, drain and mix with the same seasonings, except the bay leaf.

Prepare the rice: Bring 3 cups of water to a boil in a medium pot. Stir in the rice, turn down the heat, cover, and simmer for 45 minutes. The lid on the pot should be tight-fitting. Try not to remove it because heat and liquid will escape. When done, the rice should be firm and all the water absorbed. Remove from the heat and set aside.

Make the sauce: If using fresh tomatoes, fill a medium saucepan 3/4 full of water and bring it to a boil. Blanch the tomatoes by first slicing an X on the bottom of each and then dropping them in the boiling water until the skins start to loosen, about 2 minutes. Remove them with a slotted spoon and let cool. When cooled, peel the skin off. Squeeze each tomato over a strainer set over a bowl to trap the seeds. Chop the tomatoes and set aside the juice.

Preheat oven to 350°F.

Sauté the onion, carrots, cayenne, salt, and chili powder in the olive oil for about 2 minutes. Add the chopped tomatoes and their juice or canned purée and the stock, and cook over medium heat until the carrots begin to soften (about 10 minutes). Remove from the heat and let cool. When cool, pour the sauce into a food processor and process until it becomes smooth and has a saucelike consistency.

Lay the tortillas open on a clean work space. For each tortilla, spoon 1/4 cup beans and 1/4 cup rice in the middle. Sprinkle on top 1 tablespoon sliced scallions, 1 tablespoon salsa, 3 tablespoons grated cheese, and 1/2 tablespoon sour cream. Fold the sides in, then roll the tortillas away from you. Lay them in a baking dish with the seam side down and pour the enchilada sauce on top. Sprinkle the tops with the remaining cheese and cover the pan with foil. Bake for 30 minutes. Garnish each burrito with 1 black olive and serve.

GALLO PINTO (COSTA RICAN RICE AND BEANS)

This is a typical Costa Rican dish, often eaten with scrambled eggs for breakfast. The universal Costa Rican condiment, Salsa Lizano, which tastes like a spicy Worcestershire sauce, is used to flavor it. A combination of Worcestershire and hot pepper sauce makes a good approximation. The cilantro is an essential ingredient, adding color and an authentic Latin American flavor. Beans and rice go together in dishes from around the world. This is a particularly good one.

1 cup raw white rice

1³/₄ cups cold purified water

1 tablespoon extra virgin olive oil

1 medium onion, diced

¹/₂ red bell pepper, seeded and diced

1 jalapeño pepper, seeded and minced

2 cloves garlic, minced

1 handful chopped cilantro leaves

16 ounces canned black beans, drained

Salt to taste

1 teaspoon Tabasco sauce and 2 tablespoons Worcestershire sauce, or to taste (see *Note*)

SERVES 6

PER SERVING:

CALORIES 199

FAT 3 G
    SATURATED FAT
    0.5 G
(14% OF CALO-
    RIES FROM FAT)

PROTEIN 6.5 G

CARBOHYDRATE
    37.5 G

CHOLESTEROL
    0 MG

FIBER 3 G

❊

Wash the rice in cold water, drain, and put it in a pot with the water and a pinch of salt. Bring the rice to a boil, stir, cover, and lower the heat to a simmer. Cook the rice until the water is absorbed, about 20 minutes. Let the rice stand for 10 minutes, then fluff it with a fork.

Heat the olive oil in a skillet over medium-high heat. Add the onions and peppers and sauté, stirring, for 5 minutes. Stir in the garlic and sauté for another 2 minutes. Add the cilantro and sauté for 1 minute more.

Spoon the rice and beans into the skillet, mix well, and heat everything through. Season the dish to taste with salt and a combination of Worcestershire sauce and Tabasco sauce.

Note: You may be able to find Salsa Lizano in Latin American groceries and stores that sell a variety of hot sauces. One Website that carries it is www.mohotta.com. Pickapeppa Sauce from Jamaica also works well in this dish.

Tostadas with Salsa and Guacamole

Plan this dish for a festive evening with friends and have the beans already made. If you have the time, you can also make the salsa one day in advance. Take a casual approach and create a "tostada bar" by putting all the toppings in separate bowls. This way, everybody participates in creating their own meal, piling on whatever they want. Kids love it.

BEANS

1 1/2 cups pinto beans, soaked overnight in 6 cups of water to cover with 1 teaspoon baking soda

2 garlic cloves, peeled

1 onion, chopped

1 bay leaf

2 teaspoons dried basil

1/2 cup chopped ripe tomatoes

1 tablespoon ground cumin

1 tablespoon chili powder

1 teaspoon paprika

Sprinkling chili flakes

SALSA

1/2 cup cilantro leaves (about 1 bunch cilantro)

1 cup chopped tomatoes

1/4 cup cubed red bell pepper

1/4 cup diced red onion

1 small jalapeño pepper, seeded and minced

2 tablespoons freshly squeezed lime juice

8 corn tortillas or small flour tortillas

TOPPINGS

1 cup grated jack cheese

1 head romaine lettuce, washed and shredded

1 carrot, peeled and grated

1/2 head red cabbage, shredded

1/4 cup cilantro leaves

Fresh salsa (page 8) or a commercial brand

Fresh guacamole (page 211)

MAKES 8

PER SERVING:

CALORIES 282

FAT 6.1 G
 SATURATED FAT
 2.9 G

(18.5% OF CALO-
RIES FROM FAT)

PROTEIN 15.3 G

CARBOHYDRATE
 44.7 G

CHOLESTEROL
 12 MG

FIBER 13.8 G

Prepare the beans: Add the garlic, onion, bay leaf, and dried basil to the pot of beans that has been soaking overnight. Bring to a boil and cook for 45 minutes to 1 hour. The beans should be soft and easy to mash with the back of a spoon. When they are ready, drain any remaining water, remove the bay leaf, dump in the tomatoes, and mash the beans and tomatoes with a potato masher. Add the cumin, chili powder, paprika, and the chili flakes and mash again.

Make the salsa: Hold the cilantro under running water, making sure that all the dirt pours off. Pinch the leaves off the stems and put them in a small bowl with the remaining salsa ingredients, mixing with a spoon until everything is thoroughly melded. Serve immediately or cover and refrigerate until you are ready to use.

Lay the tortillas on a baking tray, spread 1/4 cup beans and 1 tablespoon of cheese on top, and set on the lowest rack under the broiler for 2 minutes to keep them warm until ready to serve. Put all the toppings in separate bowls so that everyone can layer their own tostada.

SALSA

SERVES 8

PER SERVING:

CALORIES 21

FAT 0.3 G
    SATURATED FAT
    0 G

(9.6% OF CALO-
    RIES FROM FAT)

PROTEIN 1.1 G

CARBOHYDRATE
4.7 G

CHOLESTEROL
0 MG

FIBER 1.1 G

Tips from Rosie's Kitchen

You've probably heard that dried pinto beans can soak for just a few hours and be ready to cook, but I always soak my beans overnight with a little baking soda. It is a fail-safe method. You can be sure they will be evenly cooked. Fill a large pot with enough water to thoroughly cover the beans, stir in 1 teaspoon baking soda, and soak. Also, salt your beans after they are cooked to flavor them. If you put salt in the water while soaking or cooking, it may cause them to remain a little hard.

To Prepare Lettuce: *To wash and shred lettuce, first pull leaves off at the end of the stalk and run them under water. Make sure all the dirt runs off. Pat them dry gently with a clean cloth, then lay them out and cut thin slices at an angle, using a sharp knife.*

To Shred the Cabbage: *Cut the head in half, then lay the half flat side down on a cutting board and make paper-thin slices, at an angle.*

You could also include the Santa Fe Chicken (page 208) in your tostada bar. It makes a great topping.

A tostada bar with baked chicken (or tofu), tortillas, salsa,
guacamole, and various toppings

USING LEFTOVERS

No one likes to waste food. It should be painful to throw out unused leftovers. I find it useful to have a plan for leftovers so that I don't wind up ignoring them until they clearly have to be discarded. Rosie agrees with me on this. In her Tips she gives numerous suggestions for using leftovers.

Orthodox Hindus refuse to eat leftovers. They try to eat only freshly prepared food for its healthful energetic qualities, which they think dissipate when food is left standing or is reheated. In my experience, some foods are just fine on reheating—bean dishes, including lentil and split pea soups, and some casseroles. Other foods definitely suffer, like pasta, most vegetables, and fish, but with some forethought they can be prepared in very satisfying ways. In some cases, recipes must be made with leftovers. It is not possible to make good Chinese fried rice with freshly cooked rice; you have to use cold, leftover rice in order to have the grains separate and absorb oil and flavor. **—A.W.**

STEAMED BROCCOLI WITH GLUTEN

I keep cans of braised gluten in my pantry and open one when I want a super-quick, satisfying meal that provides protein (derived from wheat). I like to combine it with a fresh vegetable. The name "gluten" is unfortunate; maybe "wheat protein medallions" would sound more appetizing. What's called for here is a Chinese product that is surprisingly good: the ready-to-eat medallions have a rich taste and satisfying texture that make them a delicious replacement for animal protein in stir-fries.

1 large head broccoli
1/2 cup purified water
1 tablespoon canola or grapeseed oil
Salt to taste

4 cloves garlic, chopped
10 ounces canned braised gluten (see *Note*)

Slice off the bottom ends of the broccoli stalks and cut the thick stalks away from the tops. Separate the tops into florets. Peel the fibrous stalks down to the tender inner flesh and cut them into bite-sized chunks. Place the broccoli in a saucepan with the water, oil, a bit of salt, and the garlic.

Bring the broccoli to a boil, cover tightly, and cook, stirring once, until the broccoli is bright green and very crunchy-tender, no more than 5 minutes. Do not overcook. Remove from heat, drain off all the liquid, and add the contents of the can of gluten. Stir thoroughly to break up the pieces of gluten. Heat thoroughly and serve.

Note: Braised gluten is available at all Asian grocery stores that stock Chinese canned goods. The Chinese name is *Cha' i Pow Yü,* and the best brand is Companion, from Taiwan.

SERVES 6

PER SERVING:

CALORIES 132.2

FAT 10.8 G
  SATURATED FAT
  1.7 G
  (72.4% OF CALO-
  RIES FROM FAT)

PROTEIN 7.1 G

CARBOHYDRATE
  1.8 G

CHOLESTEROL
  0 MG

FIBER 1 G

❋

CAULIFLOWER WITH CURRIED GLUTEN

Curry-flavored braised gluten is another versatile prepared-wheat protein food, so well seasoned that it can simply be combined with a fresh vegetable for a quick and easy main dish.

SERVES 6

PER SERVING:

CALORIES 106

FAT 6.5 G
  SATURATED FAT
  LESS THAN 1 G
(55% OF CALO-
  RIES FROM FAT)

PROTEIN 7.5 G

CARBOHYDRATE
  5 G

CHOLESTEROL
  0 MG

FIBER 1.8 G

❖

1 large head cauliflower
1/2 cup purified water
Salt to taste
1 tablespoon canola or grapeseed
  oil

1 medium onion, chopped
10 ounces canned curry-flavored
  braised gluten (see *Note*)
1/2 cup chopped cilantro leaves
  (optional)

Separate the cauliflower into florets and cut into bite-sized chunks. Put the cauliflower in a saucepan with the water and a bit of salt. Bring to a boil, cover tightly, and cook until the cauliflower is crunchy-tender, no more than 5 minutes. Remove from the heat and drain well.

Heat the oil in a skillet, add the onions, and sauté over medium-high heat until the onions just begin to brown. Add the contents of the can of curry-flavored braised gluten and the steamed cauliflower, stirring well to break up the pieces of gluten, and heat thoroughly. Add the cilantro if desired, cook for another minute, and serve.

Note: The Chinese name for curry-flavored braised gluten is *Curry Cha' i Pow Yü,* and, again, the best brand is Companion.

Accompaniments

(Side Dishes, Breads, and Sauces)

Pickled Vegetables

Lemon Dill Baby Carrots

Seasonal Vegetable Medley

Mashed Potatoes and Parsnips

Shiitake Mushrooms and Pea Pods

Portobello Burger

Warm Quinoa-and-Zucchini-Stuffed
Tomatoes

Wilted Spinach with Mushrooms

Brussels Sprouts for People Who Think
They Hate Brussels Sprouts

Beets in Mustard Sauce

Steamed and Roasted Baby Red Potatoes

Greens with Tangy Miso Dressing

Toasted Grain Pilaf

Fresh Applesauce

Potato Pancakes

Pear Relish

Serrano Chili and Cilantro Cornbread
Muffins

Whole Wheat Baguettes with Sun-Dried
Tomatoes and Herbs

Tomato Mushroom Sauce

Cilantro Chutney

Mint Chutney

Salsa de Nuez

COOKING TECHNIQUES

I like to cook in ways that are efficient, clean, give good results, and do not decrease the nutritional values of foods. One technique I employ frequently is steaming. It uses little energy, results in little mess, and does the least damage to nutrients. I steam many vegetables and fish. Chinese cooks will also steam dumplings, buns, and pancake wrappers encasing other foods. Another technique I like is "steam frying": that is, sautéing food briefly in a little oil, then adding water, stock, or wine, covering the pan, and allowing the food to cook until it is done. You can uncover the pan and quickly boil off excess liquid near the end of the preparation if you want to.

I often boil less delicate vegetables, like corn on the cob, potatoes, and beets. (But if you have never tasted baked whole beets, you will be surprised at how much more delicious they are.) If you boil tender vegetables, be aware that you will lose some of their nutrients to the cooking water.

Broiling, baking, and roasting use a lot of energy and often require more cleaning up, but they produce very good results. Try not to add excessive fat to foods you cook in the oven. Also try to avoid browning them excessively, especially flesh foods, which become carcinogenic when they are cooked brown or black. Be careful not to inhale the smoke from high-temperature cooking of foods containing fat and animal protein; it is also carcinogenic. Of course, these same precautions also apply to grilling. (See page 51 for more on outdoor cooking.)

I urge you not to fry foods, especially not to deep-fry them. Frying puts excessive fat into dishes and also exposes you to the health risks of chemically altered fats. Stir-frying is perfectly acceptable if you use reasonable amounts of good oils and keep them below the smoking point.

I use my microwave oven for rapid heating and defrosting of food, especially of small portions, never for serious cooking. As a cooking method microwaving just does not produce as good results as conventional baking or broiling, and it may alter the chemical composition of food in ways that could be harmful. You should also know that if you microwave food in plastic containers or wraps, the microwaves can drive plastic molecules into the food. Never put food into a microwave oven in anything other than a glass or ceramic dish, and never cover it with plastic wrap.

A word on cookware: I use enamel-coated cast-iron pots and pans that are easy to clean and conduct heat fairly well. I also like stainless steel cookware with copper or aluminum bottoms to improve conductivity. (Stainless steel by itself is not a great conductor.) High-quality nonstick pans are also very useful, because they make it possible to sauté with little or no fat, and the nonstick coating does not interact with food. Avoid uncoated aluminum cookware; the metal can get into food you cook in it, and aluminum is probably toxic. **—A.W.**

Pickled Vegetables

Pickled carrots, jicama, cauliflower, and string beans make a healthy snack to have on hand. The carrots offer a great deal of beta-carotene and iron. The jicama and cauliflower provide vitamin C and potassium, and the string beans have a good deal of antioxidants and also add some color to the combination. The vinegar here is well seasoned with the essence of mustard, dill weed, and garlic, all offset with a hint of sweet and balancing brown sugar. The pickling liquid makes an excellent dressing for any salad.

MAKES 20 1-OUNCE
SERVINGS

PER SERVING:

CALORIES 23.1

FAT 0.2 G
  SATURATED FAT
  0 G
(5.4% OF CALORIES
  FROM FAT)

PROTEIN 0.6 G

CARBOHYDRATE
  5.7 G

CHOLESTEROL 0 MG

FIBER 1.2 G

❄

1/2 pound carrots, peeled and cut in rounds on the diagonal (about 2 cups)
1/2 pound string beans
1 small head cauliflower, broken into florets (about 2 cups)
1/2 raw jicama, peeled and cut in half and cut into sticks

DRESSING

2 cups purified water
21/2 cups cider vinegar
1/4 cup olive oil
3 tablespoons brown sugar
1 teaspoon salt
1 tablespoon dill weed
6 cloves garlic
1/4 cup pickling spices or: 5 bay leaves, 1 tablespoon mustard seed, 1 tablespoon dill seed, and 1 1/2 teaspoons red chili flakes

Fill a large pot with 5 cups of water and bring to a boil. First drop in the carrots and parboil for 2 minutes, then quickly scoop them with a strainer or large slotted spoon and transfer to a pot filled with cold water and ice to shock them. Drop the string beans into the boiling water and cook just until they turn bright green (about 3 minutes), then quickly transfer them to the ice water. The cauliflower will only need to parboil for 1 minute. Let all the vegetables sit in the cold water for a few minutes to cool. Drain the cold water, remove the cooled vegetables to a big bowl, and add the raw jicama.

Put all the dressing ingredients including the pickling spices in a stainless-steel pan set over medium heat, bring it to a boil, and cook for 2 minutes. Pour the cooked dressing over the vegetables and allow them to cool at room temperature. Once cooled, put the vegetables into a 1-gallon glass jar or lidded plastic container and fill it with as much dressing as the jar will hold. Cover and refrigerate for 2 days before eating.

Tips from Rosie's Kitchen

Blanching your vegetables makes them porous enough to absorb flavor from the dressing. Cooling them rapidly shocks the vegetables and stops any further cooking; shocking them quickly keeps your pickles crisp and crunchy rather than limp and rubbery. The jicama is porous enough raw, so it doesn't need to be blanched. Each vegetable is blanched separately because some vegetables need more time than others, and we want them all to be crisp and flavorful.

Lemon Dill Baby Carrots

It really helps to know how to make a side dish that doesn't call for a lot of time or fuss. These carrots are the answer. They are healthy, take almost no time to prepare, and go great with lunch or dinner, or by themselves.

1 1/2 pounds baby carrots
1 tablespoon freshly squeezed
  lemon juice
1 teaspoon cornstarch
1/3 cup purified water
2 teaspoons chopped fresh dill

1/8 teaspoon salt (optional)
Freshly ground black pepper to
  taste

GARNISH

Fresh dill sprigs

Steam the carrots in a steamer basket in a large pot filled with enough water to reach the bottom of the basket. Steam for 6–8 minutes. The carrots should be tender yet firm.

Combine the lemon juice and the cornstarch in a large saucepan. Stir until the cornstarch is dissolved. Gradually add the water and continue to cook over medium heat until the liquid becomes thick and bubbly, stirring constantly. Remove from the heat. Stir in the dill and salt.

Drain the carrots when they are finished steaming and arrange them on a platter. Pour the liquid over the top. Garnish with a dash of pepper and fresh dill sprigs.

Tips from Rosie's Kitchen

Make sure that you prepare the grill 15–20 minutes ahead of time so that the coals are hot and the heat is consistent. This always ensures even cooking. You can grill indoors on the stove using a cast-iron pan that has ridges on the bottom of it. It sears the food much like a grill over hot coals.

Seasonal Vegetable Medley

Grilling is a summertime tradition for me. Once you grill vegetables, you will find yourself preparing them this way quite a bit. Grilling imparts a smoky, barbecued flavor that people love, especially kids. In fact, serving grilled vegetables to kids is a good way to get them to actually enjoy eating them!

Use any leftover grilled vegetables to toss into a cold pasta salad.

During the winter months, my kitchen is full of the aroma of the seasoned roasted winter vegetables baking in the oven. These are great alone or paired with simple fish or chicken dishes such as the chicken in the Simple Marinated Chicken Salad recipe (page 94), or the Seared Salmon with Orange Glaze (page 178).

GRILLED SUMMER VEGETABLES

1 zucchini, cut lengthwise into 1/2-inch slices

2 yellow summer squash, cut lengthwise into 1/2-inch slices

4 Japanese or 1 medium eggplant, sliced lengthwise into 1/2-inch slices

1 onion, sliced into 1/4-inch pieces

1 red bell pepper, sliced lengthwise into 1/2-inch pieces

OLIVE OIL SEASONING

1/4 cup olive oil

1/4 teaspoon dried oregano

1/4 teaspoon dried thyme

1 tablespoon dried basil

1/8 teaspoon cayenne pepper (optional)

1/2 teaspoon crushed fennel seeds

1/4 teaspoon salt

1/8 teaspoon coarsely cracked black pepper

1/4 cup freshly squeezed lemon juice

SERVES 8

PER SERVING:
CALORIES 185.1
FAT 9.8 G
 SATURATED FAT 1.4 G
(42.4% OF CALORIES FROM FAT)
PROTEIN 4.3 G
CARBOHYDRATE 24.4 G
CHOLESTEROL 0 MG
FIBER 9.5 G

Put all the sliced vegetables in a large bowl. Mix all the seasoning ingredients together in a separate bowl, and then pour it over the vegetables. Toss thoroughly with a big spoon until all the vegetables are completely coated.

Spread the vegetables on top of the grill over medium-low heat for 21/2 minutes. Turn them over and cook for an additional 11/2 minutes.

SERVES 8

PER SERVING:

CALORIES 107.5

FAT 6.9 G

SATURATED FAT
0.9 G

(55.5% OF CALO-
RIES FROM FAT)

PROTEIN 1.4 G

CARBOHYDRATE
11.1 G

CHOLESTEROL
0 MG

FIBER 1.8 G

ROASTED WINTER VEGETABLES

1 cup potatoes, washed and cut into 1-inch cubes

1 cup turnips or sweet potatoes, washed and cut into 2-inch cubes

1 cup carrots, peeled and sliced into 1/2-inch rounds

1 cup parsnips, peeled and cut into 1-inch rounds

1 cup onions, quartered

1/2 teaspoon caraway seeds

Preheat oven to 375°F.

Put all the vegetables in a large bowl. Mix all the above seasoning ingredients together in a separate bowl and pour them over the vegetables. Toss thoroughly with a big spoon until all the vegetables are completely coated. Using a paper towel, oil a baking sheet with olive oil. Bake vegetables on the sheet for 20 minutes. Carefully turn the vegetables over, using a spatula, to expose the other side. Bake for another 15 minutes, until the vegetables turn golden brown.

ANDY SUGGESTS

One cup of winter squash would be good in this mixture too.

Mashed Potatoes and Parsnips

Mashed potatoes make a hearty, honest dish. It has sometimes been referred to as comfort food because it evokes memories of both big, special-occasion dinners and the simple, family dinner intended for no other reason than to share a good meal. This version of mashed potatoes tastes good because it's dense with the mildly sweet flavor of parsnips and just enough butter to please, but without the extra calories you usually find in mashed potatoes.

8 medium red or white new potatoes (see Tips), washed and cubed
4 parsnips, peeled and cubed
1 cup milk
3 tablespoons butter
1 tablespoon chopped parsley
Dash cayenne pepper
Several grindings of black pepper
1 teaspoon salt

SERVES 6

PER SERVING:
CALORIES 260.8
FAT 7.5 G
   SATURATED FAT
   4.5 G
(25% OF CALORIES FROM FAT)
PROTEIN 5.6 G
CARBOHYDRATE
   45 G
CHOLESTEROL
   21 MG
FIBER 6.9 G

Put the potatoes and parsnips in a large pot with water, making sure that the water completely covers them. Bring to a boil, lower the heat to medium, then cover and simmer for 20–30 minutes, stirring occasionally with a spoon. Test the tenderness of the potatoes with a fork; they should pierce easily and be tender, yet firm. Drain any remaining liquid and mash the potatoes with a potato masher until there are no visible lumps. Add the milk and butter and continue to mash until the potatoes are smooth and creamy. Stir in the parsley, cayenne pepper, black pepper, and salt, and beat thoroughly with a wooden spoon until all the seasonings are completely mixed in. Cover and serve warm.

Tips from Rosie's Kitchen

Red or white new potatoes have softer, thinner skins and can be mashed with the skins to preserve all the nutrients they offer. However, you might want to peel potatoes such as Idahoes or other baking potatoes because of their thicker, tougher skins.

This is a great recipe because the liquid that remains from cooking the potatoes is instant stock! Save it and use it to make Cold Cucumber Soup (page 134).

SHIITAKE MUSHROOMS AND PEA PODS

Fresh and dried shiitakes are practically different mushrooms; they are so unalike in texture and flavor. But both are delightful when combined with pea pods, which provide a vivid contrast of green, sweetness, and crunchiness (if you do not overcook them). This dish makes a good accompaniment to fish and also goes well with grains.

SERVES 4

PER SERVING:
CALORIES 279 G
FAT 4 G
  SATURATED FAT
  0.5 G
(13% OF CALORIES
  FROM FAT)
PROTEIN 8.5 G
CARBOHYDRATE
  55 G
CHOLESTEROL
  0 MG
FIBER 9.5 G

❉

1 pound snow or sugar snap peas
1/2 pound fresh shiitake mushrooms
  or 1 cup dried
2 teaspoons canola or grapeseed oil
1 teaspoon toasted-sesame oil

2 teaspoons light brown or raw
  sugar
1/4 cup sake or dry sherry
2 tablespoons shoyu or other
  natural soy sauce

Trim the ends and any strings from the pea pods.

If using fresh mushrooms, trim the stem ends and discard (or save for soup). Slice the mushrooms into 1/2-inch-wide slices. If using dried mushrooms, put them in a bowl with enough cold water to cover. Place bowl in microwave, uncovered, and microwave on high for 1 minute. Let the mushrooms sit in warm water until completely softened, about 30 minutes, then drain, squeeze out the liquid (save for soup), and cut off and discard the tough stems. Cut the caps into 1/2-inch-wide pieces.

Heat the oils in a skillet and add the mushrooms. Sauté over medium-high heat, stirring, until the mushrooms just begin to brown. Sprinkle the sugar over the mushrooms and add the wine and shoyu. Cook and stir for 1 minute, then add the pea pods. Cover, reduce the heat to medium, and steam until the pea pods are just tender-crunchy and bright green, about 2 minutes.

Remove cover and continue to cook, until most of the liquid is evaporated. Serve immediately.

Shiitaki Mushrooms and Pea Pods

COOKING MUSHROOMS

Nutritionists often teach that mushrooms have little value as food, that they are useful mainly as interesting garnishes or sources of unusual flavors and textures. This view is a product of a general fear of mushrooms common in the English-speaking world. It goes along with another wrong idea, that mushrooms have no medicinal value. I am a longtime mushroom hunter, eater, and enthusiast, and I have always extolled both their nutritional and health benefits.

Mushrooms are respectable protein sources, intermediate between foods of animal origin and vegetables. (Actually, we share more DNA sequences with mushrooms than with plants and so are more closely related to them.) Their protein is of good quality and, when combined with grains, provides all essential amino acids. On a dry-weight basis, the protein content of many species approaches that of meat. The carbohydrates in mushrooms are mostly indigestible, and there is little fat—a great plus. They provide useful amounts of some B vitamins and trace minerals.

I always stress the importance of cooking mushrooms thoroughly. Cell walls of mushrooms are tough, making it difficult for the digestive system to get at the nutrients inside them. Mushrooms often contain chemical compounds that either interfere with digestive enzymes or block absorption of nutrients. In addition, even many edible species contain natural toxins. These problems all have a common solution: heat. Sufficient cooking breaks down the tough cell walls, inactivates the antidigestive elements, and destroys many toxins. It also makes mushrooms taste better, bringing out their best flavors and textures. I strongly advise against eating any mushrooms raw, whether wild or cultivated.

Many fanciers of mushrooms sauté them in lots of butter, often adding whole milk or cream on top of that. These dishes are not healthy for hearts and arteries, however good the mushrooms are to begin with. When I try a new species for the first time, I will usually sauté it in a little olive or grapeseed oil in order to determine whether it has a good enough flavor and texture to recommend it for further experimentation. If it does, I will then look for ways to prepare it to enhance its qualities without flouting principles of healthy eating.

For example, many thick-fleshed mushrooms can be grilled over charcoal and basted with a low-fat or nonfat sauce. Fresh shiitakes, grilled with a little teriyaki sauce, are universally popular at mushroom cook-and-tastes. (Mix one part dry sherry or sake, one part reduced-sodium Japanese shoyu [soy sauce], and one tablespoon of sugar for each cup of liquid to make an easy teriyaki sauce.)

In general, Asian cooking methods work very well for mushrooms, use little fat, and result in dishes that are much more healthful than most of those described in books on mushroom cookery or dishes that are served at restaurants. In addition to grilling, other methods include simmering in broth and stir-frying with vegetables.

The only innovation in mushroom cultivation in the West has been the introduction of the portobello, a large variety of the common button mushroom that is allowed to grow to maturity. When the caps expand, their flavor intensifies as spores ripen. Grilled portobello caps are thick and meaty, lending themselves to the creation of tasty vegetarian burgers.

A number of cultivated Asian varieties are now available in our markets. Fresh shiitakes are easy to find. They are more flavorful than button mushrooms and also have anticancer and cholesterol-lowering properties. Several kinds of oyster mushrooms are in cultivation. They also offer protection from cancer, and are cheaper than shiitakes, but less flavorful. Look for maitake, a newer arrival from Japan. It is meaty, tasty (especially grilled with teriyaki sauce), and one of the best-studied species for immune-enhancing effects. In the spring, wild morels are often for sale, usually for exorbitant prices; and in the fall, yellow chanterelles are available, sometimes more reasonably. You can also find several kinds of dried mushrooms in Asian and Italian groceries. Soak them in water until they soften, save the soaking liquid (after straining) for soups or sauces, and add the reconstituted mushrooms to your recipes. Dried shiitakes, maitakes, and porcinis are especially good to have on hand. —**A.W.**

Portobello Burger

SERVES 1
(1 BURGER
WITH GARNISHES)

PER SERVING:

CALORIES 471.3

FAT 33.5 G
  SATURATED FAT
  3.8 G
(63.7% OF CALO-
  RIES FROM FAT)

PROTEIN 0 G

CARBOHYDRATE
  0 G

CHOLESTEROL
  0 MG

FIBER 0 G

❀

For a simple vegetarian alternative to a meat or turkey burger, try broiling or grilling a whole portobello mushroom cap and serving it on a toasted bun with your favorite garnishes (lettuce, tomato, onion, pickle, ketchup, mustard). Choose large, firm, fresh-looking portobellos and remove the stems. Brush the caps with olive oil and place them gill-side up on a heated grill or on a sheet of aluminum foil under a hot broiler. Cook until the caps are soft and begin to brown. Sprinkle with salt and pepper, turn them over, and cook until caps brown on that side, too. Sprinkle with additional salt and pepper and slide the cooked mushrooms onto waiting buns.

Warm Quinoa-and-Zucchini-Stuffed Tomatoes

Quinoa, like other grains, is bursting with B vitamins and iron; however, it varies from other grains because it contains more protein without a lot of carbohydrates. Quinoa actually contains all 8 essential amino acids, which makes it a unique complete food. The ancient Incas honored this protein-dense food, making it a staple in their everyday diet. It is now gaining more recognition and becoming a valuable vegetarian source of protein.

1/2 cup quinoa
2 tablespoons olive oil
1 1/2 cups purified water or vegetable stock (page 122)
1/4 teaspoon salt
1/4 teaspoon freshly ground black pepper
1 teaspoon Italian seasoning
1/2 medium onion, chopped
1 cup grated zucchini
2 tablespoons currants or raisins

1 tablespoon chopped fresh parsley or basil
1/2 teaspoon ground curry (or cumin)
1/4 teaspoon paprika
2 tablespoons freshly squeezed lemon juice
6 medium tomatoes
2 teaspoons bread crumbs
2 tablespoons freshly grated Parmesan cheese

Tips from Rosie's Kitchen

If you don't have quinoa on hand, you can make this recipe using millet or amaranth. Amaranth tends to have a slightly sweet flavor, while millet and quinoa tend to taste like natural rice, with a delicate, nutlike flavor.

Stuffed Winter Squash: *You can use the stuffing from this recipe to stuff and bake squash. Buy 3 acorn squashes or 6 baby pumpkin squashes. Puncture the surface of the squash 4 times with a knife, making sure that each stab is spaced apart. Cut the squash lengthwise and scoop out the seeds with a big spoon and discard them. Lay the squash cavity-side-down in a baking pan. Add water and bake for 30–45 minutes. When it is completely cooked, the squash should be easily pierced with a fork. Remove from the oven and let it cool in the pan. Leave all the liquid from the squash in the pan, turn the cooled squash over so the cavity side is up, and spoon up 1 1/2 cups of stuffing, filling the cavity of each squash. Cover with foil and bake for 15 minutes in the preheated oven. Garnish a platter or each of 6 plates with a sprig of fresh parsley, lay the squash on top, and serve.*

SERVES 6

PER SERVING:

CALORIES 164.1

FAT 3.4 G
  SATURATED FAT
  0.7 G

(17.3% OF CALO-
  RIES FROM FAT)

PROTEIN 5.9

CARBOHYDRATE
  30.6 G

CHOLESTEROL
  1 MG

FIBER 4.2 G

❀

Preheat oven to 350°F.

In a small saucepan, toss the quinoa in 1 tablespoon olive oil, stir, pour in the water, salt, black pepper, and Italian seasoning, and bring to a boil. Cover and simmer over low heat for 20 minutes. Remove from the heat.

Pour 1 tablespoon olive oil into a nonstick pan and sauté the chopped onions, zucchini, currants, parsley or basil, curry, paprika, and lemon juice over medium heat for about 2 minutes. Scoop the quinoa into the sauté pan and mix thoroughly with a spoon until it is blended with the vegetables to make an aromatic stuffing. Remove from heat.

Create a lid for each tomato by cutting a star shape around the stem about 1/4-inch deep. Remove the top and set it aside.

Scoop out the seeds of each tomato and some of the loose pulp, being careful to leave a strong wall of tomato all around. Spoon equal amounts of the stuffing into the cavities of each tomato, filling them up generously. Put the tomatoes in a small ceramic or glass baking dish and garnish with a sprinkle of bread crumbs and 1 teaspoon Parmesan cheese per tomato. Cover the baking dish with a glass lid or foil and bake for 25 minutes. Tomatoes should be firm and easy to transfer from the baking dish to the serving plates. Garnish by putting the star-shaped tomato lids back on top of each tomato.

Wilted Spinach with Mushrooms

This is a side dish that you can call upon a lot because it complements so many entrées. In presenting the Seared Salmon with Orange Glaze (page 178), I use the Wilted Spinach with Mushrooms as a fancy bed beneath the fish, which appeals to the eye as well as the taste buds. You can also toss it with your favorite pasta to add color, flavor, and nutritional value. And you can venture out into the world of greens and use some Swiss chard or kale along with the spinach in this recipe. Just substitute the vegetable of your choice for one of the bunches of spinach. All of them offer ample amounts of vitamins A, B, and C, and minerals. I have to warn you, though, that once you start incorporating more greens in your meals, you'll be addicted—they make your body feel great!

3 cloves garlic, sliced
2 tablespoons olive oil
1 cup sliced mushrooms
3 tablespoons vegetable stock
   (page 122) or water
2 pounds (about 2 bunches)
   spinach, washed, tough stems
   removed, to yield about 12 cups
   leaves

Salt to taste
Freshly ground pepper to taste

GARNISH

6 tablespoons goat cheese or 3
   tablespoons sesame seeds
   (optional)

SERVES 3

PER SERVING:
CALORIES 84.4
FAT 7.2 G
   SATURATED FAT
   2.4 G
(73.4% OF CALO-
   RIES FROM FAT)
PROTEIN 3.5 G
CARBOHYDRATE
   2.3 G
CHOLESTEROL
   7 MG
FIBER 1.2 G

❋

Warm Quinoa-and-Zucchini-Stuffed Tomatoes

Sauté the garlic in the olive oil in a sauté pan over medium heat until it becomes soft. Add the mushrooms and cook for 1 minute, stirring once or twice. Pour in the vegetable stock or water and dump in the spinach. Rotate the spinach with tongs so that the leaves are coated in the cooking juices. When the spinach turns bright green and is thoroughly wilted, remove from the heat. Sprinkle individual servings with 1/2 tablespoon goat cheese or sesame seeds, if you wish, then season with salt and black pepper. Serve immediately.

Tips from Rosie's Kitchen

If you're using Swiss chard and/or kale, remove the leaves from the stalks and wash them well. Wash the stalks and chop them up coarsely. Cook the chard leaves and the stalks the same way as in this recipe. If you haven't used kale, you'll find that it tastes similar to cabbage; it offers an amazing amount of calcium. However, kale takes a little longer to cook, so put it in with the mushrooms to give it more time to soften.

BRUSSELS SPROUTS FOR PEOPLE WHO THINK THEY HATE BRUSSELS SPROUTS

I understand why brussels sprouts top the list of detested vegetables for many people. When they are large, old, or overcooked, they tend to have an obnoxious, barnyardy flavor that some people are sensitive to whereas others are not. You can minimize this by choosing smaller, fresh-looking sprouts and cooking them just until they are crunchy-tender and bright colored. (Do not use frozen sprouts.) The secret of this dish is balancing ingredients to mellow the strong flavor of these miniature cabbages. Olive oil, garlic, red pepper, Parmesan, and, especially, nutmeg do the trick admirably.

1 pound brussels sprouts
1 teaspoon salt
2 tablespoons extra virgin olive oil
1 teaspoon hot red pepper flakes, or to taste

5 cloves garlic, finely minced
1/4–1/2 teaspoon nutmeg, or to taste, preferably freshly grated
1/2 cup freshly grated Parmesan cheese

Trim the ends off the brussels sprouts and remove and discard any discolored outer leaves. If sprouts are large (more than 1 inch in diameter), cut them in quarters lengthwise through the stem end. If smaller, cut them in half.

Bring 2 quarts of water to a boil, add salt and the sprouts. Boil the sprouts uncovered until they are just crunchy-tender, about 5 minutes. Do not overcook them. Drain the sprouts well.

Wipe and dry the pot and heat the olive oil in it. Add the red pepper flakes and garlic and sauté for 1 minute. Add the sprouts and nutmeg and sauté for another minute. Mix in the Parmesan cheese and toss the sprouts until the cheese melts.

SERVES 4

PER SERVING:
CALORIES 162
FAT 10 G
  SATURATED FAT 3 G
(56% OF CALORIES FROM FAT)
PROTEIN 8.3 G
CARBOHYDRATE 12 G
CHOLESTEROL 8 MG
FIBER 4.5 G

BEETS IN MUSTARD SAUCE

SERVES 4

PER SERVING:

CALORIES 176

FAT 14 G

   SATURATED FAT
   2 G

(72% OF CALORIES
   FROM FAT)

PROTEIN 2 G

CARBOHYDRATE
   12 G

CHOLESTEROL 0 MG

FIBER 3 G

The sharp taste in beets is masked in this recipe by the simple mustardy vinaigrette. Be sure to allow the beets to marinate for a full day in order for the flavors to marry.

1 pound red beets

3 tablespoons prepared mustard, preferably whole grain or Dijon

3 tablespoons red wine vinegar

¼ cup extra virgin olive oil

1 medium onion, chopped

Salt to taste

Cut the tops off the beets, leaving 1 inch of stems attached. Place the beets in a pot of cold water to cover, bring to a boil, reduce heat, and boil until the beets can easily be pierced through with a sharp knife, 45–60 minutes depending on their size.

Meanwhile, put the mustard in a bowl and whisk in the vinegar. Then whisk in the olive oil in a steady stream until the sauce is smooth and creamy. Add the onions.

When the beets are done, drain them, and submerge them in several changes of cold water until they are just cool enough to handle. Cut off the roots and tops, slip the skins off, and slice the warm beets into the mustard sauce. Mix well, cover, and let marinate in the refrigerator for at least 24 hours. Before serving, mix well and add salt if desired.

Steamed and Roasted Baby Red Potatoes

Potatoes are packed with energy-enhancing vitamins C and B₆ that give your body and mind some pep. Baby red potatoes or new white potatoes are particularly good because the peel is tender, pretty, and full of minerals like iron and potassium. The basic seasonings we add truly transform the taste of a simple potato. The garlic really enhances the flavor of the olive oil, and the rosemary, pepper, salt, and paprika give the potatoes a robust, seasoned taste.

These potatoes, steamed or roasted, make a perfect complement to many dishes. They go very well with the Roasted Pepper Turkey with Orange Liqueur (page 168), or alongside Eggs Florentine with Orange and Dill Sauce (page 4) for a fancy breakfast.

18 baby red potatoes, washed, scrubbed, and halved

SEASONING FOR ROASTING

2 tablespoons olive oil
5 whole small cloves garlic

1 tablespoon fresh rosemary (1 teaspoon dried)
1 teaspoon salt
1/4 teaspoon freshly ground black pepper
1/4 teaspoon paprika

Preheat the oven to 450°F.

Steam the potatoes: Pour about 2 inches of water into a large pot and bring to a boil. Place a steaming basket in the pot raised just above the boiling liquid, put the washed and halved potatoes into the basket, cover the pot, and allow to steam until the potatoes are easily pierced with a fork (about 8 minutes). Turn off the heat and remove the steaming basket from the pot.

Roast the potatoes: Pour the olive oil and seasonings in a large baking dish or casserole pan, add the steamed potatoes, and gently toss them until they are completely coated with the mixture. Bake for 12 minutes until the outsides of the potatoes are crusty, occasionally moving them around to ensure even browning.

Tips from Rosie's Kitchen

Steaming involves cooking something at a low temperature in a covered container with a small amount of boiling liquid. If you do not have a steaming basket, pour about 1/2 inch of water into the bottom of a pot, put the potatoes into the water, cover the pot and place on low heat.

STEAMED
SERVES 6

PER SERVING:

CALORIES 270.3

FAT 0.4 G
  SATURATED FAT
  0.1 G
(1.3% OF CALORIES
  FROM FAT)
PROTEIN 7.2 G

CARBOHYDRATE
  61.5 G

CHOLESTEROL
  0 MG

FIBER 5.5 G

❁

STEAMED AND
ROASTED
SERVES 6

PER SERVING:

CALORIES 310.1

FAT 4.9 G
  SATURATED FAT
  0.7 G
(13.8% OF CALO-
  RIES FROM FAT)
PROTEIN 7.2 G

CARBOHYDRATE
  61.5 G

CHOLESTEROL
  0 MG

FIBER 5.5 G

Serves 4

Per serving:

Calories 108

Fat 4 g
   Saturated Fat
   0.6 g
(34% of calo-
   ries from fat)

Protein 4 g

Carbohydrate
   16 g

Cholesterol
   0 mg

Fiber 3 g

GREENS WITH TANGY MISO DRESSING

The tangy miso dressing for cooked greens provides an unlikely and surprising combination of ingredients and flavors—salty, sour, and sweet, plus the distinctive earthy tang of turmeric. It manages to be a perfect accompaniment to sautéed greens that are quickly prepared and is attractive to the eye.

1 cup onions, cut into thin half-moons
1 tablespoon toasted-sesame oil
1 cup seeded and julienned red bell pepper
4 cups stemmed and julienned kale
2/3 cup purified water

4 cups julienned Napa cabbage or bok choy
1 tablespoon shoyu or other natural soy sauce
8 tablespoons Tangy Miso Dressing

Miso Dressing
About 1 cup
Serves 6

Per serving:

Calories 68

Fat 3 g
   Saturated Fat
   0.5 g
(40% of calo-
   ries from fat)

Protein 2.5 g

Carbohydrate
   8.5 g

Cholesterol
   0 mg

Fiber 1 g

In a large skillet over medium-high heat, sauté the onions in the sesame oil for 5 minutes. Add the red pepper, toss, and sauté for 3 minutes. Add the kale and 1/3 cup water. Cook until the liquid has evaporated. Add the cabbage, soy sauce, and the remaining 1/3 cup water. Cook until the greens are tender, about 5 minutes.

Divide into 4 portions and spoon 2 tablespoons Tangy Miso Dressing over each serving.

Tangy Miso Dressing

1/4 cup white miso
2 tablespoons tahini
1/4 cup freshly squeezed lemon juice
1/4 cup purified water
1 tablespoon honey or brown rice syrup

2 teaspoons chopped fresh dill weed or 1 teaspoon dried
1/2 teaspoon turmeric

Stir the miso and tahini together in a bowl. Add the lemon juice and water and mix well. Stir in the remaining ingredients.

Andy with a wok full of his Greens with Tangy Miso Dressing

Toasted Grain Pilaf

SERVES 6

PER SERVING:

CALORIES 153.9

FAT 6.2 G
  SATURATED FAT
  1.0 G
(34.1% OF CALO-
  RIES FROM FAT)

PROTEIN 4.2 G

CARBOHYDRATE
  22.7 G

CHOLESTEROL
  1 MG

FIBER 3.0 G

❄

2 cups millet, quinoa, or
  amaranth or a combination
1/8 teaspoon curry powder
  (optional)
4 cups chicken stock (page 123) or
  vegetable stock (page 122), or
  more, as needed
1/4 cup sun-dried tomatoes (dried
  in a package, not in oil)

1/2 cup boiling purified water
1/2 cup shredded zucchini
1/2 cup shredded yellow summer
  squash
1/4 cup minced red bell pepper
1/4 cup chopped scallions or green
  onions
Salt to taste

Toast the millet (or other grains) in a large saucepan set over low heat, stirring it constantly until it turns a light brown color, less than 1 minute. Stir in the curry powder until it is blended in. Remove from heat and let cool for 5 minutes. Add the chicken or vegetable stock and bring to a boil. Reduce heat, cover, and simmer. Check after 20 minutes. If the stock has boiled away, add a little more. Cook until the millet has absorbed all the liquid, about 25 minutes in all.

Meanwhile, soak the dried tomatoes in the boiling water for 15 minutes. Drain them in a colander set over a bowl to reserve the liquid, then chop them. Mix the tomatoes, reserved liquid, zucchini, yellow squash, red pepper, and scallions or green onions together in a small skillet set over low heat and cook until most of the liquid is absorbed. Pour into the cooked grain and toss until everything is completely mixed together. Taste and add salt if you think it is needed. Fluff with a fork and serve.

Tips from Rosie's Kitchen

Traditionally a Middle Eastern pilaf is made with white rice, but here we use a healthful grain, toasting it first to bring out its flavor, and mixing in aromatic vegetables to create a delicious, more nutritious dish. For more about grains, see Andy's comments opposite.

You can also make this recipe with brown rice, but the cooking time would be 45 minutes.

ABOUT GRAINS

Cereal crops are cultivated relatives of grass that have sustained human life throughout the world and often define the diets of whole populations. Americans rely on wheat as their staple grain, Asians on rice, Native Americans on maize (corn), northern Europeans on rye, and so forth. Grains are very nourishing, providing a mix of carbohydrate, protein, and fat, but how we prepare and process them can influence our health in ways both good and bad.

When people first discovered grains and domesticated the plants that produced them, they made the seeds edible by simply parching them—that is, heating them in a dry pan over a fire. Parched maize is still a common snack in Peru. Some grains, if they have sufficient water content and soft enough hulls, also lend themselves to popping. Popcorn is an ancient food that remains popular today. Another simple solution is to boil whole or cracked grains into porridges and gruels; Irish oatmeal is a good example.

People also quickly developed other uses for grains, mixing them with water, grinding them, and letting them ferment into alcoholic beverages such as beer or into dough that would rise and could be baked into bread. Until the early 1800s bread was rough, dense, and chewy—peasant bread—often with visible pieces of cracked grains. Since then it has mostly been made with white flour, a product of modern food technology. White flour is pure wheat starch in the form of superfine particles that are digested very differently from whole or cracked grains; it is devoid of the fiber and fat of whole wheat. The same technology has been applied to maize and rice, and supermarkets are filled with products made from these refined starches: breads, pastries, crackers, cookies, chips, pretzels.

As I explained in the section on nutrition, increasing consumption of these refined carbohydrate foods is a major cause of the epidemic of obesity we are seeing in America and wherever American-type fast and processed foods are popular. In my opinion, it also contributes to the prevalence of cardiovascular disease and adult-onset diabetes. This does not mean that grains and carbohydrates are bad for health. It does suggest that modern ways of processing grains have dramatically lowered their nutritional qualities.

Rosie and I both like to cook grains, but we favor unrefined, less processed ones, and we enjoy experimenting with less familiar varieties. Try boiling whole wheat grains (wheatberries) until they are tender, then mixing them with sautéed vegetables or turning them into a cold salad with walnuts, dried cranberries, and a light vinaigrette. Try some of the exotic varieties of rice now on the market, including black rice and red rice, both beautiful and delicious. Use wild rice more; it is now cultivated extensively in California and is no longer an expensive luxury. Get to know buckwheat groats (kasha) and quinoa, grainlike seeds from Eastern Europe and South America, respectively, with distinctive flavors and textures.

Even if you are watching your weight and feel you are sensitive to carbohydrates, you can enjoy these nutritious foods. Well-prepared whole and cracked grains are filling and satisfying, enjoyable both as main dishes and as accompaniments to protein foods. They are also quick and easy to cook and lend themselves to endlessly varied dishes. **—A.W.**

Fresh Applesauce

When you make this applesauce, your guests and family will never forget it and you will probably never buy it in a can or jar again.

You can use any type of apple you'd like, and because apples are pretty much available year-round, you can serve it as a warm side dish in the winter, or a cold side dish, or dessert, any time of year.

6 apples, peeled, cored, and sliced (about 6 cups)
1/2 cup apple juice

1 teaspoon ground cinnamon (see Tips)

Put the apple slices and the apple juice in a saucepan with a lid. Cook, covered, over low heat, until the apples are tender and most of the liquid is absorbed, about 10–20 minutes, depending on the type of apple you are using. Break up the apples using a fork or pour the mixture into a blender and blend until smooth. Sprinkle in the cinnamon and stir until it is thoroughly integrated into the apples. Let the apples cool for a few minutes or longer, depending on whether you want to serve them warm or cold.

SERVES 6

PER SERVING:

CALORIES 94.1

FAT 0.6 G
  SATURATED FAT 0.1 G
  (4.9% OF CALORIES FROM FAT)

PROTEIN 0.3 G

CARBOHYDRATE 24.4 G

CHOLESTEROL 0 MG

FIBER 4.4 G

❋

Tips from Rosie's Kitchen

Always let your taste buds be your guide! Cinnamon, an aromatic spice, can do wonders to enhance any type of apple, as well as different pastries, curries, soups, and stews. However, if you are starting out with apples that taste great raw, you might not want to disguise their wonderful flavor with too much cinnamon. So add only as much cinnamon as you'd like to taste.

Potato Pancakes

I have a friend who gives a party featuring potato pancakes every year. He loves to toss in hot sauce or different herbs. You can be as creative as you like, but mine are simple.

MAKES 8
PANCAKES

PER SERVING:

CALORIES 246

FAT 7.8 G
  SATURATED FAT
  1.3 G

(28.3% OF CALO-
  RIES FROM FAT)

PROTEIN 5.4 G

CARBOHYDRATE
  39.1 G

CHOLESTEROL
  27 MG

FIBER 3 G

3 large Idaho or Yukon potatoes
  (about 2 pounds)
1 large sweet onion
1 cup matzo meal, medium grain
1 egg
1 teaspoon salt, or more to taste
1/4 cup olive oil

GARNISH
Low-fat sour cream
Fresh Applesauce (page 249)

Peel and grate the potatoes and onion by hand or in a food processor and put them in a large bowl. (If you grate the potatoes ahead of time, make sure to soak them in water to keep them from turning color, then drain and squeeze when ready to use.) Add the matzo meal and the egg. Sprinkle in the salt and blend everything together until the onions and potatoes are coated with the egg and matzo meal. Let stand for 5 minutes.

With clean hands, roll a ball of dough just big enough to fit into the palm of your hand, and flatten it out with your palms to make a round cake. Repeat the process until you have used up all the batter. Set a medium sauté pan over medium-high heat with 1 tablespoon of olive oil. Lay 4 pancakes in the hot fat and cook for 1 minute on each side, until they turn golden brown. Transfer the pancakes to a paper towel to soak up any excess oil. Repeat, adding more olive oil to the pan, until all pancakes are cooked. Serve with sour cream and a side of Fresh Applesauce.

Tips from Rosie's Kitchen

I sometimes add 1/4 cup chopped fresh sorrel leaves or chives to the batter. Sorrel, an herb that belongs to the buckwheat family, is in season during the spring. Its leaves are similar to spinach, and you'll want to buy the bunch that has bright green ones. Don't buy it if the leaves look wilted or pale in color.

Rosie turning her Potato Pancakes

Pear Relish

This tastes wonderful on meat or poultry. It is similar to fruit chutney and it will change the way your meal tastes. My guests love this relish. I serve it on the side with the Roasted Pepper Turkey with Orange Liqueur (page 168).

1 whole pear
1/4 cup finely chopped onion
2 tablespoons finely chopped
   yellow bell pepper

2 tablespoons finely chopped red
   bell pepper
2 cups cranberry or apple juice
2 sprigs mint, chopped

Halve the pear and scoop out the seeds using a melon scooper or a teaspoon. Peel the skin off with a paring knife, then chop into bite-size pieces.

Put the pear, onion, peppers, and cranberry or apple juice into a small saucepan and set over medium heat. Cook until the onions and peppers become limp and the pear becomes soft.

Remove from the heat, add the mint, and drizzle over your favorite poultry dish.

MAKES ABOUT
2 CUPS

PER SERVING:

CALORIES 68.1

FAT 6.2 G
  SATURATED FAT
  0 G

(2.5% OF CALORIES
  FROM FAT)

PROTEIN 0.2 G

CARBOHYDRATE
  17.2 G

CHOLESTEROL 0 MG

FIBER 0.8 G

Tips from Rosie's Kitchen

You'll encounter a variety of pears that range in textures at your grocery store throughout the year. Some pears, like Anjou, are soft raw, while others, like Bosc, are very hard raw. All pears taste good in this recipe, but the naturally hard types will take a bit longer to cook. Softer pears will take about 7 minutes to soften, and harder pears will need about 15 minutes.

Serrano Chili and Cilantro Cornbread Muffins

These muffins are moist and chewy, spicy and sweet. When you make them, they won't last long! They are excellent eaten alone warmed with some butter, or as a side dish to an entrée such as Santa Fe Chicken (page 208) or Mexican Chicken Soup (page 136).

2 small serrano chilies (or 2 ounces canned green roasted chilies)
1 1/2 cups unbleached white flour
1/2 cup yellow cornmeal
1 tablespoon baking powder
1 teaspoon salt
Pinch cayenne
2/3 cup low-fat milk or soy milk
2 large eggs
1/2 cup canola or grapeseed oil or softened butter
3 tablespoons pure maple syrup or sugar
1/4 cup chopped fresh cilantro

HONEY BUTTER TOPPING
(Optional)
3 tablespoons honey
3 tablespoons soft butter

MAKES 10 CORN-
BREAD PIECES
OR 12 MUFFINS

PER SERVING:
CALORIES 178

FAT 8.1 G
   SATURATED FAT
   0.8 G

(40.4% OF CALO-
RIES FROM FAT)

PROTEIN 4.7 G

CARBOHYDRATE
22.1 G

CHOLESTEROL
36 MG

FIBER 1.8 G

Preheat the oven to 350°F.

Put the chilies on a baking pan on the top rack under the broiler until they blister and turn black. Turn them over and repeat. Remove them from the broiler and drop them into a brown bag to cool. The skin will become loose and flaky as they cool.

Mix together all the dry ingredients in a large bowl. Whisk together the milk, eggs, oil or butter, maple syrup or sugar, and the cilantro in a separate bowl. Stir the wet ingredients into the dry ingredients with a wooden spoon until thoroughly mixed.

Take the chilies out of the bag and slice them in half, directly down the middle. Open them up, and remove the seeds and discard. Peel the skin off and discard. Cut the chilies into small pieces and stir them into the batter until they are completely mixed in.

Smear a little butter or oil on the bottoms and sides of a 9-inch square baking pan or 12 muffin molds and pour the batter in. Bake 20 minutes if using a muffin pan or 25 minutes if you're using a baking pan. Remove from the oven and let cool.

Make the Honey Butter: Simply blend the softened honey and butter together in a bowl with a fork, whipping lightly to create a creamy spread. Scoop the spread into a ramekin and serve along with the cornbread.

Make 1 slice directly down the middle of the baking pan and 4 slices across to make 10 rectangular pieces.

Tips from Rosie's Kitchen

The indigenous people of the Southwest used to roast their chili peppers over an open fire. If you're feeling really motivated and have the time to do it, you, too, can roast the chilies over a flame or over a barbecue grill, instead of broiling them. Hold the chilies 4 inches away from the flame and rotate until all sides of the pepper turn black. If you'd like to use an alternative to chili peppers, just sauté 1/2 cup onions in a tablespoon of olive oil and use them in place. When handling serrano chilies, do not touch your eyes, because these chilies will sting.

Whole Wheat Baguettes with Sun-Dried Tomatoes and Herbs

The sun-dried tomatoes and herbs really cling to the dough of this baguette, which is similar in consistency to pizza dough. It is wonderful toasted and smeared with the spread in the Goat Cheese Toasties with Sun-Dried Tomato and Basil recipe (page 83).

1 tablespoon dry active yeast
11/2 cups warm purified water
1 teaspoon salt
11/4 cups whole wheat flour
3 or more cups unbleached white
    flour
2 tablespoons olive oil
2 garlic cloves, finely chopped
1/2 cup sun-dried tomatoes soaked
    in 1 cup boiling water

1 teaspoon finely chopped dried
    rosemary leaves
2 tablespoons chopped fresh basil
    (optional)

MAKES 2 LOAVES

PER SERVING:
CALORIES 278.9
FAT 4.4 G
  SATURATED FAT
  0.6 G
(14% OF CALO-
  RIES FROM FAT)
PROTEIN 8.6 G
CARBOHYDRATE
  52.2 G
CHOLESTEROL
  0 MG
FIBER 4.6 G

Dissolve the yeast in the warm water in a large bowl. Stir in the salt, all the whole wheat flour, and about 21/2 cups of the white flour. Turn the dough out onto a floured work surface and knead, adding more flour as necessary when the dough gets sticky, until you have a smooth, elastic dough, about 8–10 minutes. Return the dough to the cleaned bowl, cover with a towel, and let rise until tripled in volume, about 2 hours.

Heat the olive oil in a small skillet and sauté the garlic over low heat 1–2 minutes

Rosie putting the baguettes
in her patio bread oven

Tips from Rosie's Kitchen

If you don't have a paddle and a pizza stone, simply slide the baking sheet into the oven to bake.

until it just begins to color. Drain the dried tomatoes from the soaking liquid and chop fine.

Punch the dough in the bowl and scatter the garlic with its cooking oil, the herbs, and the tomatoes on top and knead these ingredients into the dough until distributed. Turn the dough out onto a floured surface, cut in half, and form it into 2 baguettes by rolling the dough with the floured palms of your hands into rolls about 10 inches long. Place on parchment on a paddle or on a rimless baking sheet. Make 3 slashes with a sharp knife on the diagonal down the length of each loaf, cover with a towel, and let rise until doubled in volume, about 45 minutes.

Preheat oven to 400°F with a pizza stone, if you have one, set up on the middle rack. Slide the risen baguettes with the parchment paper beneath them onto the pizza stone. Otherwise, simply put the baking sheet on the oven rack. Bake 40 minutes. Remove to a rack to cool. Makes 2 loaves, 12 slices per loaf.

Tomato Mushroom Sauce

It's nice to make your own tomato sauce. Of course, time doesn't always permit it, but when it does, try it. This is a favorite of mine that I use quite a bit in pastas and vegetable dishes.

12 medium ripe tomatoes or 16 ounces canned peeled organic tomatoes
2 medium onions, chopped
1 green bell pepper, diced
1 tablespoon olive oil
1/2 cup white wine

1 pound mushrooms, diced or chopped
2 teaspoons oregano
1 1/2 teaspoons basil
1/2 teaspoon salt (optional)
1 bay leaf
1 tablespoon tomato paste
1 teaspoon honey

If using fresh tomatoes, bring a large pot of water to a boil. Slice an X on the bottom of each tomato, and drop them in the boiling water until the skins start to loosen, about 2 minutes. Drain and cool completely. When cool, squeeze each tomato over a strainer set over a bowl to trap the seeds, reserving the juice and the pulp. Purée the juice and the pulp in a food processor until smooth. If you are using canned tomatoes, simply scrape out the excess seeds and mash the tomatoes with their juice by hand or with a fork.

Sauté the onions with the green peppers in the olive oil in a large sauté pan for 5 minutes over low heat. Add the wine, mushrooms, herbs, salt, the tomato purée, and the bay leaf. Simmer for 1/2 hour. Remove the bay leaf. Mix in the tomato paste and the honey and cook for 10 more minutes.

MAKES ABOUT 4
CUPS
6 SERVINGS

PER SERVING:
CALORIES 146
FAT 3.2 G
  SATURATED FAT
  0.4 G
(18.9% OF CALO-
  RIES FROM FAT)
PROTEIN 4.6 G
CARBOHYDRATE
  26.2 G
CHOLESTEROL
  0 MG
FIBER 4.9 G

❋

Tips from Rosie's Kitchen

If you don't have a food processor, you can purée the tomatoes using your hands. Wash your hands very well and then squeeze each tomato over a strainer, trapping the seeds, but keeping the juice and the pulp.

If ripe, juicy tomatoes are out of season, use organic canned tomatoes that you can find in your grocery store. They come peeled, whole, crushed, and with or without herbs. Be sure to include their liquid.

CILANTRO CHUTNEY

This recipe and the variation that follows are from south India, from the region around Mysore, where "chutney" denotes more of a savory spread than the sweet-hot relishes we associate with the term. Indians make these rich condiments with freshly grated coconut meat, but that is full of saturated fat. Raw cashews taste just as good and provide monounsaturated fat, which is much better for the cardiovascular system and general health. South Indians spread these on dosas, the fabulous (and sometimes gigantic) crepes of the region, made from rice and lentils.

MAKES ABOUT 2 CUPS
SERVES 16

PER SERVING:
CALORIES 56
FAT 4.8 G
  SATURATED FAT LESS THAN 1 G
  (77% OF CALORIES FROM FAT)
PROTEIN 1.6 G
CARBOHYDRATE 2.8 G
CHOLESTEROL 0 MG
FIBER LESS THAN 1 G

❈

1 cup raw cashews
4 cups cilantro leaves, loosely packed
1 whole jalapeño or serrano chili pepper, stemmed, with seeds
Purified water
Salt to taste
1 tablespoon vegetable oil, such as canola or grapeseed
1 teaspoon black mustard seeds

Grind the cashews in a food processor to a fine powder. Add the cilantro leaves and chili pepper and process for 30 seconds. Scrape the mixture together and continue to process, pouring in just enough water to make a mayonnaiselike cream. Salt to taste.

Heat the oil in a small pan over medium-high heat. Add the mustard seeds and cook, stirring, until they start to pop. Stir the seeds and oil into the chutney.

Use as a spread for chapatis, whole wheat tortillas, or pita bread, or as a sauce for fish or vegetables. Chutney will keep in the refrigerator for several days.

Mint Chutney

Follow the above recipe, substituting fresh spearmint leaves for the cilantro.

SALSA DE NUEZ

I discovered this sauce in Oaxaca, the southern Mexican state, where Indian culture and indigenous foods abound. It is rich and highly flavored and absolutely delicious. Use it sparingly on almost anything.

2 cups pecan halves
1 tablespoon extra virgin olive oil
5 cloves garlic, peeled and crushed
1–2 tablespoons ground red chili
    pepper or more to taste
Purified water
Salt to taste

Fry the pecans in the olive oil over medium-high heat, stirring constantly, until the nuts just begin to brown. Put them in a food processor or blender with the garlic and 1 tablespoon of the red pepper and blend until the nuts form a paste. Taste and add more chili pepper, if you wish. Add just enough water to bring the consistency to a medium-thick sauce. Season to taste with salt.

Store the salsa in the refrigerator in a tightly covered container. Use it as a sauce for steamed or broiled fish and steamed vegetables and as a spread for tortillas, crackers, or bread.

MAKES ABOUT
2 CUPS
SERVES 16

PER SERVING:

CALORIES 99

FAT 10 G
   SATURATED FAT
   0.8 G

(91% OF CALORIES FROM FAT)

PROTEIN 1 G

CARBOHYDRATE
   2.8 G

CHOLESTEROL
   0 MG

FIBER 1 G

Desserts

Almond Fruit Tart

Apple Tart with Jam Glaze

Apple Strudel with Almond Sprinkles

Honey-Nut Baklava

Angel Food Cake with Fresh Berries

Banana Cupcakes with Orange Cream-
   Cheese Glaze

Peach and Blueberry Cobbler

Blueberry Pie with Lattice Top

Apple Cake Squares

Berries with Sorbet

Pistachio Dream

Lemon Sponge Cake

Lemon Yogurt Sorbet

Ginger Cookies

Orange Oatmeal Cookies

Poached Pears

Figs in Wine

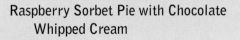

Raspberry Sorbet Pie with Chocolate
    Whipped Cream

Rice Pudding

Apple-Cranberry Crisp

Apricot Mousse

Dark Chocolate with Fruit

SUGAR AND OTHER SWEETENERS

Human beings are born with an innate craving for sweetness, because sugar represents almost instant energy. Long ago, our ancestors were only likely to encounter sugar in the form of ripe fruit or an occasional honeycomb; today it is everywhere—not only on every table but hidden in the ingredients of many pre-pared foods, from soups to ketchup. Some nutritionists say that sugar is a dietary evil, the cause of mood swings, hyperactivity in children, and systemic yeast infections in adults. Others tell us that refined white sugar is the problem and urge us to use honey and other more "natural" sweeteners in its place. And today, a large number of people are using artificial and nonnutritive sweeteners in place of sugar, a significant change in eating habits.

You will find sugar, honey, and maple syrup in some of the recipes in this book. Neither Rosie nor I think that sugar is evil, but we worry that most Ameri-cans eat much too much of it and feel that it should be consumed consciously and in moderation. Sugary foods and drinks certainly contribute to obesity in our society and to dental decay. They may raise the glycemic index of meals, putting a burden on the pancreas and raising the risk of insulin resistance and its attendant problems (see page xx).

I do not think there is much difference between sugar and other natural sweeteners. Honey, maple syrup, molasses, and sorghum contain trace miner-als and have novel flavors, but to the body they are all sugar to be converted to glucose for metabolic fuel. Until recently, all so-called raw or natural sugars were actually white sugar colored and flavored with the addition of some molasses (the residue of concentrated sugar cane juice after removal of most of its content of sucrose). In other words, they were the same as light- and dark-brown sugars. Today, real raw sugar is on the market; one brand calls itself "evaporated cane juice." It is straw-colored with a rich flavor that I prefer in many dishes to that of white sugar. Of the other natural sweeteners, my per-sonal favorite is maple syrup. I love it. As for honey, I much prefer the flavor and texture of raw varieties to those of cooked ones.

Some nonnutritive sweeteners are natural: sorbitol and xylitol, for exam-ple, which are made from wood pulp and are used in sugarless chewing gum, candy, and toothpaste. But be aware that they can cause flatulence and can aggravate irritable bowel syndrome. Stevia is also in this category. It is the leaf of a South American shrub, from which a very sweet compound, stevioside, can be isolated. This is so sweet that it is best dissolved in water and dispensed from a dropper bottle. It has a licorice flavor that I do not find agreeable, but it might be worth trying if you are diabetic or intolerant to sugar.

Artificial sweeteners are of more concern to me as a physician. In the first place, there is no evidence that they help anyone lose weight, although that is why people use them. (I love watching people put artificial sweeteners in their coffee after they have downed rich desserts.) Second, most of them taste funny. And, most important, the highly popular ones may be harmful. Saccharin, which has been around the longest, may increase risks of bladder cancer and other forms of the disease. Aspartame (NutraSweet) may damage brain cells; many people note symptoms that appear to correlate with their use of it: headaches, for example, or intensification of menstrual problems. If you must use an artificial sweetener, I recommend the newest one on the market, sucralose, sold under the brand name Splenda. It tastes better than aspartame and appears safer.

Because sugar can add to the pleasure of food and eating, it should be part of the optimum diet. The dessert recipes in this book offer some examples of using it wisely. **—A.W.**

BUTTER AND BUTTER SUBSTITUTES

I do not cook with butter and do not keep it in my house, because it provides too much saturated fat for me. I like good cheese and get enough butterfat from it. On the very rare occasions that I make muffins, pie crust, or topping for a fruit crisp I prefer to substitute healthier fats for butter. In many cases neutral-tasting oil will do, such as grapeseed oil or expeller-pressed canola oil. (Expeller-pressed oil is pressed mechanically at relatively low pressure and temperature rather than extracted with high-pressure, high-temperature methods or with solvents. The oil suffers less damage as a result.) I make a great crumb pie crust with graham crackers, sesame tahini, and maple syrup. And occasionally I use Spectrum Spread as a butter substitute. Unlike margarine, this product contains no hydrogenated or trans-fats. It uses a mechanical process to emulsify oil and water to make a spread that has the flavor of butter and good baking qualities. I introduced Rosie to it and she has included it as an option in recipes calling for significant quantities of butter. You will find Spectrum Spread in the refrigerated sections of stores that sell natural foods.

—A.W.

Almond Fruit Tart

This is a less rich rendition of the popular French tart. It makes a lovely complement to a shared pot of freshly brewed tea.

SERVES 12

PER SERVING:

CALORIES 249.9

FAT 10.9 G
  SATURATED FAT
  4.8 G
(42.3% OF CALO-
  RIES FROM FAT)

PROTEIN 4.1 G

CARBOHYDRATE
  329 G

CHOLESTEROL
  36 MG

FIBER 2.7 G

PASTRY

1 cup oat flour
1 cup unbleached white flour
1/4 cup skinned ground almonds
1 tablespoon freshly squeezed
  orange juice
4 tablespoons diced cold butter or
  Spectrum Spread
4–5 tablespoons cold purified
  water

FILLING

1/4 cup pine nuts
3 tablespoons butter
2 tablespoons brown sugar
1/4 cup unbleached flour
1/4 cup frozen orange juice
  concentrate
1 egg yolk
2 egg whites
2 tablespoons Amaretto

JAM GLAZE AND FRUIT TOPPING

1/2 cup all-fruit strawberry or
  apricot jam or jelly
3 tablespoons purified water
2 kiwis, peeled and sliced
1 1/2 pints (3 cups) raspberries (or
  Poached Pears, page 294)

Preheat oven to 350° F.

Make the pastry: Put all the ingredients for the pastry, using 3 tablespoons water, in a food processor and pulse briefly about 6 times, just until smooth, about 30 seconds. If the dough seems very dry, add 1 or 2 more tablespoons water and pulse briefly again. Cut a piece of parchment paper that measures 10 × 10 inches, roll the dough into a ball, wrap it in the paper, and chill it in the refrigerator for 10 minutes. The parchment paper may seem large for the dough ball, but you will be using it later in the recipe.

After the dough has chilled, unwrap it and roll it out on the parchment paper with a rolling pin, making a circle that stretches about 1¹/2 inches beyond the edges of a 9-inch pie pan. Flip the parchment paper over onto the pie pan and peel off the paper. Press down on the dough with your fingers, molding it to the bottom and sides of the pie pan. Trim excess dough with a knife so that it is flush with the edge of the pan. Refrigerate, covered, for 15 minutes.

Remove the pan from the refrigerator and bake for 15 minutes in the preheated oven until the crust is dry in the center. You can test for dryness by inserting a toothpick in the center; when the toothpick comes out dry, the crust is done. Let it cool for 15–20 minutes.

Make the filling: Process all the filling ingredients in a food processor until smooth and pour into the crust. Bake for 20 minutes in the preheated oven, until the top puffs up and is golden brown. Let cool.

Make the glaze: Heat the jam and water together in a saucepan on low heat until syrupy. Strain the glaze through a wire mesh strainer over a bowl. Brush the syrup over the tart.

Arrange the kiwi slices around the perimeter of the tart and the fresh raspberries (or Poached Pears) in the middle. Brush another layer of jam glaze over the raspberries and kiwi to make the fruit shine and to hold them together. To serve, quarter the pie, then cut each quarter into 3 pieces.

Apple Tart with Jam Glaze

Serves 8

Per serving:

Calories 276.5

Fat 8.9 g
  Saturated fat
  5.4 g
(28.5% of calo-
  ries from fat)

Protein 3.6 g

Carbohydrate
  46.8 g

Cholesterol
  23 mg

Fiber 38 g

Tarts are a dessert that can be served for any occasion after any meal. I like to make tarts during the holidays because they have such a dressy presentation.

CRUST

3/4 stick (6 tablespoons) cold
  butter or Spectrum Spread
2 cups unbleached white flour,
  plus 2 tablespoons for dusting
1/2 tablespoon sugar
1/4 teaspoon salt
4–5 tablespoons cold purified
  water

3 Granny Smith apples, peeled
  and sliced vertical and thin
2 tablespoons sugar
1 teaspoon cinnamon

GLAZE

1/2 cup apricot jam
3 tablespoons purified water

Preheat oven to 350°F.

Cut the butter into small pieces. Put the butter, flour, sugar, and salt in a food processor and pulse on and off about 10 pulses, until crumbs start to form. Slowly add the cold water and pulse again. If you don't have a food processor, cut into the mixture with 2 knives simultaneously. Turn the dough out and shape into a ball. Wrap the dough ball in parchment paper and chill it in the refrigerator for 15 minutes or in the freezer for 10 minutes.

Sprinkle a little bit of flour on a piece of parchment paper and using a floured rolling pin roll the ball of dough out until it is flat and larger than a 9-inch pie pan. If it tears, pinch it back together. Turn the parchment paper over directly on top of a 9-inch pie pan. Trim off any of the dough that hangs over the side of the pan.

Tips from Rosie's Kitchen

The pastry can be made ahead of time and placed in the tart pan covered with plastic and frozen until ready to use.

Arrange the apples in rows in the tart pan, slightly overlapping them on top of each other. Combine the sugar and cinnamon and sprinkle over the apples. Bake uncovered for 30 minutes, then cover them with foil and bake an additional 35 minutes. The apples should be soft and juicy. Remove from the oven.

Heat the jam with the water in a small saucepan until it becomes thick. Using a pastry brush, brush the glaze over the tart. Let cool for 15 minutes or so but serve warm (reheat if necessary).

ANDY SUGGESTS

I like topping this off with something creamy, like some low-fat sour cream with a bit of maple syrup and vanilla.

Apple Strudel with Almond Sprinkles

Strudel is usually made with apples, but cherries also make a terrific filling when they're in season (see Tips). Granny Smith apples are my favorites but use whatever good, flavorful apples are in season when you make this strudel.

Like the Honey-Nut Baklava recipe that follows, this strudel calls for clarified butter. Clarified butter can be made a couple of days in advance (see Tips) or the night before. It is one of those ingredients that is great to have on hand in the refrigerator because it is a good substitute for oil when sautéing and can be used in making phyllo-dough dishes.

SERVES 9

PER SERVING:

CALORIES 306.9

FAT 17.1 G

SATURATED FAT

8 G

(48.7% OF CALO-

RIES FROM FAT)

PROTEIN 2.8 G

CARBOHYDRATE

37.7 G

CHOLESTEROL

31 MG

FIBER 2.8 G

❊

FILLING

2 tablespoons clarified butter
3 cups peeled, cored, and thinly
  sliced wedges of apples
1/3 cup maple syrup
1 tablespoon cinnamon
1 teaspoon freshly squeezed
  lemon juice
3 tablespoons cornstarch
1/4 cup water
2 tablespoons honey
1/4 cup currants

Pinch almond extract (less than
  1/8 teaspoon)
1 tablespoon pure vanilla extract
1 teaspoon lemon zest

1/2 cup clarified butter or walnut
  oil
6 phyllo sheets (preferably natural), defrosted
1/2 cup finely chopped almonds or
  almond meal
1/4 cup sugar

Preheat the oven to 400°F.

Put 2 tablespoons of the clarified butter and the apples in a sauté pan and add the maple syrup, 2 teaspoons of the cinnamon, and the lemon juice. Sauté over medium heat for 2–3 minutes until the apples are tender. Mix the cornstarch with the water together in a small bowl until pasty. Stir into the apples, and simmer, covered, on low heat until the mixture becomes thick. Stir in the honey, currants, almond extract, vanilla, and lemon zest. Remove from the heat to cool. While the apple mixture cools, begin preparing the pastry.

Warm the 1/2 cup clarified butter (walnut oil does not need to be warmed).

Working quickly, lay 1 phyllo-dough sheet on a piece of parchment paper and lightly brush the dough with a generous tablespoon of the clarified butter. Combine the prepared almond meal with the 1/4 cup sugar. Sprinkle about 1 1/2 tablespoons of the almond-sugar mixture evenly over the phyllo and lay a second sheet on top.

Brushing the phyllo dough with
clarified butter

Tips from Rosie's Kitchen

Clarified Butter: Melt 3/4 cup (1 1/2 sticks) unsalted butter (clarifying reduces the butter to 1/2 cup) in a small, heavy saucepan over low heat for 20 minutes. The butter-fat will separate and sink to the bottom of the pan and foam will start to accumulate on the surface. Skim the foam off the top and throw it away. Let the liquid that remains in the pan cool for about 5 minutes. Strain the milky residue through a fine sieve. Pour the completely cooled golden liquid that remains into a small bowl, jar, or plastic container. Cover and refrigerate. If you don't have the time to prepare the clarified butter, you can purchase walnut oil and use it straight out of the bottle.

You will need a pastry brush and parchment paper, which you can find at any supermarket.

Chop the almonds in a food processor, or see instructions on grinding almonds in blender (page 34) because you need to create a finely ground meal. Or buy almond meal.

Spooning the filling to one side of the length of the dough. (In this instance, Rosie is using her cherry filling. See Tips, page 272.)

Brush clarified butter evenly over the surface and sprinkle on another 1 1/2 tablespoons of almond sugar. Repeat the process until all 6 sheets have been lightly brushed with the clarified butter, sprinkled with the almond-sugar mixture, and stacked on top of each other. Spoon the apple filling along the length of the top layer, leaving about a 2-inch border on each long side, and gently roll the phyllo dough up lengthwise so that the filling remains inside.

Brush the top of the pastry with the remaining clarified butter and sprinkle the remaining cinnamon and almond-sugar mixture on top. Put a piece of parchment paper on a baking sheet and lay the pastry roll, seam side down, on top. Bake for 20 minutes until the top is golden brown. Remove from the oven and let it cool a bit. Slice into 9 pieces while it is still warm and serve.

Rolling up the strudel

Brushing the top of the strudel, now placed on parchment paper and ready to bake

Tips from Rosie's Kitchen

Cherry Strudel: If you'd like to try this recipe with cherries instead of apples, you'll need to make the following substitutions: 3 cups fresh (or frozen) pitted cherries instead of apples, and 1/2 cup softened cream cheese instead of the currants. Begin by blending the cream cheese, honey, vanilla, and lemon zest in a small bowl until smooth. Then just follow the rest of the directions.

Honey-Nut Baklava

Layers of flaky pastry sheets lightly brushed with butter and capped by a thick honey-and-nut spread are what make this native dish of Greece so popular around the world.

Plan to start the baklava one day in advance because the phyllo dough needs to be defrosted in the refrigerator overnight and the clarified butter should be prepared the night before and refrigerated until you are ready to use it.

1/2 cup walnut pieces
1/2 cup almond pieces
2 cups honey
1 tablespoon pure vanilla extract
1/2 cup clarified butter (see Tips, page 271)

9 sheets phyllo pastry (preferably natural), defrosted
1/2 cup chocolate chips

MAKES 36 PIECES

PER SERVING:

CALORIES 145.3

FAT 7.3 G
   SATURATED FAT
   3.3 G
(42.5% OF CALO-
   RIES FROM FAT)
PROTEIN 1.4 G

CARBOHYDRATE
   20.7 G

CHOLESTEROL
   11 MG

FIBER 0.6 G

Preheat oven to 400°F.

Process the nuts in a food processor to chop them up. Pour the honey and vanilla into a medium bowl and stir with a wooden spoon until the vanilla is completely drawn into the honey. Add the nuts and mix with the wooden spoon until they are completely coated with the honey. Grease a baking sheet, then lay parchment paper over it and cut to fit.

Warm the clarified butter in a small pot.

Open the defrosted phyllo-dough package and spread the dough out on the counter. Remember to work fast as dough dries quickly, making it less responsive. You will eventually create 2 separate stacks of phyllo dough placed on top of each other on the baking sheet. The first stack consists of 6 sheets of phyllo dough, which you will cut in half. The second stack consists of 3 sheets, which you will fold in half.

Prepare the first stack (6 sheets), keeping the remainder covered with a large piece of foil. Quickly brush the clarified butter on each sheet with a pastry brush, one at a time, layering one on top of the other. Using clean kitchen scissors, cut the stack in half and lay 1/2 on the baking sheet. Spread 1/2 of the honey-and-nut mixture evenly on

Spooning the filling into the pan lined with phyllo dough

that half. Lay the other half on top of the honey-and-nut mixture. Spread the remaining 1/2 of the honey-and-nut mixture on the top. Next, coat the second stack of phyllo dough (3 sheets) with the clarified butter and fold all the sheets in half. Lay them on top of the earlier stack that's already on the baking sheet. Place the filled sheet in the oven and bake until the top is golden and the honey is bubbling, about 20 minutes. Remove the baking sheet from the oven and let cool. Making 6 even slices, cut the entire pastry horizontally first, then make 6 even slices at a 45-degree angle from top to bottom to create 36 triangular pieces.

Melt 1/2 cup chocolate chips in a stainless-steel double boiler. Stir until the chocolate is smooth. Remove from the heat. Working quickly, dip a fork into the chocolate and drizzle it horizontally across the cooling baklava.

Cherry Strudel and Honey-Nut Baklava for tea

Angel Food Cake with Fresh Berries

Angel food cake can be eaten so many ways. Here, it is served with fresh fruit, but it can be served topped with vanilla ice cream, Chocolate Whipped Cream (page 296), or any fruit combination of your choice. Because it isn't overly sweet, but just sweet enough, sometimes I just cut a small piece and eat it plain.

1 cup cake flour
1 1/2 cups granulated sugar
12 egg whites (room temperature) or dried egg white (see Tips)
1/2 teaspoon cream of tartar
1/4 teaspoon salt
1 teaspoon pure vanilla extract
1/4 teaspoon almond extract

FRESH FRUIT TOPPING

2 cups sliced strawberries
1/4 cup freshly squeezed orange juice
1 tablespoon honey
1 pint blueberries

MAKES 1 BUNDT CAKE OR 12 MUFFINS SERVES 12

PER SERVING:

CALORIES 257

FAT 0.3 G
  SATURATED FAT
  0.1 G
(0.9% OF CALORIES FROM FAT)

PROTEIN 4.7 G

CARBOHYDRATE
  61.6 G

CHOLESTEROL
  0 MG

FIBER 1.3 G

Preheat oven to 325°F.

Mix the cake flour and sugar together in a bowl. Whip the egg whites and the cream of tartar in a mixer until they become firm and peaks begin to form. Sift 1/3 of the flour-sugar into the bowl with the whipped eggs and slowly fold the mixture into the whites. Repeat by sifting and folding another 1/3 of the flour-sugar into the whites, and finally the last third. Fold in the salt, vanilla, and almond extract until everything is combined.

Spoon the batter into the ungreased bundt pan or muffin mold, scraping the bowl with a spatula to get all of it. Bake for 1 hour (30 minutes for muffin molds) until the top becomes light brown. Remove from the oven and cool for 1 hour on a cooling rack. When completely cooled, slide a knife around the edge of the molds to loosen the cake or muffins. Turn them over onto a platter. Mix together the strawberries, orange juice, honey, and blueberries and spoon this fresh fruit topping on top.

Tips from Rosie's Kitchen

I serve angel food cakes as birthday cakes. I give them a little flair by using the Apricot Mousse recipe (page 300) as filling, substituting strawberries for the apricots. When the cake is completely cooled, I cut it in half horizontally and spread the strawberry mousse in the center. It adds some flavor without a lot of calories.

You also have the option of using muffin molds instead of a bundt-cake pan, but this will reduce baking time, so you'd have to keep a close eye on it while baking.

Using dried egg whites will make this recipe a bit easier for you if the thought of beating fresh egg whites seems daunting. Simply add 1 1/2 cups of water to the mixture of dried egg whites and cream of tartar and follow the rest of the recipe. It is very important that the bowl in which the egg whites are whipped is clean and not at all greasy or it will cause them to flop.

Banana Cupcakes with Orange Cream-Cheese Glaze

Using very ripe bananas is the key to giving these cakes such abundant flavor. Alternatives to the traditional cupcake mold are mini-loaf pans or a standard bread pan or baby bundt-cake molds. The latter gives the cakes a dressier presentation. Whatever you choose, the combination of bananas and ginger, along with carrots or zucchini, make for a healthy bread with a distinctive flavor.

ORANGE CREAM-CHEESE GLAZE

1 cup softened low-fat cream
   cheese
1/4 cup freshly squeezed orange
   juice
1/4 cup honey
1/2 teaspoon pure vanilla extract
1/2 teaspoon orange zest

GARNISH

12 whole walnuts

CUPCAKE BATTER

2 cups whole wheat flour

1/2 cup oat or wheat bran

1 tablespoon baking soda

1/4 teaspoon salt

1/8 teaspoon ground cloves or
   pumpkin spice

1/8 teaspoon dried ground ginger

4 ripe bananas, mashed

1/2 large carrot or 1/2 zucchini,
   grated

6 tablespoons softened butter

1 cup brown sugar

2 eggs

1/4 teaspoon pure vanilla extract

1/4 cup chopped walnuts

MAKES 12 CUP-
CAKES, 12 BABY
BUNDT CAKES,
4 MINI-LOAVES,
OR 1 STANDARD
LOAF
SERVES 12

PER SERVING:

CALORIES 354

FAT 14.6 G
   SATURATED FAT
   6.3 G

37.1% OF CALO-
   RIES FROM FAT)

PROTEIN 7.9 G

CARBOHYDRATE
   53.4 G

CHOLESTEROL
   60.6 MG

FIBER 4.4 G

Let the cream cheese for the icing soften at room temperature while you prepare the cupcake batter.

Preheat oven to 375°F.

Make the batter: Mix the flour, bran, baking soda, salt, and spices together in a bowl. Mash the bananas in a separate bowl with a fork until all fruit chunks are completely squashed. Drop in the grated carrots or zucchini, and stir thoroughly with a spoon until they are completely covered in bananas. In a medium bowl, cream together the softened butter, brown sugar, eggs, and vanilla with an electric mixer, or by hand with a whisk, until smooth, with no sign of lumpy sugar granules. Add the walnuts and stir with a spoon until they are completely coated. Slowly mix in the dry ingredients for 1 minute, using a wooden spoon or electric mixer set on low, until all ingredients are thoroughly blended. Pour in the mix of mashed banana and grated carrot or zucchini and stir everything with a big wooden spoon until the bananas are completely blended into the batter.

Spray the baby bundt pans with nonstick cooking spray, making sure to coat all of the fluted sides, and pour in the batter, scraping the bowl with a spatula to get it all.

Bake the cupcakes, baby bundt cakes, and the mini-loaves for 20 minutes; the large loaf will take 45 minutes. Remove from the pans and let cool before frosting.

To make the glaze: Whisk together the softened cream cheese, orange juice, honey, vanilla, and orange zest in a bowl until the glaze becomes smooth and thick. For cupcakes, use 1 tablespoon of glaze per cake. For mini-loaves or baby bundt cakes, use 1/4 cup for each loaf. For a standard loaf, use 1/2 cup. Garnish each cake or loaf with a walnut in the center.

Peach and Blueberry Cobbler

This is an old-fashioned dessert that most people thoroughly enjoy eating. The baked fruit filling is crowned with a thin biscuit topping. It can be eaten warm or cold, plain or topped with vanilla ice cream.

FILLING

5 peaches, peeled and sliced
1 cup fresh blueberries
1/4 cup freshly squeezed orange juice
1/2 cup sugar
Pinch nutmeg (less than 1/8 teaspoon)
2 teaspoons cornstarch

BISCUIT TOPPING

5 tablespoons softened butter or Spectrum Spread
2 cups flour plus 1/4 cup flour for rolling out
1 tablespoon sugar
1 tablespoon baking powder
1/2 teaspoon salt
3/4 cup milk

GLAZE

2 tablespoons sugar

SERVES 10

PER SERVING:
CALORIES 241.8
FAT 6.9 G
  SATURATED FAT 4.1 G
(25% OF CALO-RIES FROM FAT)
PROTEIN 3.9 G
CARBOHYDRATE 42.3 G
CHOLESTEROL 19 MG
FIBER 2 G

❋

Preheat oven to 400° F.

Bring all the filling ingredients to a boil in a large saucepan, then turn down heat and simmer until the filling becomes thick. Spoon the thickened fruit filling into a medium (at least 10 × 8–inch) baking or casserole dish, and spread it around evenly until it meets all sides of the dish.

Using clean hands, pinch the butter and the flour together between your thumbs and forefingers until the flour and butter become crumbly. Mix in the sugar, baking powder, and salt and slowly stir in the milk to make a soft dough. Sprinkle a work surface with the 1/4 cup flour, knead the dough lightly a few turns on the floured surface, and roll out to a perimeter approximately the size of your baking dish. With a cookie cutter or a glass cut out 10 biscuits and lay them slightly overlapping on top of the fruit filling, using scraps of leftover dough to fill in any uncovered spots. Sprinkle the top with the

Peach and Blueberry Cobbler

sugar. Bake in the preheated oven for 20 minutes until biscuit topping turns golden brown. Cool for 10 minutes. To serve, scoop out a biscuit and fruit filling and transfer to a dessert bowl or plate.

Tips from Rosie's Kitchen

The topping on our cobbler tastes delicious baked on its own as scrumptious herb biscuits.

__To Make the Herb Biscuits:__ Just replace the sugar with fresh herbs (I use 1 teaspoon fresh parsley, 1 teaspoon fresh oregano, 1 teaspoon fresh thyme, and a pinch of cayenne). Prepare the dough as you would for the cobbler, form 6 biscuits, lay them on a greased baking sheet, and bake in a preheated oven for 12 minutes at 400°F.

Blueberry Pie with Lattice Top

Blueberries are in season during July and August. As a child, I picked blueberries during walks through our back woods to make pie, but collecting enough blueberries for the pie was impossible because they made their way to my mouth instead of the basket! Frozen blueberries can be substituted for fresh as long as they're drained.

CRUST

11/2 sticks cold butter or Spectrum Spread

21/2 cups unbleached white flour, plus 1/4 cup for dusting

1 tablespoon sugar

1/2 teaspoon salt

8–10 tablespoons cold purified water

FILLING

3 cups washed and drained blueberries
1/2 cup maple syrup
2 tablespoons flour
1 tablespoon cornstarch
1 teaspoon lemon zest
2 tablespoons freshly squeezed
   lemon juice (about 1/2 lemon)

GARNISH

2 tablespoons sugar

SERVES 8

PER SERVING:

CALORIES 386.8

FAT 17.7 G

   SATURATED FAT
   10.9 G

(40.6% OF CALO-
   RIES FROM FAT)

PROTEIN 4.8 G

CARBOHYDRATE
   53.5 G

CHOLESTEROL
   46 MG

FIBER 2.9 G

Preheat oven to 350°F.

Cut the butter into small pieces. Put the butter, flour, sugar, and salt in a food processor and pulse on and off about 10 pulses, until crumbs start to form. Add the cold water and pulse again. If you don't have a food processor, cut into the mixture with 2 knives simultaneously. Turn the dough out and shape into 2 equal-sized balls, and press each mass together to adhere. Wrap the dough balls in parchment paper and chill them in the refrigerator for 15 minutes or in the freezer for 10 minutes.

Sprinkle a little bit of flour from the remaining 1/4 cup on a piece of parchment paper and roll one of the balls of dough out using a floured rolling pin until it is flat and larger than a 9-inch pie pan. If it tears, pinch it back together. Turn the parchment paper over directly on top of the 9-inch pie pan. Trim off any of the dough that hangs over the side of the pan. Toss the blueberries with the maple syrup, flour, cornstarch, lemon zest, and lemon juice in a bowl, then pour it all into the pie shell.

Roll out the second piece of dough on a flour-dusted surface, until it is flat and a little larger than the top circumference of the pan. Cut 1/2-inch strips on the diagonal and lay them across the blueberries, spaced a little bit apart, using the longer ones for the middle part of the pie pan. Lay the remaining strips down in the opposite direction, creating a woven "lattice" look. Press the dough into the side of the pie shell, using a fork, so that the strips are secured in place.

Bake for 1 hour. When the pie is done, remove from the oven and sprinkle the top with 2 tablespoons of sugar.

Apple Cake Squares

The bonus of this cake is that it's fast to make. It's a moist cake with a mellow cinnamon-apple taste. You can serve it for dessert or you can wrap slices up to take to school or to the office.

1 cup whole wheat pastry flour

1/4 teaspoon salt

3/4 teaspoon nutmeg

1 teaspoon baking soda

1 teaspoon cinnamon

3 tablespoons sugar

3 tablespoons softened butter or Spectrum Spread

2 eggs

2 cups peeled, cored, and finely shredded apples

1/4 cup finely chopped dates

1/4 cup confectioners' sugar

GARNISH (Optional)

1/4 cup finely chopped walnuts

1/4 cup maple syrup

SERVES 9

PER SERVING:

CALORIES 201.2

FAT 7.5 G
  SATURATED FAT
  2.9 G

(39.9% OF CALO-
  RIES FROM FAT)

PROTEIN 3.6 G

CARBOHYDRATE
  31.6 G

CHOLESTEROL
  58 MG

FIBER 1.4 G

Preheat oven to 350°F.

Mix the flour, salt, nutmeg, baking soda, and cinnamon together in a medium bowl and stir thoroughly. Cream the sugar and butter together in a large bowl. Beat in the eggs and whisk until smooth. Stir in the shredded apples and dates until they are completely distributed throughout. Slowly stir in the dry ingredients and mix thoroughly into the batter. Spray the bottom and sides of a 9-inch square baking pan with nonstick cooking spray, or grease it with 1/4 teaspoon of butter and pour in the batter. Bake in the preheated oven for about 45 minutes.

Put the confectioners' sugar in a sifter and dust it over the cooled cake a few times until all the sugar is gone. If you want to garnish, mix the walnuts with the maple syrup and drizzle over individual serving plates. Cut the Apple Cake into 9 squares and arrange each one on top of a decorated plate and serve.

Blueberry Pie with Lattice Top

BERRIES WITH SORBET

For this simple but very light and satisfying dessert, use raspberries, blackberries, blueberries, organic strawberries, or a mixture of these. Look for high-quality fruit sorbets with a minimum of ingredients. This is perfect after a heavy meal and provides a good measure of protective phytochemicals in the red and purple pigments of the fruit.

2 pints fresh berries
2 pints fruit sorbet (one or more
    flavors)

Wash the berries, drain them, and distribute them in 6 serving bowls. Let guests add their own sorbet. Serve with cookies, if you wish.

SERVES 6

PER SERVING:

CALORIES 63.1

FAT 0.4 G
  SATURATED FAT
  0 G

(4.8% OF CALO-
  RIES FROM FAT)

PROTEIN 0.6 G

CARBOHYDRATE
  16 G

CHOLESTEROL
  0 MG

FIBER 2.3 G

PISTACHIO DREAM

The combination of pistachios, sugar, almond extract, and rosewater is an exotic and irresistible flavor signature of the Near East. This is a nondairy frozen dessert, essentially a frozen, flavored nut milk, made practical by the welcome availability of natural, shelled pistachios, now grown in abundance in California and Arizona. I use a hand-turned Donvier ice cream maker, which is very simple to operate. You need only serve small portions of this dessert, perhaps accompanied by simple cookies.

1 1/2 cups cold purified water
1/3 cup sugar
1 cup raw, unsalted, shelled pistachio nuts

Pinch salt
1/2 teaspoon pure almond extract
1 teaspoon rosewater (see *Note*)

Mix the water and sugar in a saucepan. Cover and heat to boiling. Reduce the heat and boil for 1 minute. Remove the saucepan from heat and uncover.

Place the pistachios in a blender and grind to a fine powder, stopping the motor occasionally to stir in any large pieces.

Add half of the hot sugar water in a stream and blend at high speed for 1 minute, stopping occasionally to stir in any unblended nuts. Add the remaining sugar water and blend at high speed for 1 minute more. Pour the mixture through a fine sieve, pressing the residue with the back of a spoon to extract as much liquid as possible. Discard the residue. Stir in the pinch of salt, almond extract, and rosewater, and chill in the freezer until cold.

Pour the mixture into the chilled container of a frozen-dessert maker and freeze it according to the manufacturer's directions.

Serve the frozen dessert in small chilled cups with fresh fruit or cookies.

Note: Rosewater is available in groceries that stock Middle Eastern or Indian foods.

SERVES 4

PER SERVING:
CALORIES 250
FAT 15.5 G
  SATURATED FAT
  2 G
(56% OF CALO-
  RIES FROM FAT)
PROTEIN 6.5 G
CARBOHYDRATE
  24.5 G
CHOLESTEROL
  0 MG
FIBER 3.5 G

Lemon Sponge Cake

Finally, a recipe that uses the whole egg! We use the egg whites in the Sponge Cake to make it a fluffy complement to our creamy, lemony custard, where we use the egg yolks. These counterparts may taste familiar, as they are used in classic desserts like lemon meringue pie.

I serve this cake with Spiced Tea (page 42) when I'm having some friends over for a casual afternoon tea.

MAKES 8
SERVINGS

PER SERVING:

CALORIES 251.5

FAT 5 G
   SATURATED FAT
   1.9 G
   (17.7% OF CALO-
   RIES FROM FAT)

PROTEIN 8.8 G

CARBOHYDRATE
   43.5 G

CHOLESTEROL
   17.7 MG

FIBER 0.6 G

SPONGE CAKE

4 egg whites (set out at room
   temperature for 1 hour)
1/4 teaspoon salt
1 tablespoon pure vanilla extract
1/2 cup sugar
1/2 cup white or unbleached flour
1/2 cup almond meal (finely
   ground skinned almonds)

LEMON CUSTARD

1/2 cup sugar
2 tablespoons cornstarch
1 cup milk (or water for lighter
   recipe)

Pinch salt
2 egg yolks
1/4 cup freshly squeezed lemon
   juice
1/2 teaspoon lemon zest
3 tablespoons confectioners' sugar

GARNISH

1 cup berries (blueberries,
   raspberries, blackberries, or
   combination)

Preheat oven to 325°F.

Crack the eggs, keeping the yolks separate from the egg whites, each in their own bowls. Whip the egg whites with the salt until they become stiff. Fold in the vanilla extract. In a separate bowl combine the sugar, flour, and almonds. Mix thoroughly and fold carefully into stiffened egg whites.

Lay a piece of parchment paper on an ungreased 8 × 12–inch baking pan. Scrape the batter onto the paper and spread it out evenly into a rectangle about 6 × 10 inches. Bake for 15 minutes.

Meanwhile, put the sugar and the cornstarch into a medium saucepan set over low heat. Gradually stir in the milk (or water) and keep stirring until smooth. Turn up the heat to medium, and using a whisk, mix in the salt and the egg yolks, and bring to a boil. Whisk in the lemon juice and lemon zest and continue to boil for 1 minute more. Let cool 10 minutes before spreading it on the sponge cake.

Remove the cake from the oven and let it cool for 10 minutes. Lay a clean piece of parchment paper down and sprinkle the confectioners' sugar over it. Invert the cake on top of the sugar sprinkled parchment paper. Trim the edges. Spread a thin layer (about 1 1/4 cups) of cooled lemon custard over the surface. Starting at the long end near you, roll the cake up and wrap it securely in the parchment, twisting the ends of the paper to keep it closed (some custard might ooze out of the sides of the cake). Chill in the refrigerator for 3 hours.

Slice just before serving into 2-inch-thick slices, and place each slice on a plate with a dollop of remaining custard. Sprinkle about 1 tablespoon berries over each and serve.

Tips from Rosie's Kitchen

Almond meal is simply blanched, finely ground almonds that you can buy at a health-food store. If you want to make your own, just grind 1/2 cup blanched and skinned almonds in a food processor.

You will find that you use only about half the custard for the filling. But it is lovely to have extra on hand to serve with fruits and berries. If you want you can make only half the amount.

Lemon Yogurt Sorbet

A simple combination of mellow fruit and tangy citrus, this lively dessert can complete a meal or serve as a palate cleanser between courses. An appealing way to serve this sorbet is to scoop it into a hollowed-out lemon-peel cup.

SERVES 12

PER SERVING:

CALORIES 49.7

FAT 0.7
   SATURATED FAT
   0.4 G
(11.1% OF CALO-
   RIES FROM FAT)

PROTEIN 0.8 G

CARBOHYDRATE
   11.3 G

CHOLESTEROL
   2 MG

FIBER 0.4 G

❈

32 ounces plain yogurt
1/2 cup freshly squeezed lemon
   juice
1/2 cup chopped crystallized
   ginger
1 teaspoon lemon zest

1/2 cup honey
1/2 cup raspberries
1/2 cup green grapes

GARNISH

1 sprig mint

Blend all the ingredients together, except the berries and the grapes, in a blender or by hand. Pour the blended fruit-honey mixture into a big bowl, cover with plastic wrap, and put it in the freezer until thoroughly chilled, about 30 minutes. Pour into an ice cream machine and freeze according to manufacturer's instructions. Center a scoop of sorbet on top of the fresh raspberries and the green grapes. Garnish with mint.

Alternate Method

If you don't have an ice cream maker or sorbet machine, simply freeze the blended ingredients in a covered, stainless-steel bowl until they are crystallized, about 3 hours. Place crystallized ingredients in a food processor and pulse for 30 seconds. Return to the bowl and cover with plastic wrap and freeze until solid.

Tips from Rosie's Kitchen

To Make Your Own Yogurt: *Use 1 quart of fresh whole milk (or low-fat milk, if you prefer) and 1 tablespoon plain yogurt. Bring the milk to the boiling point, stirring constantly. Pour the milk into a bowl and let cool, until it becomes cool enough so that you can stick a finger in and hold it there comfortably. Whisk 1 tablespoon of yogurt into the warm milk and mix well. Cover the bowl and set at room temperature overnight. If your kitchen is cold, just set it in a turned-off oven, or on the stovetop over the pilot light. When the yogurt has thickened, refrigerate for 6 hours and up to 1 week.*

Lemon Yogurt Sorbet with
heart-shaped Ginger Cookies

Ginger Cookies

Ginger cookies are fun to make and kids will love to be involved in the cutting and decorating. I like heart-shaped cookies, but you can use any shape cookie cutter including those that make gingerbread men. Whatever cookie cutter you use, you're sure to enjoy these soft, scrumptious cookies.

MAKES ABOUT 32 COOKIES (3 INCHES EACH)

PER SERVING
 (1 COOKIE):
CALORIES 96.9
FAT 1.8 G
 SATURATED FAT
 0.1 G
(1.6% OF CALO-
 RIES FROM FAT)
PROTEIN 1.6 G
CARBOHYDRATE
 19 G
CHOLESTEROL
 0 MG
FIBER 0.5 G

2/3 cup molasses or sorghum
1/3 cup softened butter or Spectrum Spread
1/4 cup frozen concentrate apple juice, thawed
1 teaspoon pure vanilla extract
2 egg whites
4 cups unbleached all-purpose flour
1/2 cup sugar
2 teaspoons powdered ginger
1 teaspoon cinnamon
1/4 teaspoon powdered cloves
1/4 teaspoon allspice

1/2 teaspoon salt
1 teaspoon baking soda
1/2 teaspoon baking powder
1/8 teaspoon grated orange zest

GLAZE

1/4 cup frozen concentrate apple juice, thawed

Preheat the oven to 350°F.

Mix the molasses, butter, apple juice concentrate, and vanilla together in a large bowl. Beat the egg whites in a separate bowl for 3 minutes, and then whisk them into the wet ingredients.

Mix all the dry ingredients together, including the orange zest, in a separate, large bowl. Slowly add the dry ingredients to the wet ingredients, using a wooden spoon to mix everything together until the dough becomes stiff. Knead the dough with clean hands for a couple of minutes, and then divide it in half. Flatten each half into 2 round disks, wrap them in plastic wrap, and put them in the freezer until they are completely chilled, at least 2 hours, or overnight.

After the dough has thoroughly chilled, roll it out on a floured surface. Sprinkle the dough with a little more flour. Roll it out into 1/8-inch-thick slabs, and then cut it into shapes with a cookie cutter. Using a pastry brush, lightly brush the cut cookie shapes with the apple juice concentrate.

Smear the baking sheet with 1/4 teaspoon of butter and arrange the cookies on top. Bake for 10–12 minutes until they turn a light golden brown. Remove the cookies from the oven and let them cool for a few minutes before transferring to a cooling rack.

Tips from Rosie's Kitchen

Ginger cookies don't have to be plain. You can liven them up by using dried cranberries, cherries, citrus zest, sunflower seeds, almond slices, or raisins. Let the cookies cool after baking until they become warm and gently press the dried fruit or nuts into the soft cookie.

In order to glaze the cookie before baking, you will need a pastry brush that you can buy at any grocery store.

Sorghum, also called sorghum molasses, is made from the cereal grass called sorghum. The juice from the stalk is squeezed out and then boiled to make syrup. Sorghum molasses is often used as a sweetener in baking or as a syrup for pancakes and waffles.

If you want to involve kids in baking, these cookies are a great place to start. During the holiday season, you can use gingerbread cookie cutters and let the kids make their own gingerbread man. Children love cookies no matter what shape they are cut into, especially if they have a hand in adorning them with delicious, edible, bite-size decorations.

Orange Oatmeal Cookies

These cookies are excellent because of the orange flavor, the banana mixed into the batter, and the clumps of raisins or chocolate chips. They taste less like just a sugary mass of oatmeal and more like a real cookie: dense with genuine flavor and satisfying. I like to freeze these cookies in a sealed plastic bag because they are refreshing and delicious when cold!

MAKES 16 LARGE COOKIES

PER SERVING:

CALORIES 205.3

FAT 14.2 G
    SATURATED FAT
    6 G

(53.9% OF CALORIES FROM FAT)

PROTEIN 3.1 G

CARBOHYDRATE
24.1 G

CHOLESTEROL
29 MG

FIBER 2.9 G

1/2 cup (1 stick) butter, room temperature, or Spectrum Spread (8 tablespoons)
1 egg
1/4 cup mashed ripe banana (about 1/2 banana)
1 teaspoon pure vanilla extract
1/2 cup brown sugar
1 1/2 teaspoons orange zest
1 cup whole wheat pastry flour
1/4 teaspoon salt
1 teaspoon baking powder

1 1/2 cups old-fashioned rolled oats (or 1 cup oatmeal plus 1/2 cup 4-grain cereal)
1/4 cup unsweetened shredded coconut
1/2 cup chopped walnuts
1/2 cup golden raisins (or 1/2 cup chocolate chips)

Preheat oven to 350°F.

Cream the butter and egg together until it is well blended and smooth. Gradually beat in the banana, vanilla, and brown sugar. Add the orange zest. Mix well with a wooden spoon until all the ingredients are thoroughly blended.

In a large bowl mix the flour, salt, baking powder, oats or 4-grain cereal, coconut, walnuts, and raisins or chocolate chips. Use a wooden spoon to combine the dry ingredients until they are blended well and evenly distributed. Stir the dry ingredients into the wet ingredients and mix thoroughly until there is no sign of dryness.

Smear 1/4 teaspoon of butter on a baking sheet, drop heaping tablespoonsful of the dough onto the greased baking sheet 2 inches apart, and press down lightly against the dough to flatten. Bake for 20 minutes until lightly browned. Cool on a wire rack.

❈

Tips from Rosie's Kitchen

If you want to turn these cookies into a treat that provides more roughage, replace 1/2 cup of the rolled oats with 1/2 cup of 4-grain cereal. Rolled oats are included in the 4-grain cereal so you don't lose the benefits of vitamins E, B_1, and B_2 that oats provide. Cracked wheat, cracked rye, and cracked barley make up 3 grains that pack a lot of fiber.

Packaged coconut is available sweetened or unsweetened. I like to use the unsweetened because it adds enough flavor and a bit of texture without the extra sugar.

Poached Pears

There are many versions of poached-pear recipes using various liquids. I poach pears in fruit juices because the juice from the pears when combined with apple or cranberry juice has a delicately sweet flavor. Choose pears that are ripe and firm. Poaching pears that are too ripe will make them mushy.

If you have leftover pears you can use them in making Pear Relish (page 252), to drizzle over warm turkey, or any other type of poultry dish.

3 pears, sliced in half
2 cups cranberry or cranapple
   juice
2 cinnamon sticks
3 whole cloves

GARNISH

6 mint leaves

SERVES 6

PER SERVING:

CALORIES 143.7

FAT 1.3 G
  SATURATED FAT
  0.2 G
(7.1% OF CALO-
  RIES FROM FAT)

PROTEIN 0.7 G

CARBOHYDRATE
  36.4 G

CHOLESTEROL
  0 MG

FIBER 5.6 G

Scoop the seeds out of the pears using a melon scooper or a teaspoon. Peel the skin off with a paring knife.

Put the pears and the fruit juice with the cinnamon sticks and cloves in a saucepan over medium heat. Make sure the pears are entirely covered by the juice and cook them until they are soft. If the pears are already very ripe, cook them for 7 minutes; for harder pears, cook them for about 15 minutes. They should be easily pierced with a fork. Remove the pears, using a slotted spoon, and cool them on a clean cloth. Lower the heat and cook the remaining poaching liquid for 45 minutes until it is reduced to a third of the original amount of liquid. When it becomes thick and syrupy, remove it from the heat.

Lay each pear half with the flat side down on each of 6 plates. Cut 6 thin slices at the wide end of each pear half. Fan the slices out and drizzle the syrup on top. Serve warm or chilled. Garnish each with a mint leaf and serve.

FIGS IN WINE

This is an unusual and healthful dessert, full of flavor and devoid of fat. You want the figs to swell up and become very tender as they absorb the wine. To do so they must be moist and pliable to begin with. Very hard, dry figs will not do the job.

2 cups dried white figs (Turkish or
    Calimyrna), the softer the better
2 cups red wine, such as Merlot or
    Pinot Noir
Zest of 1 large, organic orange
    (optional)

Put the figs in a glass or ceramic bowl and pour the red wine over them to cover. Cover the bowl with plastic wrap and refrigerate for 24 hours until the figs are very soft.

    Drain the figs and toss them with the optional orange zest.

SERVES 6

PER SERVING:

CALORIES 236

FAT 0.8 G
    SATURATED FAT
    LESS THAN 1 G
    (3.5% OF CALO-
    RIES FROM FAT)

PROTEIN 2 G

CARBOHYDRATE
    47 G

CHOLESTEROL
    0 MG

FIBER 6.5 G

Raspberry Sorbet Pie with Chocolate Whipped Cream

Chock full of berries embraced by a thin, crunchy chocolate crust, these miniature frozen pies are loaded with heavy flavor without being a heavy dessert. They make the perfect light and gratifying way to end a great meal.

SERVES 8

PER SERVING:

CALORIES 323.8

FAT 15.1 G

SATURATED FAT
6.5 G

(49% OF CALO-
RIES FROM FAT)

PROTEIN 3.4 G

CARBOHYDRATE
40.3 G

CHOLESTEROL
32 MG

FIBER 2.3 G

❊

PIE SHELL

3 tablespoons canola oil
12 chocolate graham crackers (to make 1 1/2 cups crumbs)
1 egg white

SORBET FILLING

10 ounces packaged unsweetened frozen raspberries with juice, slightly thawed
10 ounces packaged unsweetened frozen strawberries, slightly thawed, or 1 cup fresh strawberries
1 cup blackberries
1/2 cup sugar
1/2 cup apple juice

CHOCOLATE WHIPPED CREAM

1/2 cup heavy cream
2 tablespoons confectioners' sugar
1 tablespoon unsweetened chocolate cocoa powder
1/2 teaspoon pure vanilla extract

GARNISH

Fresh strawberries
8 sprigs mint

Preheat oven 350°F.

Make the pie shells: Lightly grease the bottom and sides of 8 small tart pans or ramekins with 1 tablespoon of the oil. Process the chocolate graham crackers in a blender or a food processor to make fine crumbs. Mix the remaining oil, the egg white, and the cracker crumbs in a bowl, then distribute even amounts of the chocolate crumb mixture among the 8 pans. Press down on the crumbs with your fingers to create even shells. Bake for 10 minutes, then remove from the oven and chill while you prepare the filling.

Process all the filling ingredients in a blender or food processor until smooth. Strain the seeds out of the filling, using a spoon to push the purée against the strainer; discard seeds. Scoop the purée into the cooled pie shells. Freeze the filled pans for 2 hours.

Make the Chocolate Whipped Cream: Whip the heavy cream in a clean, stainless-steel bowl, using a standing electric mixer set on high, or whisk it by hand. Whip until the cream becomes thick, about 3 minutes. Add the confectioners' sugar, cocoa powder, and vanilla and whip for 1 more minute until it becomes fluffy and light. Cover and set aside.

Pull the Raspbery Sorbet Pies out of the freezer, garnish with a dollop of Chocolate Whipped Cream, fresh strawberries, and mint.

Tips from Rosie's Kitchen

If you want to make this an entirely dairy-free dessert, use Andy's almond milk (page 34) as a garnish instead of the Chocolate Whipped Cream. Pour a thin stream on a plate around the tart and sop it up with forkfuls of the tart.

Rice Pudding

This eggless rice pudding is not as sweet and heavy as traditional rice pudding. I like to use jasmine rice because I think it tastes sweeter. Basmati rice has a nuttier flavor and is a finer grain. They both make a fine rice pudding; it just depends on what flavor of rice appeals to you. I serve this light dessert after a salad entrée or a light meal.

MAKES 6

PER SERVING:

CALORIES 349

FAT 4.2 G
   SATURATED FAT
   3.3 G
(13.4% OF CALORIES
   FROM FAT)
PROTEIN 8 G
CARBOHYDRATE
   72.6 G
CHOLESTEROL
   6 MG
FIBER 1.2 G

FRUIT SAUCE

2 peaches, peeled and sliced
1 cup freshly squeezed orange
   juice
2 tablespoons honey

RICE PUDDING

3 cups 1 percent low-fat milk
1 cup jasmine rice or brown
   basmati

1 teaspoon lemon zest
1 teaspoon pure vanilla extract
1/8 teaspoon grated nutmeg or
   mace
1/2 cup honey
1/2 cup evaporated skim milk
1/2 cup unsweetened shredded
   coconut

Make the fruit sauce: Put the peaches, orange juice, and honey in a bowl and toss well until the peach slices are completely coated with the honey and juice. Cover and refrigerate until ready to use.

Preheat oven to 325°F.

Bring the milk and rice to a boil in a large saucepan. Reduce the heat and simmer, covered, for 15 minutes, until all the liquid is absorbed. Remove from the heat. Stir in the lemon zest, vanilla, nutmeg or mace, honey, and evaporated milk. Add the coconut. Use a fork to mix everything together and break up the granules of rice. Spoon the mixture into 6 ramekins and cover each with foil. Arrange them in a baking pan with warm water that comes about 2/3 of the way up the sides of the ramekins. Bake in the preheated oven for 30 minutes, and then carefully

Tips from Rosie's Kitchen

If you want to make this a completely dairy-free dessert, substitute either rice milk or vanilla soy milk for the cow's milk called for here. Use the same measure and cook it the same way.

remove the foil. Bake for another 15 minutes until the tops of the puddings puff up. Remove from the oven and let cool.

When completely cooled, slide a knife along the inside edge of the ramekins to separate the pudding from the sides of the dish. Turn each ramekin over onto a plate and spoon equal portions of chilled fruit sauce on top of each pudding.

APPLE-CRANBERRY CRISP

Cranberries give this crisp a delightful color and tartness. A moderate amount of oil replaces the large amount of butter usually called for in toppings for this kind of dessert. It is best served warm.

12 large green apples, peeled, cored, and sliced
8 ounces fresh or frozen cranberries
Juice of 1 lemon
1/3 cup brandy
1/3 cup light-brown sugar, packed
1 teaspoon cinnamon
2 tablespoons whole wheat pastry flour

TOPPING

1 1/2 cups old-fashioned rolled oats
1/2 cup toasted wheat germ
3/4 teaspoon salt
1 1/2 teaspoons cinnamon
1/2 cup light-brown sugar, packed
1/3 cup canola or grapeseed oil
1/3 cup maple syrup

SERVES 12

PER SERVING:
CALORIES 279.5
FAT 7.7 G
  SATURATED FAT
  0.8 G
(24.8% OF CALORIES FROM FAT)
PROTEIN 4.1 G
CARBOHYDRATE
  48.7 G
CHOLESTEROL
  0 MG
FIBER 5.8 G

❁

Preheat oven to 375°F.

Toss the sliced apples in a large bowl with the cranberries, lemon juice, brandy, 1/3 cup of light-brown sugar, 1 teaspoon of cinnamon, and the whole wheat pastry flour. Pile the apple mixture into an 8 × 10–inch baking dish.

Mix together the ingredients for the topping and spread over the apples. Cover the baking dish with aluminum foil and bake for 20 minutes. Uncover and bake for 40 minutes more until the apples are soft.

Apricot Mousse

You will have a hard time refusing seconds with this dessert. You can taste every bit of fruit in it, from the apricots to the raspberries. Every foamy, sweet, and savory bite melts in your mouth.

SERVES 6

PER SERVING:

CALORIES 103.3

FAT 0.3 G
  SATURATED FAT
  0 G
(2.2% OF CALO-
  RIES FROM FAT)

PROTEIN 2.5 G

CARBOHYDRATE
  25.7 G

CHOLESTEROL
  0 MG

FIBER 1.7 G

❄

3 tablespoons agar-agar (vegetar-
    ian gelatin)
1 1/2 cups cold purified water
2 cups fresh, peeled apricots, or 1
    cup dried apricots (unsulfured)
1 tablespoon honey
2 cups apple juice
2 cups frozen vanilla yogurt

GARNISH

About 6 tablespoons plain low-fat
    yogurt
1 pint fresh raspberries
1 lime, thinly sliced

Dissolve the agar-agar in 1 cup of the water in a small bowl.

Drop the apricots into a second bowl. Bring remaining 1/2 cup of water to a boil in a small pot, then add the honey and stir. Pour the liquid over the apricots to hydrate and sweeten them.

Bring the apple juice to a boil, then stir in the dissolved gelatin and continue to cook, while stirring, for 5 minutes. Strain the apricots through a colander or vegetable mill, then add them to the boiling juice mixture. Stir again a few times and remove from the heat. Let cool for 1 minute, then pour into a glass bowl. Chill, covered, until the jellied apricots set overnight, or at least 2 hours.

After the jelly has set, blend it with the yogurt in a blender or food processor until it is whipped. Scoop it into glasses. Garnish with a dollop of yogurt, a sprinkling of fresh raspberries, and a slice of lime.

Tip's from Rosie's Kitchen

Agar-agar is a natural gelatin made from dried seaweed. It is a strong setting ingredient and you can find it at any health-food store.

Though you can chill the ingredients for 2 hours to set the gelatin and it works fine, I always chill the jelly overnight. Whatever you choose, you'll need to plan accordingly.

This recipe is actually two recipes in one because you have the option of serving it simply as fruit jelly, or you can blend it into a mousse. If you must, you can drop a small glob of Cool Whip or real whipped cream on top as an alternative to the yogurt. This dessert is exceptionally easy to make, requiring minimal ingredients, and the bonus to your friends and family is that it's preservative-free.

CHOCOLATE

Most people love chocolate; many are passionate about it. Some say dessert is either chocolate or something other than chocolate. But this food of the gods, enjoyed as a sacred drink by natives of ancient Mexico and Meso-America, has gotten a bad reputation in our times. Considered a "guilty pleasure," it has been demonized because of its fat content and is said to have no place in a good diet. Some health-food producers have even come up with a wretched imitation of it—carob—that they use to make "nutritious" fake chocolate candies, cakes, and cookies. In fact, chocolate not only beats carob hands down in both the taste and health categories, it has many attributes that recommend it for inclusion in an optimum diet.

Cocoa butter, the fat in chocolate, turns out not to be so bad. Although it is a saturated fat, the body turns it into monounsaturated fat, processing it like olive oil. Chocolate appears to be neutral, at worst, in regard to cardiovascular health and may actually lower serum cholesterol. In addition, chocolate has strong antioxidant activity, equivalent to that of red wine and green tea. It is a stimulant because it contains theobromine, a relative of caffeine, but, for unknown reasons, it is also, for many people, a rapid-acting antidepressant.

The best form of chocolate from a health standpoint is high-quality, plain, dark chocolate. I say "high-quality" because cheaper brands contain less actual chocolate, often replacing expensive cocoa butter with unhealthful hydrogenated vegetable oils. The first ingredient on a bar of high-quality chocolate should be chocolate—usually indicated as "chocolate liquor," "cacao," or "cocoa." It should not be sugar. The brands I like best contain 70 percent cocoa. (Bitter baking chocolate is 100 percent cocoa; more than 80 percent is too bitter for most people to enjoy.)

I say "plain" because chocolate candies often contain butter and cream, sources of highly saturated animal fats, as well as other ingredients much less good for us than the natural constituents of cocoa beans. And I say "dark" because milk chocolate contains much less cocoa and more butterfat and sugar.

When I want a sweet, I usually go for a piece (or chunk) of high-quality dark chocolate, which I regard as a pleasure, but not one I need to feel guilty about. I often serve dark chocolate with fruit as a dessert (the recipe follows) and keep dark chocolate sorbet in the freezer. In moderation, these treats are not fattening, provide important nutrients, are perfectly fine for people following low-carbohydrate diets—and they certainly add to the pleasure of eating.

—A.W.

SERVES 6

PER SERVING:

CALORIES 302

FAT 13.4 G
  SATURATED FAT 7.6 G

(40% OF CALORIES FROM FAT)

PROTEIN 2.4 G

CARBOHYDRATE 51.9 G

CHOLESTEROL 0 MG

FIBER 6.5 G

DARK CHOCOLATE WITH FRUIT

This couldn't be simpler, and your guests will love it. Serve an assortment of fresh fruit that is perfectly ripe and flavorful. Also serve some high-quality dark chocolate broken into pieces, and let people help themselves.

1¹/2 ounces chocolate
1 pear or apple

Rosie's Tips on Planning Menus

The menus Andy and I have designed here should give you an idea of how to mix and match our dishes to create a healthy diet throughout the week. As well, we offer two exciting menus for celebratory meals.

But often, menu planning is and should be prompted by the season—what the weather is like and what fresh produce is in the market. Also, keep in mind what you may have left over from a meal so that you can use it in a creative way the next day or so. I even plan for leftovers, deliberately making more so I have something to work with—which saves me time. As a general rule, I serve my meals with something fresh, like a slice of melon or 1/4 cup spring salad mix. I also like to use edible flowers, such as nasturtiums, geraniums, pansies, and lavender, as a garnish. It's good to have these items available because they taste good and dress up the plate.

A spring meal after a visit to the farmers' market (or, if you're so fortunate, your own garden), where you find baby lettuce greens and small spinach leaves, might feature Mixed Greens with Potato Crouton Salad (page 101). The Vegetable "Quiche" (page 11), served hot or cold, would be perfect with the salad to complete a lovely light spring lunch.

In summer, you can enjoy the breeze while grilling outside. Sip on a glass of iced Berry Herbal Tea (page 41), while you prepare Thai Shrimp Brochette (page 67), having set up a Tostada Bar (page 217) for a casual dinner get together. The Spanish Seafood Cocktail, Gazpacho-Style (page 64) would make a pleasant chilled appetizer that goes well with the Spanish Tostada. Both dishes use salsa and other common summer ingredients, which you can prepare ahead of time. I usually like to end a meal with a cup of herbal tea and/or fresh fruit. On the weekends, when you have more time, you may want to make a special treat, like a Blueberry Pie with Lattice Top (page 280), to make the most of the delicious seasonal berries.

On a chilly fall evening when it's nice to have the oven warming up the kitchen, you could prepare ahead some Apple Cake Squares (page 283), that would make a fine ending for a dinner starting with Baked Curried Sea Bass (page 188) accompanied by Stuffed Winter Squash (page 236), instead of Grilled Summer Vegetables (page 156).

In the winter months, again it's nice to warm up the kitchen on a leisurely Sunday afternoon by baking an Apple-Cranberry Crisp (page 299) and roasting at the same time the Savory Roasted Cornish Hens (page 150). The whole roasted heads of garlic that are part of that recipe are delicious over Mashed Potatoes and Parsnips (page 231), another winter treat. In the middle of that pleasant day of cooking, you might stir up some simple Miso Soup (page 125) for a wholesome lunch or snack.

So I have added some additional seasonal menus that make the most of the year's changing bounty.

NOTE: The nutritional analyses for these menus are not written in stone—there will inevitably be slight variables in the kind of fruit or cheese or bread or nuts you might choose. But they serve as guidelines for planning a healthy diet through the week and allow for some additional rounding out of the meals, as you see fit, since the calorie counts come in well under the recommended guidelines. The holiday and special dinners are more indulgent, but we all need to celebrate on occasion and you can simply cut back on the rest of the day's intake or adjust your meals accordingly on the ensuing days.

Daily Menus

Monday

BREAKFAST

Scrambled Eggs with Fresh Salsa
Sunrise Orange Grapefruit Juice
Toast

SNACK

Pineapple Almond Shake

LUNCH

Lebanese Salad
Whole Wheat Baguette
Fresh Fruit

DINNER

Grilled Fish with Tropical Relish
Lemon Dill Baby Carrots
Brown Rice
Figs in Wine
Berry Herbal Tea

❃

Tuesday

BREAKFAST

Frosted Orange Ginger Fruit Salad
Frittata

SNACK

Orange Oatmeal Cookie

1 SERVING

CALORIES 1534.8

FAT 37 G
  SATURATED FAT
  9.6 G

(26.3% OF CALORIES FROM FAT)

PROTEIN 71.3 G

CARBOHYDRATE
  104.9 G

CHOLESTEROL
  204 MG

FIBER 12.3 G

1 SERVING

CALORIES 1474

FAT 49 G
  SATURATED FAT
  14.7 G

(31.9% OF CALORIES FROM FAT)

PROTEIN 31.9 G

CARBOHYDRATE
  196.1 G

CHOLESTEROL
  224 MG

FIBER 43.1 G

LUNCH

Mixed-Bean Minestrone Stew

Cheese and Crackers

DINNER

Baked Spicy Tofu with Bean Thread Noodles,
 Corn, and Mango
Shiitake Mushrooms and Pea Pods
Berries with Sorbet

❈

1 SERVING

CALORIES 1394.3

FAT 54 G
 SATURATED FAT
 12.9 G

(34.4% OF CALO-
 RIES FROM FAT)

PROTEIN 106.3 G

CARBOHYDRATE
 125.7 G

CHOLESTEROL
 246 MG

FIBER 18.9 G

Wednesday

BREAKFAST

Muesli or Granola

SNACK

Frozen Fruit Smoothie

LUNCH

Tabbouleh Salad
White Bean Spread
Pita

DINNER

Escarole Soup
Grilled Salmon with Mustard Sauce
1 Slice Baguette
Wilted Spinach with Mushrooms
Grapes and Cheese

❈

Thursday

BREAKFAST

Two-Colored Fruit Gazpacho

Applesauce Muffins

SNACK

Honey Ginger Lemonade

A Handful of Nuts

LUNCH

Vegetable Nori Rolls

Broccoli Salad with Avocado

DINNER

Tomato, Corn, and Basil Soup

Turkey Burgers or Portobello Burgers

Lemon Yogurt Sorbet and

    (optional) Ginger Cookies

❋

WITH TURKEY
BURGERS
1 SERVING

CALORIES 1512.8

FAT 50.1 G
  SATURATED FAT
  8.4 G

(27.9% OF CALO-
RIES FROM FAT)

PROTEIN 55.5 G

CARBOHYDRATE
235.2 G

CHOLESTEROL
110 MG

FIBER 36.9 G

WITH PORTOBELLO
BURGERS
1 SERVING

CALORIES 1552.3

FAT 70.3 G
  SATURATED FAT
  9.5 G

(38.5% OF CALO-
RIES FROM FAT)

PROTEIN 29.9 G

CARBOHYDRATE
222.4 G

CHOLESTEROL
20 MG

FIBER 30.9 G

Friday

1 SERVING

CALORIES 2008.2

FAT 70.4 G
  SATURATED FAT
  13.7 G

(18.2% OF CALO-
  RIES FROM FAT)

PROTEIN 56.6 G

CARBOHYDRATE
  305.1 G

CHOLESTEROL
  54 MG

FIBER 37.3 G

BREAKFAST

Scrambled Tofu with Fresh Salsa
Slice of Melon
Whole Wheat Toast

SNACK

Spiced Tea

LUNCH

Cold Vegetable Pasta Primavera
Fresh Fruit

DINNER

Grilled Fish Tacos
Spanish Rice
Dark Chocolate with Fruit

Saturday

1 SERVING

CALORIES 2088.1

FAT 52.2 G
  SATURATED FAT
  11.3 G

(21.3% OF CALO-
  RIES FROM FAT)

PROTEIN 51.3 G

CARBOHYDRATE
  383 G

CHOLESTEROL
  30 MG

FIBER 54.3 G

BREAKFAST

Pancakes or Waffles with Fruit Compote

SNACK

Citrus Mango Freeze

LUNCH

Roasted Winter Squash and Apple Soup
Hummus Pinwheels with Raw Veggie Crudités

DINNER

Vegetable Lasagna
Green Bean Salad
Poached Pears

Sunday

B R E A K F A S T

    Eggs Florentine with Orange and
        Dill Sauce
    Fresh Fruit

S N A C K

    Low-Fat Vanilla Shake

L U N C H

    Cold Cucumber Soup
    Thai Shrimp and Papaya Salad

D I N N E R

    Tofu Fajitas
    Greek Salad with Mild Red-Chili Dressing
    Blueberry Pie with Lattice Top

CALORIES 1659.1

FAT 73.5 G
  SATURATED FAT
  23.6 G

(38% OF CALO-
RIES FROM FAT)

PROTEIN 64.6 G

CARBOHYDRATE
205 G

CHOLESTEROL
366 MG

FIBER 31.6 G

Menus for Special Occasions

HOLIDAY DINNER
WITH TURKEY,
1 SERVING

CALORIES 1099.9

FAT 49.6 G
  SATURATED FAT
  10.7 G
  (24.9% OF CALO-
  RIES FROM FAT)

PROTEIN 211.3 G

CARBOHYDRATE
  125.9 G

CHOLESTEROL
  87 MG

FIBER 20.2 G

HOLIDAY DINNER
WITH FISH,
1 SERVING

CALORIES 1417.2

FAT 49.5 G
  SATURATED FAT
  9.7 G
  (30.1% OF CALO-
  RIES FROM FAT)

PROTEIN 51.4 G

CARBOHYDRATE
  207 G

CHOLESTEROL
  29 MG

FIBER 40.6 G

Holiday Dinner

Miso Paté

Spinach Toasts

Roasted Pepper Turkey with Orange Liqueur,
    or Fish with Spinach *En Papillote*

Vegetarian Shepherd's Pie with Sweet Potato
    and Lentil Filling

Andy's Brussels Sprouts

Jicama and Carrot Salad

Pistachio Dream and Cookies

Apple Strudel

Cranberry Barley Tonic

❋

Dinner Party for Friends

Smoked Fish with Horseradish Sauce

Goat-Cheese Toasties with Sun-Dried Tomatoes
    and Basil

Mediterranean Stuffed Grape Leaves

A. Celery, Artichoke, Hearts of Palm, and Shrimp Salad,
    or B. Mixed Greens with Potato Croutons and
    Tarragon Dressing

A. Savory Mushroom Lobster Crepes,
    or B. Eggplant Rollatini with Spinach and
    Cheese Filling

A. Apple Tart,
    or B. Raspberry Sorbet Pie

❋

DINNER FOR
FRIENDS WITH
MAIN AND
DESSERT COURSE
SELECTIONS A

1 SERVING

CALORIES 1511.8

FAT 72.2 G
  SATURATED FAT
  17.8 G

(41.7% OF CALO-
RIES FROM FAT)

PROTEIN 78.8 G

CARBOHYDRATE
148 G

CHOLESTEROL
102 MG

FIBER 24.8 G

DINNER FOR
FRIENDS WITH
MAIN AND
DESSERT COURSE
SELECTIONS B

1 SERVING

CALORIES 1692.7

FAT 69 G
  SATURATED FAT
  23 G

(36.8% OF CALO-
RIES FROM FAT)

PROTEIN 116.4 G

CARBOHYDRATE
150.3 G

CHOLESTEROL
527 MG

FIBER 15.6 G

Seasonal Menus

1 SERVING

CALORIES 618.5

FAT 19.6 G
  SATURATED FAT
  9.2 G
(27.8% OF CALO-
  RIES FROM FAT)

PROTEIN 18.1 G

CARBOHYDRATE
  96.2 G

CHOLESTEROL
  193 MG

FIBER 4.4 G

Spring Brunch

Vegetable Quiche with Radish Rosettes
Herbal Biscuits (made from leftover cobbler dough)
Angel Food Cake with Fresh Berries

❈

1 SERVING

CALORIES 601

FAT 20.8 G
  SATURATED FAT
  3.4 G
(28.5% OF CALO-
  RIES FROM FAT)

PROTEIN 21.6 G

CARBOHYDRATE
  95.7 G

CHOLESTEROL
  1 MG

FIBER 18.6 G

Summer Garden Party

Chicken Satay with Peanut Dipping Sauce
Warm Quinoa-and-Zucchini-Stuffed Tomatoes
Greens with Tangy Miso Sauce
Apricot Mousse

❈

Summer Dinner

Grilled Summer Vegetables
Lemon Grilled Halibut with Papaya Salsa
Spanish Rice
Two-Colored Fruit Gazpacho

✺

1 SERVING

CALORIES 503.8

FAT 16.8 G
  SATURATED FAT
  2.3 G

(29.4% OF CALO-
RIES FROM FAT)

PROTEIN 43.8 G

CARBOHYDRATE
47.0 G

CHOLESTEROL
54 MG

FIBER 17.1 G

Fall Dinner

Warm Mediterranean Stuffed Grape Leaves
Baked Curried Sea Bass with Lentils
Greek Salad with Mild Red Chili Dressing
    or Green Salad
Lemon Sponge Cake

✺

1 SERVING

CALORIES 298.5

FAT 8.3 G
  SATURATED FAT
  1.2 G

(23.8% OF CALO-
RIES FROM FAT)

PROTEIN 14.8 G

CARBOHYDRATE
44.9 G

CHOLESTEROL
0 MG

FIBER 14 G

Winter Dinner

Roasted Winter Squash and Apple Soup
Cornish Game Hens with Roasted Garlic
Apple Cranberry Crisp

Any-Time-of-Year
Vegetarian Menu

Miso Soup
Teriyaki Sampler Plate
     with Scallion "Firecracker" garnishes
Rice Pudding

A Note About the Authors

Rosie Daley was born in New Jersey to a large family. She trained as a chef at Cal-a-Vie Spa just north of San Diego, then relocated to Chicago to work as the personal chef for Oprah Winfrey for five years. She is the author of *In the Kitchen with Rosie,* published in 1994. Since then she has been busy teaching cooking classes to small and large groups, promoting healthy eating. She now lives in California with her son, Marley.

Andrew Weil, M.D., a graduate of Harvard College and Harvard Medical School, is Clinical Professor of Medicine at the University of Arizona and director of the Program in Integrative Medicine at that institution. Dr. Weil produces a monthly newsletter, *Self-Healing,* maintains a popular Web site, DrWeil.com, and writes a monthly column in *Prevention* magazine. He is a frequent guest on radio and television and lectures widely on nutrition and natural medicine. This is his ninth book.

A Note on the Types

Rosie's text was set in a typeface called Méridien, a classic roman designed by Adrian Frutiger for the French type foundry Deberny et Peignot in 1957. Adrian Frutiger was born in Interlaken, Switzerland, in 1928 and studied type design there and at the Kunstgewerbeschule in Zurich. In 1953 he moved to Paris, where he joined Deberny et Peignot as a member of the design staff. Méridien, as well as his other typeface of world renown, Univers, was originally created for the Lumitype photoset machine.

Andy's text was set in Meta Plus. Heralded as the Helvetica of the nineties, the definitive sans serif face Meta was originally commissioned for the German Post Office (Bundespost) in 1984. Although the project was eventually canceled in favor of staying with Helvetica, Erik Spiekermann completed the design as a digital font in 1989, and it was published in 1991 by FontShop International. Since that time, the family has been expanded to its current comprehensive state of twenty weights and has been warmly embraced by the international design market.

Composition and color separation by North Market Street Graphics,
Lancaster, Pennsylvania
Printed and bound by R. R. Donnelley, Crawfordsville, Indiana
Designed by Virginia Tan